# Confident Parents, Confident Children

## Policy and practice in parent education and support

Gillian Pugh, Erica De'Ath and Celia Smith

Published by the National Children's Bureau
8 Wakley Street, London EC1V 7QE
Telephone 071-278 9441

Registered Charity no. 258825

© National Children's Bureau 1994

ISBN 1 874579 37 7

Typeset by Books Unlimited, Rainworth, Notts, NG21 OJE
Printed by Biddles Ltd, Guildford
Cover designed by Wave Design 0424 715 754
Photo credits: David Gibson; Sebastian Buccherie; The National Youth Agency

The National Children's Bureau was established as a registered charity in 1963. Our
purpose is to identify and promote the interests of all children and young people and
to improve their status in a diverse society.

We work closely with professionals and policy makers to improve the lives of all
children but especially young children, those affected by family instability, children
with special needs or disabilities and those suffering the effects of poverty and
deprivation.

We collect and disseminate information about children and promote good practice
in children's services through research, policy and practice development,
publications, seminars, training and an extensive library and information service.

The Bureau works in partnership with Children in Scotland and Children in
Wales.

# Contents

# Acknowledgements

Many organisations and individuals responded to our request for information for this book and they are listed in Appendix 1. We are most grateful to them for their time and ideas.

Colleagues to whom we are particularly grateful for their contribution to our first draft are John Coleman, Trust for the Study of Adolescence; Janet Paraskeva, National Youth Agency; Joan Sartain HMI; and Rachel Thomson, Sex Education Forum. We would also like to thank them for their comments on the final draft of the book, and to thank others who have commented on all or part of the draft: Alan Beattie of Lancaster University, Dorit Braun of Northamptonshire Health Authority, Margaret Buttigieg of the Health Visitors Association, Barbara Hearn of the National Children's Bureau, Eileen Hayes of the National Society for the Prevention of Cruelty to Children, Judy Perrett and Alison Skinner of the National Youth Agency, Ceridwen Roberts of the Family Policy Studies Centre, Philippa Russell of the Council for Disabled Children, and Sheila Wolfendale of the University East London.

Many other people have also contributed to the development of this book, for it builds on the three-year study published in 1984 as *The Needs of Parents: policy and practice in parent education* and the discussions that informed that.

The book would not have been possible without grants from the Calouste Gulbenkian Foundation and the Department of Health, and we are most grateful to them for their support.

Gillian Pugh, Erica De'Ath and Celia Smith
April 1994

# The authors

Gillian Pugh is the Director of the Early Childhood Unit at the National Children's Bureau. Her recent work includes consultancy, training and publications in the fields of policy development at national and local level, coordination of services, curriculum development in the early years and parent education and support. She is author and co-author of many books including **Contemporary Issues in the Early Years** (ed.) (Paul Chapman), **Working with Children: developing a curriculum for the early years** (National Children's Bureau and NES Arnold, 1989) and with Erica De'Ath, **Working Towards Partnership in the Early Years** (National Children's Bureau, 1989) and **The Needs of Parents: practice and policy in parent education** (Macmillan, 1984).

Erica De'Ath is Chief Executive, National Stepfamily Association. Her recent work includes consultancy, training, policy analysis and publications on issues relating to remarriage and stepfamily life and their impact on children. She has previously worked for The Children's Society and the National Children's Bureau on studies of parent education and partnership between parents and professionals. She is co-author with Gillian Pugh of two of the books listed above.

Celia Smith has worked in the field of child care in both statutory and voluntary sectors. Recent reports and publications include **A Family Support Model of Day Care: a study of pre-school projects in Barnardo's London Division** (National Children's Bureau, 1993) and, forthcoming with Jeni Vernon, **Nurseries at the Crossroads: how nurseries are meeting the challenge of child care in the nineties** (National Children's Bureau, 1994).

# Introduction

This is a book about being a parent in the last decade of the twentieth century. It looks at the kind of society in which parents are bringing up their children, and at the kinds of families in which children are growing up, but its chief concern is with what could be done to make being a parent and bringing up children easier, more enjoyable and more satisfying than it is for many parents at present. Parenthood today is a demanding and at times stressful, lonely and frustrating experience; if society continues to put high expectations on parents, then it must also provide sufficient support to enable them to fulfil their obligations with knowledge, understanding and enjoyment.

Ten years ago *The Needs of Parents: policy and practice in parent education* by Gillian Pugh and Erica De'Ath reported on a three-year development project, based at the National Children's Bureau from 1980-1983, which had sought to paint a national picture of preparation, education and support for parents in the UK. The project took a lifecycle approach to parent education, examining the role of schools, colleges and youth services in preparing young people for family life; at antenatal education; at support services for families within the community; and at the role of the media in parent education. During the course of the project a considerable amount of information was collected and analysed, and discussion of the key issues was promoted through conferences, seminars and working parties.

*The Needs of Parents* was widely used and quoted from, but by 1993 it was unavailable. In any case, over the intervening ten years the context of family life had changed in many respects, and much of the information had become out of date. The issue of parent education, however, was as topical and important as ever. As Britain joins countries throughout the world in celebrating International Year of the Family in 1994, the spotlight turns again on to parents, and questions are asked about whether Britain really is a 'family friendly society'.

For those parents in employment the challenge is how to balance the responsibilities of work with bringing up children; for many other families the challenges are of how to manage on benefits or low incomes, as the numbers of children growing up in poverty continues to increase. The combination of changing patterns of work and changing family patterns – the increasing incidence of divorce and remarriage, and of children growing up in lone parent families – has led some commentators to voice concern about parents' ability to bring up their children satisfactorily. There are, of course, no easy answers to these challenges, but there are many ways in which support and education can be provided which will enable all parents to do 'well enough' by their children – and this is the focus of our book.

This new book is the result of a small scale review of current practice in the field of parent education, funded by the Gulbenkian Foundation and the Department of Health. We did not have the resources to embark on a national consultation exercise as we did in the early eighties, but we were able to contact 160 organisations and individuals who are working in the area, either by individual letter or through a number of short articles in the national and professional press, and they are listed in Appendix 1. Many of these gave detailed responses to our letter seeking information and views on what was needed to adequately prepare young people for family life, and provide support and education for parents, and who should provide it. When we quote from these responses in the text, we refer to them as 'response to enquiry'.

Our definitions of parent education are discussed in chapter 3, but we summarise them here. The overall term **parent education** we use to encompass approaches at each stage of the life cycle, and we define it as:

---

**A range of educational and supportive measures which:**

- **help parents and prospective parents to understand their own social, emotional, psychological and physical needs and those of their children and enhance the relationship between them; and**
- **create a supportive network of services within local communities and help families to take advantage of them.**

---

Within this overall term, work with young people before the conception of children we call **family life education** or **education about parenthood and family life**; support during pregnancy and the transition to parenthood we call **preparation for family life;** and work with parents and their children we call **support for parents** or, when it is very specifically educational, **parent or parenting education.**

We hope the book will provide a useful resource for all those working with and for parents and their children, and will highlight the urgency of creating an environment in which parents and children feel better valued and supported than many do at present. Bringing up children is a lifelong responsibility, and the most important task that most of us perform. The extent to which the next generation become responsible, fulfilled and productive citizens, will depend to a considerable degree on the quality of the relationships they have today with their parents, and to the levels of support that parents receive from their own families and the wider community.

# How the book is organised

The material in this book is presented with three main objectives in mind:

- to contribute to the current debate on parent education and parental responsibilities by presenting for discussion a framework for examining the skills needed for successful parenting, and the needs of individuals in order to develop their full potential as parents;
- to present a revised and updated overview of what help parents and prospective parents in Britain might find in their local schools, health clinics and communities under the general umbrella of 'parent education and family support';
- to encourage the many people working with parents and their children, whether as professional or voluntary workers, to re-examine what their own contribution might be to the network of supportive and educative services, and to question the nature of their relationship with parents.

Part one examines what it is like to be a parent in the 1990s. Chapter 1 looks at the context in which parenting is taking place, at changes in employment patterns and at changes in family roles and structures. Chapter 2 examines what we mean by 'parenting' – at the skills and attributes needed to be a 'good enough' parent, at fathering and mothering, and at the cultural and social context of child-rearing. Chapter 3 defines what we mean by 'parent education', examines the principles upon which it should be based, the form that it might take at different stages of the life-cycle, and the different methods and approaches used.

Part two presents an analysis of current initiatives across the country, using published documents and research, and information gathered by a short questionnaire survey of individuals and organisations working in the field, as noted above. Chapter 4 looks at the role of schools, colleges and the youth service in preparing young people for family life. Chapter 5 discusses antenatal clinics and classes and postnatal education in supporting the transition to parenthood. Chapter 6 describes a wide range of support and education, some services available for all parents, and some more specialist help for particular groups of parents, for example lone parents and parents whose children have special needs.

Part three summarises the evidence presented throughout the book to suggest a coherent approach to parent education and support. We make a number of specific recommendations and look at the implications of these for policy-makers and practitioners alike, reflecting on the extent to which our recommendations of ten years ago have been implemented.

## The 'Job for Life' project in Hampshire

There is one particular initiative that has informed our thinking and our recommendations. Following the publication of *A Job for Life* (Pugh and others, 1982) – the theoretical framework that preceded *The Needs of Parents* – proposals were drawn up to put the theory of a life cycle approach to parent education into practice. Two or three local authorities were to be identified where there was already considerable activity and interest in parent education and support, in order to develop a comprehensive and continuous network of services on the *Job for Life* model. In the event it proved possible to work only in Hampshire, and the three year development project that was set up in Winchester, funded by Hampshire County Council and Winchester Health Authority, is described in *Parenting as a Job for Life: a local development project in Hampshire* (Pugh and Poulton, 1987).

Over the course of the three years Lin Poulton, the development officer, set up a whole range of initiatives at each stage of the life cycle, in such a way that each one could be taken on by local parents and professionals when the project funding came to an end. Lifeskills groups were set up with ten and 11-year-olds in the community primary school; with 13-year-olds at the secondary school; and with sixth formers at the sixth form college. Groups were set up for pregnant women and new mothers (the NEST group – Newborn Early Support Team); for parents and toddlers; and a toy library (Play and Learn Library). Parents were trained over the course of the project to take over leadership of these groups. A home teaching programme was also introduced. Groups were set up for the parents of children in the 'Lifeskills' groups, and a 'Booklook' group was introduced with librarians from the city library.

Other initiatives involved bringing together the many professionals working in the community – a resource list compiled during the project listed 41 different agencies involved. Groups were set up at three levels: a project advisory group at county level; a fieldwork managers group covering the area in which the project was based; and an educare group, attended by between 20 and 30 local practitioners. A child assault prevention resource group was also established in association with the police and social services, and a 'listening ears' group of local resource people, trained by the local Marriage Guidance Council to offer counselling and support when needed.

The evaluation showed that the project was remarkably successful during its three year lifespan (Pugh and Poulton, 1987) and many of the groups and initiatives are still in operation today. The primary school (granted community status during the course of the project) proved to be the ideal base for the project, and the only group that failed to establish itself was the youth club. The Lifeskills work in schools was particularly successful. Parents were able and willing to be trained to act as group convenors; and the project led to greater multi-agency cooperation at county, district and local level. The catalyst in all of this was obviously the development officer, whose skills at times combined community work, social work, adult education and counselling. If this project is replicated – as we very much hope that it will be – the direction taken will again depend on the skills and interests of the development worker appointed. In chapter 3 we estimate what it would cost to establish schemes such as this on a national basis.

# Part I: Why parent education?

# 1. Parenting in context

## Introduction

> It is generally agreed that the impact of parenting is felt throughout
> one's lifetime and for succeeding generations. No other form of human
> interaction can boast such power and longevity. (Bavolek, 1990)

Bringing up children is perhaps the most challenging and important
task that most of us perform. It is a lifelong commitment – sometimes
described as the only job we have for life – and how well we do it is
likely to have a continuing impact on future generations, playing a
significant part in shaping the values and attitudes that young people
take into their own adult relationships and their approach to being a
parent.

All parents want the best for their children, but the growing
emphasis on individualism, and changes in family patterns and in
social circumstances, make it increasingly difficult for many to know
just what is expected of them and how they are supposed to match up
to those expectations. Mothers and fathers in the 1990s may also find
themselves confronted with a range of issues that were less prominent
or even unknown when they themselves were children. While today's
children have a wide window on the world through virtually universal
access to television, they may also have access to computer
pornography and videos portraying unacceptable levels of violence.
Whilst the majority of children live in families who have access to a
car, the levels of traffic and fears of accidents or abduction mean that
many parents feel that it is not safe for their children to play in the
street or local park, or to ride their bikes, or to walk to school on their
own. There are concerns about the quality of the environment – about
high levels of air pollution and levels of lead in drinking water; and
about the ready availability of drugs and the extent of reported alcohol
and substance misuse amongst young people. And if young people are
not to be out on the streets or sitting in front of the television, then
what should they be doing?

There are too the traditional concerns of generations of parents:

that children should be healthy and have access to a good education, developing skills that will enable them to get a job and become independent adults, at a time when the availability of jobs is less and less certain.

Most children in Britain today still grow up with both their own birth parents, most of whom will be married to each other or living together in permanent relationships. But, if current trends continue, an increasing number will live for a time in a family household with a lone parent, or with a parent and step-parent. These children will accumulate different sets of extended family members – new step-grandparents, step-relationships, half-siblings as well as the original extended family networks with whom many, but not all, children will remain in contact.

Despite a number of significant changes in legislation with wide ranging repercussions for children and families, and the recent announcement that the Secretary of State for Health is to take on responsibility for family issues, there is still no overall coordination of government policies affecting families. Ironically, many families are actually financially worse off in the 1990s than in previous decades. There is concern that the gap between what parents are expected to provide for their children and the means available to them to do this is growing wider.

In trying to understand some of the challenges facing today's parents we can turn to the 16,000 children of the 1958 National Child Development Study (NCDS) cohort, the majority of whom are now parents. At the time of the last sweep for information in 1991, when they were 33-year-olds, 67% had children. Men were more likely than women to be raising children within a first marriage (87% and 72% respectively). One in eight of the mothers was without a partner and one in eleven of the mothers was in a second or subsequent marriage. Further analysis of the life histories of these individuals who have been so closely monitored through their childhood, adolescence and early adult years may give us greater insight into the impact of public issues as well as private family matters on being a parent. Perhaps the most striking factor is the number of profound social, economic and political changes that have occurred particularly during the 15-year period when they were aged 18 to 33:

> The labour market has been dominated by two major recessions sandwiching a consumer-led boom; unemployment has risen to levels unprecedented in the life-time of the cohort. Family life has become increasingly characterised by change and diversity, largely as a result of steep rises in cohabitation, divorce and the birth of children to single mothers. The position of women has changed, especially in terms of

their labour market and other extra-familial roles. The housing scene has been characterised by contrasting trends, with marked rises in both owner occupation and in homelessness. The moves towards ameliorating economic and social inequality, which took place during the childhood of the NCDS (National Child Development Study) sample have been reversed in recent years, and the changes noted above have been accompanied by a developing cultural ethos which emphasises individualism, self-reliance, and private enterprise and ownership. (Ferri, 1993, p 3)

The value of helping parents and their children to cope better in changing and often stressful situations and the conditions needed to support them have been widely acknowledged. Research studies have attributed the resilience and success of some socially disadvantaged children who have succeeded despite adverse social and economic circumstances and stressful experiences, to their child-centred parenting and their parents' interest in and aspirations for their education (Osborn, 1990; Pilling, 1990). Other studies of multiple deprivation have also suggested that the 'quality' of parenting is likely to be an influential factor in children's development (Kolvin and others, 1990; Utting and others, 1993).

## Changing attitudes to marriage and parenthood

The Eurobarometer Survey of 1990 indicates that whereas all other European countries see the most important role for families as 'bringing up and educating children' less than one in four in the UK endorsed this view. In contrast, more UK respondents felt that the most important role of the family was 'to provide love and affection'. This emphasis on companionate marriage with the concept of togetherness based on a satisfactory intimate and emotional relationship means there is a greater possibility of disappointment (Dormor, 1992). It is not a coincidence that Britain has the second highest marriage rate in Europe (after Portugal) and the second highest divorce rate (after Denmark); there are more people both embracing marriage and finding that it does not match their expectations.

There appears to be a British ambivalence about marriage, parenting and children. The 1989 British Social Attitude (BSA) Survey found 73% of men and 68% of women agreed that 'people who want children ought to get married'. But there is a marked age difference within responses to this survey with only 50% of the under 25s agreeing that people should marry if they want children.

Returning to the 33-year-olds in the NCDS cohort cited above, seven out of ten of the sample agreed with the statement that 'It is alright for people to have children without getting married.' (Ferri, 1993). This suggests that in future couples may not feel they need to marry when they become parents.

Current trends suggest that young people are postponing marriage and living as cohabiting couples prior to deciding to have a child. In the 1960s and 1970s almost all young people married, and over 90% of those born in 1946 were already married by 1976 at the age of 30 years (Kiernan, 1989). Compare this to the NCDS cohort born 12 years later in 1958, where 90% had lived as a couple at least once by the age of 33 but only 63% had married (Ferri, 1993) The social acceptance of cohabitation, often as a prelude to marriage, is now a majority practice (Kiernan and Estaugh 1993). Whilst considerable numbers of cohabiting mothers do marry, often several years after the birth of their child, reasons given by long-term cohabiting mothers for not getting married are fear of divorce, the high cost of weddings and objections to the institution of marriage (McRae, 1993). There are also significant differences: cohabiting couples with dependent children, on average, have lower household incomes, are more likely to receive income support and housing benefit, to live in local authority housing, and the male partner is likely to be unemployed or in semi-skilled or unskilled occupations, than are married couples with dependent children (Kiernan and Estaugh, 1993).

The perception of a move away from marriage as an institution towards marriage as a relationship has implications for parenthood as well as partnership. The 1662 Book of Common Prayer states that the primary purpose of marriage is the procreation of children, whereas the more recent 1980 Alternative Service Book states the primary purpose is for mutual comfort, help and fidelity. If we consider the views expressed by the British public, then it appears that parenthood is no longer seen as the purpose of marriage, although the majority of cohabiting couples do get married when they plan to become parents. This shift in equating parenthood with marriage appears to have been acknowledged in recent legislation, such as the Children Act 1989 and the Child Support Act 1991, both of which put an emphasis on parental rather than marital status in stating the duties and responsibilities of parents. Some marriages and remarriages will be based on a partnership relationship rather than on becoming parents, and some couples will become parents but will cohabit rather than marry.

# Changes in society and changing family patterns

The diversity of contemporary life not only creates opportunities for challenge and change but can also increase anxiety, insecurity and instability in family life. Social acceptance has influenced patterns of behaviour such as cohabitation, pre-marital sex, and children being born out of wedlock. Changes in legislation recognise such social changes, for example in relation to divorce, abortion, equal rights and opportunities, forbidding discriminatory practices and removing archaic concepts, such as illegitimacy. Values and attitudes are also influenced by changes in technology, from contraception on the one hand to computers on the other. Being a parent no longer means you are wiser by virtue of being older; it can in fact mean knowing the wrong 'outdated' information. Economic and employment trends can alter the expectations and patterns of family life; for example it is now becoming easier for women, mothers and daughters, to get employment in some areas than it is for men, fathers and sons.

Bringing up children cannot be seen in isolation from these wider influences and patterns of family life. The population of Great Britain is changing. The 1991 Census shows a declining birth rate with 20.1% of the population being children aged under 16, compared to 22.3% in 1981. There has been a slight shift towards a higher proportion of elderly people, from 17.7% of pensionable age in 1981 to 18.7% in 1991. There has also been a marked increase in the numbers of people living alone. Only 5% of families reflect the traditional nuclear family model, although this refers only to those family households with dependent birth children in which the parents are married, the father is in paid work and the mother is at home not doing paid work. The impact of parental cohabitation, male unemployment, working mothers, young adults remaining at home with their parents, parental separation and re-partnering means that families today are much more varied and diverse than this traditional model.

Early motherhood is now less common in most developed countries than it was in the 1970s, partly due to the increase in abortion (Phoenix, 1991). Britain, however, has the highest teenage pregnancy rate in western Europe, with 103,000 under-20s pregnant in 1991. Although the majority of teenage mothers are 18 and 19 and legally adults, during the decade from 1980 to 1990 conception rates among the under-16s rose steadily. The 1992 White Paper, *The Health of the Nation*, set a target to halve the conception rate of under-16s by the year 2000 to no more than 4.8 per 1,000. In fact, OPCS figures have shown that teenage conception rates did drop from 10.1 per 1000 young women in 1990 to 9.3 per 1000 in 1991, although that trend is by no means certain to continue. In 1991, 83% of teenage mothers were single, compared with the figure of 30% for mothers of all ages (Ineichen and Hudson, 1994).

## Family households

Some 25% of all households in 1991 were a married or cohabiting couple with dependent children, compared to 31% in 1971. A further 36% were married or cohabiting couples either with no children or non-dependent children who have grown up and left home. When we look at the number of people involved, however, we see a different perspective. Although only a quarter of households are made up of a couple with dependent children, this constitutes over 41% of the population as a whole.

The majority of children do still grow up in a two adult family. In 1971 this applied to over nine out of ten families; in 1991 it was eight out of ten families, the mean number of dependent children being 1.8. However, in one in 12 of those two adult families there is a parent and step-parent and the mean number of dependent children is 2.1. The 1991 Census highlights a major change in living arrangements of young adults over the 1980s with an increased tendency for young people in their twenties, especially women, to remain in the parental home (Teague, 1993).

The 1991 Census was the first in Great Britain to include a question on ethnic group. Slightly over three million people, 5.5% of the population, described themselves as belonging to an ethnic group other than white (Teague, 1993). About a third of the minority ethnic population are under 16 years compared with a fifth of the white population. The three largest groups are: Indian, constituting 1.5% of the total population and 27.9% of the minority ethnic population as a whole; three black categories (black Caribbean, black African and black Other) together formed 1.6% of the total population and 29.5% of the minority ethnic population; and Pakistanis formed 0.9% of the total population and 25.8% of the minority ethnic population (Teague, 1993). Married couples with dependent children account for 45% of this population. The vast majority of Indian, Pakistani, Chinese and Arab families with children are headed by a married couple, with the mean number of dependent children per family of 2.1 (where family head is Indian), 2.9 (Pakistani) and 3.3 (Bangladeshi). Within West Indian and Guyanese families 6 in 10 are headed by a married couple, with 1.8 children, and in African families around 7.5 in 10, with 2.0 children (Haskey, 1989).

## Marriage, cohabitation and births

The majority of children, seven in ten of all births, are still born inside marriage but clearly a major change has occurred. An increasing number of children are born outside marriage, 31% in 1992, many of them to cohabiting parents, with over half (55%) jointly registering the birth. The proportion of births outside marriage to teenage mothers has actually decreased from 39% in 1971 to 28% in 1990 although, as mentioned above, we still have the highest rate of teenage pregnancies in western Europe. Families have also become smaller: the average is now 1.8 children, except for stepfamilies with an average of 2.1 (which may include combinations of his, or her, or his and her children with their own children of the new relationship). A growing number of children (8% of all live births) are being born into second and subsequent families. Over half (52%) of the stepfamilies with dependent children, have at least one child of the new partnership. Women in general have been having babies later and the average age for a first child has risen from 24.5 years in 1971 to 27.9 years in 1992, the highest since 1957 (OPCS, 1994). Not only are women having children later but those children in turn are staying at home longer.

## Lone parent families

Lone parent families now make up around 19%, or one in five, of all families with children. This has attracted considerable attention from the press and politicians as the number has more than doubled since 1971. In 1991 there were 1.3 million lone parent households with 2.2 million dependent children (Haskey, 1993). This is a very varied group headed by single, separated, divorced or widowed lone mothers or lone fathers, although nine out of ten are women. It is the increase in the single, never married women in their early twenties that causes the politicians most concern because of anxieties about costs to the welfare state in benefits and the presumption that the child has no resident father. There are differences between the various ethnic groups with a very small proportion of lone parent families in the Indian, Pakistani and Chinese communities; African-Caribbean groups have a higher preponderance of lone parent households (24%) with the highest being West Indian/Guyanese with 42% (Haskey, 1989) but often supported by more complex familial and friendship networks than are found in other communities.

## Parental separation and divorce

It is a sad fact of life that the separation or divorce of parents is increasingly seen as a feature of family life in Great Britain. The number of divorces has increased from 145,713 in 1981 to 158,745 in 1991 (LCD, 1993) and has remained at about the same figure over recent years. One in four children will see their parents divorce before they are aged 16. Three quarters of the children experiencing the separation or divorce of their parents each year are aged under ten. There is also an unknown number of additional children who are affected by the separation of parents who are not married and these children are not reflected in the formal divorce statistics.

Whatever the economic or social circumstances, with or without conflict, parental separation is likely to be stressful and upsetting for the children and adults involved. The prevailing wisdom in the 1980s was that the first two years after the disruption were frequently a period of crisis but that children gradually adapted to new roles, relationships and other changes in family living (Demo and Acock, 1988: Dyson and Richards, 1982). This view has now been challenged in a study of 76 children whose families had undergone a series of disruptions and changes where it was found that such children are more likely to experience social, educational and health problems than a comparable group of 76 whose families remain intact (Cockett and Tripp, 1994) A review of research looking at the outcomes for children of family disruption points out that the effects of lone parenthood and family disruption are complex, that social class, age and gender are major influences on outcomes but cautions that it cannot be assumed divorce will always be a negative experience or intact family life a positive one (Burghes, 1994). Elliott and Richards also caution that in looking at children's behaviour we cannot simply assume that the problems observed before and after family disruption have the same cause (1991). What is clear is that many children are not adequately prepared for or supported during such family transitions and that although many parents turn to the various helping professionals for advice and support they do not receive the help they need in coming to terms with the marital breakdown or understanding how to cope with the distress of children or their own vulnerability (Cockett and Tripp, 1994; Mansfield and others, forthcoming).

The differences in the average outcome for children stem more from the number and form of disruptions in the family that children experience, such as bereavement, divorce, transition into a stepfamily, than the type of family itself. For example, the difference in the average outcomes for children of widowed lone parents and intact two parent families is often not very great. Those in separated lone parent and repartnered households on average do less well educationally and behaviourally, especially the girls (Cherlin, 1991). Research shows that some of the effects upon children are evident before the event (Chase-Lansdale and Hetherington, 1990; Richards and Elliott, unpub). It is also evident that the more family transitions children experience, the more likely they are to report difficulties with school, friendships and family relationships (Cockett and Tripp, 1994). Parental conflict brings distress to children whether in intact, separated or repartnered families (Richards, 1993) and the more intense the conflict and the longer it lasts the greater the psychological and behavioural consequences (Chase-Lansdale and Hetherington, 1990). We should, however, be more careful in interpreting results from previous studies and certainly in applying them to today's children (Burghes, 1994).

Separating and divorced parents struggling to reconcile their own needs as adults with those of their children have been described as having 'diminished parenting capability' (Wallerstein and Kelly, 1980). The parents' own distress may mean that either or both parents are 'preoccupied and psychologically unavailable' to their children (Chase-Lansdale and Hetherington, 1990).

Whilst the research shows there is no inevitable path of disadvantage and under-achievement for any individual child who experiences family disruption, it does show that 'on average' children do less well. There are examples of young people dropping out of school, early pregnancies and early home leaving which may jeopardise their chances of higher education and a job as well as the personal risks for those living on the streets, with no financial support from the state or parents, because of problems at home (Kiernan, 1992). Clearly, there is no room for complacency and the development of mediation services for parents and children and greater awareness of children's needs at the time of separation and divorce are essential to lessen the trauma and help build cooperative parenting relationships to support their children emotionally.

## Repartnering and remarriage

In 1992, four out of ten marriages was a remarriage for at least one partner. Second and subsequent marriages for both partners have more than doubled from 8% in 1971 to 17% in 1992. A substantial proportion of these will be divorced parents: 72% of fathers and 57%

of mothers remarry within five years of the divorce (OPCS, 1989). If current trends continue it is predicted that 'by 2010 the majority of couples would cohabit before getting married and the majority of marriages would end in divorce, followed by remarriage' (Northcutt, 1991, p 310). The General Household Survey 1991 (OPCS 1993) provides the first formal statistics on some of these repartnered households indicating that 8% or one in 12 of families with dependent children are composed of a birth parent and new partner creating full-time stepfamilies.

There is some evidence that same-sex step-relationships (stepfather-stepson, stepmother-stepdaughter) may be more problematic for adolescents in stepfamilies (Ferri, 1984), the most stressful areas being divided loyalties and discipline (Lutz, 1983) and that this may result in some stepchildren leaving home earlier (Kiernan, 1992). However, step-parents can bring greater objectivity to the parenting process and be an important extra adult in a child's life (Ihinger-Tallman and Pasley, 1987; Burgoyne and Clark, 1984).

Remarriages are at greater risk of breakdown than first marriages. The highest risk of breakdown occurs in those marriages where both husband and wife are remarrying and both have children from previous marriages (White and Booth, 1985). Clearly there is a particular need to provide support to these parents and step-parents to ensure the children maintain links with both parents and are able to build a new family stability within the stepfamily (De'Ath and Slater, 1992). Stepfamilies are challenging and complicated and the psychological adjustments required of both adults and children are different from and greater than for intact families.

> The fact that many couples end their stepfamilies is the result not only of the difficulties of merging two families with all the complex issues of parenting and wider family relationships, or that they are compared to an idealised picture of a 'normal' family; but there are also the factors which contribute to the ending of the first marriages. (Robinson and Smith, 1993, p.210)

The stepfamily has often been hailed by politicians as the route out of poverty for lone parents and a means of re-establishing the two adult family household presumed to be best for children. The stepfamily should not be seen as either the idealised re-establishing of the traditional family nor the selfish pursuit of adults to form a new relationship at the cost of their childrens' needs. Like all families, some work better than others, and over 50% of stepfamilies do survive despite the difficulties.

# The social context of parenting

Parenting cannot be seen in isolation. Many parents, particularly when their children are young, experience loneliness, and lack of adult company, and considerable numbers of women experience post-natal depression (Cummings and Davies 1994). Poverty and other external stresses also create considerable difficulties for some parents. A study of the ten-year period 1979-89 (Kumar, 1993) makes very chilling reading. The gap between the income of the rich and poor has widened; the relationship between infant mortality and morbidity with social class is stronger; homelessness has increased sharply; children in deprived urban areas make less progress educationally than their peers in less deprived areas; and poverty amongst children is significantly higher for children from minority ethnic groups.

For black and minority ethnic parents there may be other stresses: racism and racial harassment; conflicts as they bring up their children in a culture different from their own; language barriers; and lack of appropriate of services. There are often particular problems for Asian teenage girls around issues of gender-appropriate behaviour and arranged marriages (Grant, forthcoming).

Key factors putting pressures on many parents are patterns of work and unemployment, poverty, housing and homelessness, and we now turn to each of these in turn.

## Patterns of work and unemployment

Over the last decade there has been a dramatic increase in the number of women who are combining motherhood and employment. In 1992 some 63% of married mothers and 40% of lone mothers with dependent children had paid jobs (OPCS, 1994). There has been a marked rise in the number of employed mothers of young children, with a higher uptake of maternity leave by both first time mothers and those with a subsequent birth (McRae, 1991). The number of mothers working with a youngest child aged four or under has increased from 25% in 1973 to 47% in 1990, including those seeking work (OPCS, 1994), the greatest increase being in part-time work. With the majority of mothers with dependent children now working, arranging child care is a major issue in many households. This is discussed later in this chapter.

Joshi (1991) estimates that parenthood has little effect on men's participation or pay but the combination of part-time work, downward occupational mobility and lost work experience reduces opportunities and rates of pay (by 15%) for the majority of mothers relative to women without children. Certainly, the most common pattern for families with children is now one where both parents have a job. Work patterns are often not supportive of family life: it has been estimated that the 'average' father works 40-49 hours, with 36% putting in over 50 hours a week and that this is more likely to be when his children are younger when the need for additional income is greatest (Moss, 1992a).

There are substantial variations between employment patterns in the UK and other European countries. Virtually all women with children in Denmark, Norway and Sweden (Leira, 1993) are economically active, and around two-thirds of mothers in Portugal, Belgium and France (Moss, 1992a). The opportunities for paternity and maternity leave, and the availability of appropriate and affordable child care are key facilitating factors in these countries. A significant difference in the UK is that while the majority of mothers in two adult households are working, the majority in lone parent households are not, often because of the lack of affordable child care, lack of training and employment opportunities and low salaries. In 1987, only 27% of lone parents had earnings as their main source of income compared to 86% of two parent families (Kiernan and Wicks, 1990)

The UK government has recently brought in a number of measures designed to introduce some incentives to lone parents to take up paid employment including replacing Family Income Supplement with Family Credit, reducing the number of working hours for eligibility, introducing a child maintenance disregard for those on family credit but not on income support, and more recently a disregard of child care costs, again only for those on family credit. However, without access to training, job opportunities and greater provision of child care such incentives have limited practical value and there has been criticism that many lone mothers are still worse off financially in paid employment. There has also been some questioning of the presumption that lone mothers should be seeking employment rather than giving their time and attention to looking after their children at home. What most parents want, whether in one or two parent households, is the choice of whether to take up paid employment to provide for their families or for a parent to stay at home and look after the children.

Other factors relating to work patterns also have an impact on parenting. The call to the unemployed to 'get on your bike' to find a job has had mixed results, with commuter parents working and living in one part of the country during the week and separated from their family during that time. Little research has been undertaken on the possible stress and disruption to children whose fathers or mothers work away from home, returning only at weekends, a concept known as 'weekending' amongst the armed forces, Members of Parliament and other commuting parents. There are many other occupations, for example, oil rig workers doing a 'three week on, three week off shift', where children may be separated from one of their parents for varying lengths of time, which has implications for the parenting role of both parents. It has long been recognised (through educational allowances, and free or assisted places) that boarding schools could provide stability for children whose parents were regularly on the move, such as clergy, the armed forces or diplomatic services and some senior managers in multinational companies. However, there is little information on the effect on children or on the relationships between the parents, or between parent and children, of possible family disruption caused by the regular separation and return of parents. Concern has been expressed at the high divorce rate within the armed services.

Whilst difficulties in balancing the demands of employment with the responsibility for family life are a challenge for many parents, for others the chances of a job seem very remote. In January 1993 unemployment levels topped three million, the highest total since 1986. Unemployment amongst men in their thirties, many of whom will be fathers, has increased dramatically by 93% to 474,600, roughly one fifth of the total. The probability of the long term unemployed man having a young family appears to be particularly high, partly because of the concentration of low-skilled workers amongst the unemployed and partly because low-skilled workers tend to have larger families (Irwin and Morris, 1993). A study in the late 1970s found also that couples with an unemployed husband were more likely than married couples in general to have pre-school children (Wood, 1982).

In households with a long-term unemployed male spouse, 83% of women aged under 25 were already parents, as were all women aged between 25 and 29. Women married to unemployed men are also less likely to be working, partly because of the disincentives through the benefit system which creates a structural division between 'work poor' and 'work rich' households (Irwin and Morris, 1993). In a study of couples, 60% of women with employed husbands were in paid employment, in contrast to 33% of women with unemployed husbands (Davies and others, 1991). It is unclear the extent to which young adults most extensively hit by the recession of the 1980s are now building families and what impact that may have on their role as

parents. Within the NCDS cohort 4% of the 33-year-olds were unemployed at the time of the survey in 1991 but 23% had experienced
some unemployment, with the men more likely to be unemployed
than the women and to be unemployed more often (Ferri, 1993).
Amongst minority ethnic groups, unemployment is particularly high,
comprising 13% compared to 7% for the general population
(Campling, 1993).

## A European perspective on work and family

The European Community has been consistently concerned about
equal opportunities for women and men in the labour market and
believes reconciliation of employment and family responsibilities is
fundamental to achieving this objective. Key issues that need
reconciling have been recognised as follows:

- increasing employment among women with children is not
  matched by changes in employment patterns of men with children
  which continue to be dominated by long hours which ignores the
  position of men in relation to employment and family
  responsibilities;
- solutions to work-family issues depend heavily on parents' ability
  to buy services or on employment benefits, so the extent and
  growth of inequalities both in jobs and income have major
  implications for the access of children and parents to services and
  other support measures;
- families are increasingly diverse and many workers may experience
  a period as a lone parent with implications for household income,
  and availability of time and support;
- most workers have responsibilities for children but increasing
  numbers will also have responsibilities arising from the care of
  dependent adults, especially elderly relatives;
- focusing on 'time at work' rather than a focus on outputs and
  outcomes. (Moss, 1992b; Simpson and Walker, 1993)

As a result of the work of the European Commission Childcare
Network, the Council of Ministers has adopted a Recommendation on
Childcare. Member states have been recommended to take or
encourage initia- tives in four areas to 'enable women and men to
reconcile their occu- pational, family and upbringing responsibilities
arising from the care of children':

- provision of child care services for children while parents are
  working, following a course of education or training;

- leave for employed parents;
- making the environment, structure, timing and organisation of work responsive to the needs of workers with children;
- promoting increased participation by men in the care and up-bringing of children.

The UK government must respond to this Recommendation by 1995 although it has consistently opposed European initiatives such as the introduction of parental leave and continues to view the provision of child care for children under five as the responsibility of parents (Moss, 1992b).

## Poverty and low incomes

A major issue for many parents is poverty. Government figures for 1990-91 reveal that nearly a third of children in the UK (3.9 million) were living on income below half the average (after housing costs) and that well over one-fifth of all children in the UK (2.7 million) were living on income support (DSS, 1993a: DSS, 1993b). Families with children have been particularly disadvantaged:

> During the 1980s, children bore the brunt of the changes which occurred in economic conditions, demographic structure and social policies in the UK. Most children were living in low income families and financial poverty doubled. Inequalities became more widespread. (Bradshaw, 1993)

In many households this is because one or both parents are un-employed. In others it is the low rates of pay or the growth of part-time as opposed to full-time jobs, which increases the need for both parents to take up paid work. Children of lone parents are particularly at risk of poverty because they are trapped on benefits, often unable to take up paid work because of the lack of appropriate or affordable child care. Families are grappling not only with financial poverty, but also 'fuel poverty' and 'water poverty' – reduced or no access to these commodities because of the cost of pre-payment meters and increased charges. It has been argued that a Code of Practice is needed to protect children from the increased health risks of dysentry now being observed as water, gas and electricity are cut off from families who can no longer afford them (SSAC, 1990; PUAF, 1990). The pressure on parents who are raising children with candles for lighting, oil stoves for heating and no running water for washing or toilet facilities must be very considerable.

Living in poverty inevitably creates social and material hardship and restricts the activities in which children can participate. A study to estimate the cost of living for families in the 1990s drew up three budgets. The low-cost budget, representing a very frugal level of living, cost £36 *more* per week than the Income Support scales. It was suggested that the government should review this low-cost family budget for claimants and identify which items they believe they should do without (Bradshaw, 1993). Many parents who have had to provide for their family on low incomes for long periods talk of suffering from stress, despair, ill-health and isolation. A child in a poor family is nearly twice as likely as a child in a well-off family to die before the age of one, a gap that has widened during the 1980s (Oppenheim, 1993; OPCS Mortality Statistics, 1988, 1989, 1990).

Coping on very little money often puts an extra stress on the relationship between parents and between parents and children. The links between poverty and poor physical and mental health have been well documented. A recent study of poverty and health concluded that whilst

> all parents, regardless of income, ethnic/cultural background or social class appear to start off holding very positive attitudes to child care and child health ... poverty and poor access to material resources have a powerful influence on the child care practices of parents. (Blackburn, 1991, p 146)

Whilst all parents share similar goals for their children, Blackburn and Mayall (1986) argue that material constraints affect their ability to realise their goals. A recent review of the changing financial circumstances of households with children notes that changes in the distribution of income, increasing unemployment, and changes in the social security system have resulted in a high level of unmet need and debt among parents caring for children on low incomes.

> For an increasing number of mothers, it appears that parenthood is structured around an unending conflict between caring enough and economising enough, trying to be a good enough mother who simultaneously meets and denies her family's needs. (Graham, 1994)

Minority ethnic families are likely to experience particular disadvantage.

> Overall, to be born into an ethnic minority in Britain – particularly a minority whose origins are in Bangladesh, the Caribbean or Pakistan – is to face a much higher risk of leading a life marked by a low income, repeated unemployment, poor health and housing, working for low wages with few employment rights and being forced to rely on social security benefits than someone who is white. For an Afro-Carribbean

or Asian women, the chances of being poor are even greater. (Amin, 1992)

For parents in paid employment the financial situation has also become worse. Families with young children have had an increased tax bill since April 1994, paying a higher proportion of their income than a single person to the Inland Revenue. The lack of a policy of financial investment in children and family life through an integrated tax and benefit system exacerbates the poverty trap for many. Some parents find themselves financially poorer when they take up paid employment because of tax and national insurance deductions, withdrawal or reduction of some benefits previously available to them in addition to the extra costs of actually going to work and arranging for child care. Such poverty clearly makes good parenting even more difficult, a point made by the Commission on Social Justice who argue that public policy must create the conditions that make it possible for both men and women to fulfil their parental responsibilities (Hewitt and Leach,1993).

The implementation of the Child Support Act 1991 has had a severe financial impact on both lone parents and many stepfamilies. Information from nearly 3,000 forms submitted to Citizens Advice Bureaux across the country suggests that lone parents and their children are not benefiting as much as the government had suggested they would when introducing the legislation (National Association of Citizen's Advice Bureaux, 1994) and some lone parents are actually worse off. A study by the Child Poverty Action Group (1994) argues that it is the Treasury rather than children who have benefited and that the incomes of many families have been reduced to benefit level and below. The initial lack of any phasing-in period, the delays incurred through the Child Support Agency and the apparent disregard of past agreements has plunged many stepfamilies – where men (primarily) have undertaken new family responsibilities, often for stepchildren as well as children in the new family, in good faith that a divorce settlement had been agreed – into debt and created tensions between ex-spouse, new partners and the children. The three year timetable for introducing this legislation has left some step-families assessed in 1993 for child support going out of the family but having to wait until 1996 for an assessment for child support coming into the family for stepchildren.

## Housing and homelessness

Having a warm, comfortable place to call home, a physically safe place for children to grow up is a basic requirement for all families. Significant changes have occurred in the housing scene since 1981, most of which will have affected families with children. Owner occupation has risen from 54% to 67% but the housing market slump, high rates of unemployment, redundancies and a deep economic recession has created pressures on many families, with increased risks of mortgage arrears, repossession, negative equity (owing more than the house was worth if sold) and being unable to sell, all reducing mobility or the ability to clear debts. During the 1980s there was a considerable reduction of accommodation in the private rented sector and a decrease in the number of local authority housing projects started. At the same time there was a sharp increase in rent levels in both the private sector and local authority. Clearly, higher rents will drive tenants who are low paid or unemployed into a deeper poverty trap. The UK has the lowest level of investment in housing of any EC country except Portugal. The Housing Act 1980 restricted the use of revenue from the sale of council accommodation and the only increase in social housing came following the 1988 Housing Act with the increased role of housing associations.

Research on housing issues reflects the desperate shortage of available accommodation and the increasing need. A study of the housing consequences of divorce, for example, estimated that 80,000 new homes are needed every year to keep up with the demand created by current divorce rates (Walker and others, 1991). The shortage of public sector housing has resulted in the law on homelessness being applied inconsistently, especially in response to women made homeless by domestic violence (Hague and Malos, 1993). The development of large new estates which house seriously disadvantaged tenants on low incomes is creating unbalanced communities in many areas with child densities three to six times the level recommended by the Department of Environment and the Home Office (Page, 1993). Young people are finding it particularly difficult to find and afford independent housing and the ability of parents to help young people financially is much lower than has been assumed (Pickvance and Pickvance, 1992). The withdrawal of state support for young people has put an additional burden on families as young people find it increasingly difficult to find a job, somewhere to live and make the transition to young adulthood independently. Some young people find the pressures at home unbearable and leave for an uncertain future on their own, often on the streets, jeopardising not only their prospects of higher education or a job but also for a minority running the risk of becoming involved in prostitution or crime in order to survive. A study of 400 young people who had left home showed 41% had spent time living on the streets before age 16. Although half had experienced some form of family breakdown, most cited 'arguments' rather than parents' separation, divorce or death as their specific reason for leaving (Stockley and Bishopp, 1993)

The number of families placed in temporary accommodation while waiting for permanent housing has risen sharply. There were over 55,000 households in this situation in the second quarter of 1991, 63% of whom had dependent children with a further 20% where the woman was pregnant (DoE, 1991). The prospects for these parents and children are grim and far removed from the 'permitting circumstances' which we discuss later in chapter 2 as necessary for healthy child development:

> Their families are often placed in overcrowded and poor living conditions, with a lack of basic amenities and playspace, resulting in strained family relationships and social isolation, and frequent ill-health and accidents. (Edwards, 1992)

They may also have poor access to health, education and other services (Conway, 1988).

# Who is looking after the children?

If so many mothers and fathers are working, and many families are evolving from two parent, to lone parent to stepfamily, who is looking after the children?

## Parents in employment

A recent survey of 14,000 parents revealed that their major source of anxiety was how to combine work and parenthood (Katz, 1994).

The majority of working parents rely on an informal network of friends and family to provide child care, which may include each parent providing child care while the other works (Cohen, 1990). Although there are more three and four generation families where grandparents and great-grandparents can help out, many grandparents are themselves working. Full time day care is not widely available, with places for less than 1% of children under five in publicly funded care and just over 1% in private day nurseries, with few places for children under 18-months-old. The greatest number of child care places are with registered childminders who provide places for just under 7% of children under five (National Children's Bureau, Early Childhood Unit, 1993). Forty seven per cent of children aged three to four years are in nursery education and primary schools and 35% in playgroups but these are almost all part-time and are not designed to meet the needs of working parents for child care. The Children Act 1989 encourages the development of family centres but these are more likely to provide programmes for parents and children together and support for vulnerable families rather than child care for working parents.

Such expansion as there has been in the last decade has been largely in the private day care sector, but without subsidies the costs are prohibitive to parents on low incomes. Although the shortage of day care is widely recognised, few employers have set up workplace nurseries because of the high cost as well as the limited number of employees who benefit. In 1990 only 3% of employers provided some form of child care with 2% offering child care allowances. Examples of employer-led initiatives include linked childminding schemes, a family advice and new parents project, job shares, career breaks and flexible working hours, and a community-based child care information and development service (Hogg and Harker, 1992). A grant of £45m has been made available through the TECs for the establishment of out-of-school schemes for school-age children and this is considerably expanding provision in this area.

Many European companies have found that family friendly policies make business sense as well as benefiting employees. Although there are different approaches to work and family issues there is some consensus on what it means to be 'a family friendly employer':

> One that recognises that the workforce is comprised of individuals with full and complex lives outside the workplace. A family friendly employer asks employees about their experiences and involves them in forming and implementing policies through effective communication and training. (Hogg and Harker, 1992, p 136)

Sadly, UK employers have been slow to adopt family friendly policies. Parents find they are expected to make their own arrangements and are pilloried if these are not judged suitable. A reminder of the barriers facing many parents is provided by the case of the lone mother, no longer able to afford a childminder but desperate to keep her job, who left her young child unattended all day whilst she went to work. She was subsequently jailed without apparent thought for the additional separation and distress that was being caused to her child. The particular stress on lone parents trying to be independent through paid employment should be an issue for public concern rather than one which parents are expected to cope with alone. The needs of children must also be addressed, as Leach points out:

Babies and young children have to be cared for by committed adults in suitable environments for 24 hours of every day. Society expects all able-bodied citizens of working age to earn the money they need and the satisfaction they crave at specialised all-day jobs in special, distant and unsuitable places. People cannot be in two places at once; ergo one person cannot be simultaneously a solvent, self-respecting citizen and an actively caring adult. (Leach, 1994)

## Separated parents sharing the care of their children

Married parents both retain parental responsibility for their children after separation or divorce. Although there is a presumption of co-operation between parents over the continuing care of their children, each can act independently of the other when the children are with them. The Children Act has provided the opportunity for many unmarried fathers to seek a parental responsibility order and establish their parental status and contact with their child. It is clear from recent research (McRae, 1993) that many cohabiting couples are unaware that an unmarried father does not automatically have parental responsibility unless he seeks to acquire this and there is a need for more public information on this issue. Although there are possibilities for shared residence orders the Courts have indicated it is important that a child should make a settled home with one of the parents and not pass to and fro between them, particularly where there are differences between the parents (Children Act Advisory Committee, 1993). We may be expecting too much from separated parents that they should share the care of their children in a cooperative way. Many manage 'parallel' parenting where they communicate very little with each other but provide as best as they can for their children whilst in their care. More research will be needed to see what the likely implications of such separate parenting may be upon children.

Since the majority of stepfamilies are created after separation and divorce rather than death, at least half of these parents will, in addition, be sharing the care of their child with their ex-partner. It is often this multiplicity of roles and responsibilities, which are rarely clear in terms of 'what you are supposed to do', that makes stepfamily life so difficult for so many (Robinson and Smith, 1993).

## Substitute care of children

On any one day in 1990 there were 13,200 children being looked after by social services departments in residential homes, and 34,000 in foster homes (National Children's Bureau, 1992). In addition some 115,000 children were at mainstream boarding schools, and approximately 30,000 at special boarding schools for pupils with special educational needs. Although fewer children are in residential care now compared to 20 years ago the average age of those being looked after is getting higher.

For children who have spent part of their childhood being looked after by people other than their own parents, families are still important and the majority will return home rather than move into independent living, even if they do not stay long and use the family as a bolt-hole or spring-board (Stein and others, 1993). The emphasis in the Children Act on parental responsibility and sharing care with families makes it even more important that parents are given adequate support by social workers, not only in keeping in touch with their children when they are in care, but in easing their return home. As Bullock and others (1993) point out, there is often a need to renegotiate family roles, to compromise and share territories, often with new adults and rival children, which can make returning home very stressful.

## The impact of recent legislation on parenting

There have been many changes in child, family and other social welfare legislation over the last ten years that have direct implications for parents. The most significant is the shift in emphasis signalled in the Children Act 1989 towards parental status rather than marital status, and towards parental responsibilities rather than rights. Four key factors contributed to the consensus around the Children Act 1989: the presumption of non-intervention in public and private matters; state paternalism and child protection, strengthening the powers of local authorities to provide more family support services; defence of the birth family and parents' rights; and children's rights (Fox Harding, 1991).

The Act is comprehensive, bringing together for the first time public and private law relating to children; it has a new philosophy of partnership and an emphasis on parental responsibilities which replace parental rights; and it embraces a wider range of children, including those with disabilities, in long term hospitals and independent boarding schools. All members of the family are acknowledged – the status and position of children, unmarried fathers, grandparents and other relatives are all enhanced, parents never lose their parental responsibility and are expected to behave responsibly and resolve disputes amicably. But there are still concerns. Some believe that the presumption of non-intervention and the emphasis on provision for child protection rather than for children in need leaves many parents and children without help and support when they need it. There is also a growing concern over false allegations of abuse made by children against adults, whether in a parental or professional capacity. Step-parents still have no legal recognition of their role even when providing daily parental care (Dimmock, 1992), although proposals within the Adoption Law White Paper (DOH, 1993) do propose access to a parental responsibility order for step-parents.

The Act requires separating parents to agree their own arrangements for the residence and continuity of contact with their children. The Courts will only become involved when the parents are unable to do so. It may be that the emotional and psychological stress parents experience at such a stage, in addition to the practical and financial problems, has been under-estimated. We may be expecting too much from parents to maintain a cooperative and conflict free relationship at the point when they have decided they cannot tolerate living with each other any longer (Walker, 1992). Some parents may be able to work together amicably and keep the children's interest foremost in their minds but many more are finding it extremely difficult especially where there is a history of violence, and may need advice and support through the separation process and a mediator to help them draw up arrangements for the children. We know from research that it is important for children to maintain continuity with both parents (Mitchell, 1985; Walczak, 1984) but to involve fathers as well as mothers in playing an active role in their children's lives, including parental responsibility through contact and financial support, may be unrealistic and too stressful for many parents unless more help is provided through mediation and contact centres.

This shift towards parental responsibility for children rather than rights over them has been matched with a commitment to children's rights. The UN Convention on the Rights of the Child emphasises that there should be a presumption in all policies and decisions concerning children to be guided by the principle of 'the best interest of the child'. Since implementation of the Children Act, children being looked after by the State have a legal right to be consulted on all decisions affecting them. Children whose parents are separating and divorcing should also be consulted about arrangements being made for contact and residence. There is however still considerable confusion amongst children and parents on certain issues, for example, whether girls under 16 years can be prescribed contraceptives without notifying their parents, and whether young people can be given advice and information on their sexuality by teachers or youth workers.

Another significant shift in the status of parenthood arises in relation to the adoption process. The White Paper (DOH, 1993) defines afresh the balance between the rights and interests of the child, the adoptive parents and the birth parents, in particular, ensuring that children are aware of their adoptive status, making arrangements to keep open the possibility of continuing contact between a child and birth parent, and supporting the new family relationship. There still appears to be concern amongst some social work personnel about the viability of continuing contact. This is sometimes to do with a misunderstanding of terms, of what might be arranged and much can be learned by giving more attention to how children in other situations cope, for example, step-parent adoptions where contact is maintained with the separated parent (Triseliotis, 1991).

The emphasis on parental responsibilities is reflected across recent and current government thinking and legislation. The view that parents need to have their responsibilities enforced if necessary is also manifested. The 1991 Criminal Justice Act amendment proposes that parents be fined £1000 if their children do not meet the requirements of the courts or probation orders. The Child Support Act 1991 has introduced a fixed formula to determine financial responsibilities for child support, on the assumption expressed by one Minister that 'men who remain financially involved with their children will be more likely to stay emotionally involved with them' (cited in Willetts, 1993). There have even been proposals to link child benefit to compulsory training in parenting skills (Ball, 1994), and for divorce to be made more difficult for those with children (Lord Chancellors Department, 1993).

In addition, there are assumptions within legislation that parents will and should take responsibility not only for the development and behaviour of their children but also for the running and provision of some services. The Education Act 1988 and subsequent education legislation gives parents new rights as well as new responsibilities. Parents are requested to vote on a range of issues, such as whether the school should opt out of local education control, or on matters such as sex education within the curriculum, or the election of parent governors. Since the Children Act requires head teachers to know who has parental responsibility in order to exercise it, this has raised issues over which parental figures and how many may be involved on an individual child's behalf.

The guidance to the NHS Community Care Act 1990 makes assumptions about the amount, duration and level of care that could or should be provided by families to disabled children or adults. Whilst this Act does not relate to children in general it clearly has implications for many ordinary families, as the presumption of family care may be impractical and impossible if the assumed carer is also a parent of dependent children and a paid worker. The Health of the Nation Strategy (DOH White Paper, 1992) expects parents to take responsibility for ensuring healthy surroundings and healthy life-styles for their children, but there is no right or access to affordable housing and adequate income to do this. Most parents know how to provide a nutritious diet but many items are not available at local shops and some just cannot afford them (Bradshaw and Holmes, 1989).

There has been a significant change in attitude and legislation away from support for families through the welfare state system to an expectation that families are responsible for their own welfare. But this belief that the nuclear family alone should care for all its members (young and old), to provide financially (both now and for their future) and to participate in local community provision and delivery of services is not feasible for many parents. Whilst increased rights and greater choice for parents are to be welcomed, parents also need additional support whilst raising children, not simply more responsibilities.

## Alternative routes to parenting

Alternatives routes to natural birth parenting have also changed. In 1977 there were 13,000 child adoptions. In 1991 not only had that total nearly halved to just over 7,000 but the proportion of step-parent adoptions increased and accounted for half of all adoptions, reducing the number of children adopted from outside the family to around 3,500 per year. The selection of adopters has also changed, reflecting the emphasis on children's rights and developmental needs rather than parents' desire for a family. For some prospective adopters or foster parents this may mean rejection because of their age, marital status, sexual inclination, personal habits or beliefs about child-rearing or apparent or alleged lack of racial awareness or religious tolerance.

For those who remain childless, developments in artificial insemination, embryo transfer, the use of aborted foetal tissue, infertility treatment and in vitro fertilisation, as well as surrogate motherhood and womb leasing, have progressed to such an extent that there is now growing concern over the substantial ethical issues being raised. These are not only about 'designer babies' where the colour, sex and other attributes can be determined, including the possibility for post-menopausal women to give birth, but there is also concern for the true genetic inheritance of some of these children. The bewildering array of choice and possibilities may reinforce the painful reminder of 'failure' to many who cannot conceive or bear a much-wanted child and for others a long and sometimes painful process before realising the dream of parenthood.

Where children require substitute parents other rights and responsibilities have been raised. The Children Act requires that a child's 'race, religion, language, and cultural background' be considered when making a placement with a fostering or adoptive family. There has been less clarity on how substitute parents will be selected or meet the needs of the child who may be of mixed ethnicity, religion or culture. What about a child with Catholic and Protestant parentage, or a black child of a Muslim and Anglican union? What will be considered the predominant factors in seeking a new family? The context of the resources, both financial and staff, available on the one hand (often an excuse for not seeking out a wider range of family placements) and the ideologically driven purists on the other (who insist particular selection criteria are always paramount over others) should never be allowed to obscure the needs of the particular child for a family household in which to develop as an individual (Smith and Berridge, 1994). More recent debates about whether childminders or substitute parents (either foster or adoptive) should be allowed to smoke or to smack has highlighted the tension between institutional care, substitute care and parental care. How a child is disciplined at home and the freedom to pursue personal pleasures such as smoking, are seen by many to be purely private matters, rather than a public concern for the protection of all children from both physical punishment and an unhealthy environment.

## Parents and professional experts

Most parents want to do their best for their child and worry about doing the 'right' thing. An unintended pressure on parents can be the relationship between parents and the considerable number of specialists, experts and professionals in the field of child care and family support they encounter through their child's life. A recurring theme in research reports, parents' discussion groups and descriptions of self-help and parent befriending schemes is that the attitudes of many professionals are tending to undermine parents' self-confidence and their belief in their own abilities, particularly where there may be misunderstandings over different social or cultural traditions of child-rearing. The increasing emphasis on parental responsibility for their child's behaviour and performance, and the number of different people who may have a parenting role for an individual child, is making some parents feel even more apprehensive about seeking help for fear of being criticised and judged. The finding of the Court Committee is as timely now as when it reported in 1976:

> The growth in the number and variety of professions connected with child rearing, however necessary in our kind of society, has in some measure undermined the self-confidence of parents....Professionals tend to gather a mystique to themselves which can be predicatory on the proper role of the layman....There is a case to be made at this stage of development of our society for stating the true relationship that should exist on behalf of children between their parents and other caring adults who affect the child and the family. Besides doctors and nurses, this applies to teachers, especially as nursery education develops, and to social workers. We feel especially keenly that services for the very young child must not be allowed to become over-professionalised: instead they should seek to work through the family, encouraging its strengths and helping in its shortcomings. There is overwhelming evidence that measures that do not involve parents achieve only short term gains. (Committee on Child Health Services 1976)

Whilst parents may feel outnumbered by professionals on the one hand, many say there seems to be little or no help at hand when they need it. All parents seek help from a range of different professionals at some point, whilst some parents continue to seek help as their children grow older and new areas of advice or information or forms of support are needed. However, it can be all too easy for professionals, especially when under stress from increasing case loads, to pathologise families under stress rather than recognise the normality of difficulties in child rearing and the value and effectiveness of offering family support services before a crisis. Frustration has been expressed that the high hopes for a range of family support services heralded by the Children Act 1989 for families with children in need, appear in many areas to be limited to those families in crisis where children have experienced or are likely to be at risk of physical or sexual abuse (Children Act Advisory Committee 1993). This is further compounded by competing local authority priorities, including child protection work, and an overall lack of resources to meet the intentions of the Children Act. The debate about family support has tended to polarise between universal child care to allow parents to be independent and work on the one hand, and social services family centres designed to prevent family breakdown and provide child protection on the other, with community based family centres usually run by voluntary organisations somewhere in the middle. There is evidence that day care may well be the most effective way of supporting some families through enabling parents to work (Gibbons, 1990). These issues are explored further in the chapters that follow.

# The way forward

One of the assumptions behind the welfare state was that parents required certain economic and social conditions in which to raise their families, the next generation. In particular, such conditions would include suitable housing, access to medical facilities, appropriate day care, an adequate family income through employment or welfare benefits, the opportunity for education and training. There are wider aims as well: insurance against risks like illness and unemployment; redistribution towards those with greater needs; smoothing out the level of income over the life cycle; and stepping in where the family 'fails' (Hills, 1993). Fundamental questions are now being asked about what kind of welfare state the UK should have and what can be afforded. Direct government spending on the main welfare services (education, housing, health, personal social services and social security) reached nearly £160 billion in 1992-93 (Treasury, 1993). The welfare state is already targeted on those with lower incomes and the debate now is not about whether to target but how to do so and how to avoid the side-effects, such as the poverty, unemployment or savings traps. The debate on tax-benefit integration continues with revised models for providing a guaranteed minimum income for most of the population (Atkinson, 1993).

Legislation, whilst giving new rights as well as new responsibilities to parents, is still dominated by a model of the traditional family of working father and mother caring for the children that is no longer the norm. The criticism and punitive measures towards lone parents and single mothers suggested by some politicians not only ignore the needs of their children but conflict with recommendations from research and practice in the child care field that parents need additional support rather than less when raising children alone. It may be unsettling to know that increasingly couples are choosing to have babies without being married, to separate and divorce, and to create new partnerships or remarry but legislation cannot make people marry, or love one another, or be good parents or stay together until the children are young adults. Legislation and good policies can, however, enhance the status of parenthood and value parenting by ensuring that families are supported in their role through family friendly employment practices, tax and benefit allowances that reflect the costs of child upbringing, housing policies, child care and nursery education provision, personal and social development in the school curriculum, sex education which can reduce unwanted pregnancies, community support and preventive health and welfare services.

Family matters and successful parenting are major political issues. In the Foreword of *The Citizen's Charter*, John Major wrote:

> The Citizen's Charter is about giving more power to the citizen. But citizenship is about our responsibilities – as parents, for example, or as neighbours – as well as our entitlements. (1991)

If opportunities and entitlements for some parents are eroded it is more difficult for them to meet their increasing responsibilities.

As the Audit Commission report (1994) on community child health and social services for children in need reminds us, whilst the prime responsibility for the well-being of children rests with parents, the state provides support at three levels: universal services; select support for families needing rather more help (because of poor housing, ill-health, anxiety, stress, low income or unemployment); and, occasional intervention to protect children's welfare. Legislative changes – the NHS and Community Care Act 1990, the Children Act 1989, and the 1990 GP contract (and one may add the 1988 and 1993 Education Acts, though education was not considered by the Audit Commission) – are now requiring major adjustments in the way agencies discharge their responsibilities and relate to each other, and to families. The way in which professionals relate to parents, and the ability of health, education and social services to work collaboratively towards shared objectives, are both essential ingredients in a coherent programme of preparation, education and support for parents.

The preamble to the UN Convention on the Rights of the Child stresses that:

> The family, as the fundamental group in society and the natural environment for the growth and well being of all its members and particularly children, should be afforded the necessary protection and assistance so that it can fully assume its responsibilities within the community.

The model of partnership between parents and the State reflects a recognition of the social responsibility which all citizens carry for children and acknowledges the need for social support to enhance the opportunities of all children within their family wherever possible. Article 18.2 states that the government must provide 'assistance to parents ... in the performance of their child rearing responsibilities and shall ensure the development of institutions, facilities and services for the care of children.' The following chapters will indicate how and where such provision is developing.

# 2. Parents and parenting

> ...in order to raise a child well one ought not to try to be a perfect parent, as much as one should not expect one's child to be, or to become, a perfect individual. Perfection is not within the grasp of ordinary human beings. Efforts to attain it typically interfere with that lenient response to the imperfections of others, including those of one's child, which alone make good human relationships possible. (Bettelheim, 1987 p ix)

Most children live in small family households with their parents and perhaps one or two siblings, but who is actually looking after the children, doing and sharing the parenting, may vary considerably between families. Responsibility may be shared between the two parents, one of whom may not be living in the family home anymore, or shared with a childminder, a nanny, a friend or relative, or a step-parent. Although it will be clear who is and is not a child's biological parent, it may not always be clear who is and is not doing the parenting. The experience of parenting an individual child is also different according to the age, gender, personality, particular characteristics and abilities of both the child and parent and the relationship that develops between them and with others. And circumstances do make a difference: a parent living alone has all the day to day responsibility and maybe no-one with whom to share the good times and the bad ones; a mother or father who is not at home when children return from school may regret missing the immediacy of hearing of the day's events.

Just what does the job of being a parent entail? To do any job well it helps to know what is expected, an understanding of why the job is important, the skills to do it and the bare necessities and circumstances to get started. Despite the entreaty of Bruno Bettelheim that we should not strive to be perfect this is exactly what many parents feel they **are** doing. Society does expect a great deal from parents and the media, politicians and others are quick to criticise when parents are seen to fall short of that ideal. If we were to advertise the position of parent it might well look like this:

**WANTED:** *A responsible person, male or female, to undertake a life-long project. Candidates should be totally committed, willing to work up to 24 hours daily, including weekends during the initial 16-year period. Occasional holidays possible, but may be cancelled at no notice. Knowledge of health care, nutrition, psychology, child development, household management and the education system essential. Necessary skills: stress management and conflict resolution, negotiation and problem solving, communication and listening, budgeting and time management, decision making, ability to set boundaries and priorities as well as providing loving support. Necessary qualities: energy, tolerance, patience, good self-esteem, self-confidence and a sense of humour. No training or experience needed. No salary but very rewarding work for the right person.*

How many of us would apply for the job? We all want children to have the best start in life but is it possible for parents to match up to the high hopes that often surround parenthood? Surely it is not realistic to expect everyone to be the perfect parent any more than we would expect every child to be perfect. The key issue is how parents can feel confident that they are 'good enough' in helping their children develop appropriate skills, knowledge and qualities, in the light of the many constraints and influences within families. The most critical of these factors will be firstly, the effect of the parent's own childhood experiences, and secondly the social, environmental and economic circumstances in which mothers and fathers are trying to raise their children. Parents need to be supported and valued by society, as well as feeling that looking after their children is a valuable and rewarding job in itself.

Although there may be no universal definition of what constitutes a 'family' there are common values and norms that parents aim to uphold in a variety of diverse ways to provide a stable and secure upbringing for their children. There are thus many ways of organising family life that will reflect social and cultural differences; family patterns are changing and it is important not to make unjustified assumptions about what is and is not appropriate.

## From partners to parents – the challenges of becoming a parent

Individual life chances, childhood experiences, career development and personal relationships obviously vary. However, the birth of a first child is a highly significant event and it has been suggested that the transition to parenthood can produce a crisis for many couples (Lemasters, 1959). Certainly there is research that shows pre-marital pregnancy and the conception of a child soon after marriage are predisposing factors towards subsequent marriage breakdown (Rutter and Madge, 1976; Thornes and Collard, 1979). Other research shows an association between the presence of children and a deterioration in the quality of the parents' marriage especially in the early years (Michaels and Goldberg, 1988; Moss and others, 1986) and as Clulow (1982) observes 'even wanted children can throw marital partnerships into disarray.' A study of 100 first time fathers indicated that the men had little awareness of the extent to which a baby would change their lives; they failed to appreciate the impact of the loss of the woman's earnings; and they grossly underestimated the direct costs of babies and children (Jackson, 1984). Clearly there is a need to prepare couples for the practical reality of parenthood.

Are some partnerships and marriages more able to cope with the tensions and stress of becoming parents? Bernard (1976) pointed out that any marriage has two perspectives – his and hers. Clulow and Mattinson (1989) also show that while it is possible for men and women to contract an equal partnership in marriage, while they have only themselves to consider, the situation changes radically when there are children: 'Marriage and parenthood are two distinct institutions, and parenthood works to reassert traditional divisions of labour between the sexes.' A recent comprehensive review of changes in marriage and family life by sociologists describe some couples as having a 'companionate' marriage with many shared interests and a high degree of satisfaction from these shared activities, and others as having 'differentiated' marriages where roles are separately defined and spouses find satisfaction primarily from activities and relationships outside the marriage (Clark, 1991). It would appear that those with differentiated marriages fare better in the transition to parenthood where, as noted above, parenthood works to reassert divisions of labour rather than shared activities.

The need to be able to adapt to changing demands, whether from the couple themselves, from external factors or by the arrival of children, is highlighted in a study of 65 young couples begun in 1979 to observe their pathways into marriage and different forms of partnership (Mansfield and Collard, 1988). A different study with a group of couples expecting their first child began at the same time in California (Cowan and Cowan, 1992). The findings have been remarkably similar. Where the baby was planned the transition to parenthood was smoother. Where one or both partners were ambivalent the relationship began to be affected. Wives felt different once they became mothers and their lives as husbands and wives started to diverge. The different levels of involvement inside and outside the home led couples to feel more distant, less together. Almost all the British couples found the transition to parenthood stressful: a quarter were 'managing well', a half were 'coping', and a quarter were 'surviving'. The couples who managed best already had partnerships founded on parenting, a differentiated marriage where they actively renegotiated their partnership in relation to the demands of children and the practical realities of earning a living and keeping a home (Mansfield and others, forthcoming).

Whilst research on fatherhood is limited there have been a number of studies looking at fathers' attitudes towards pregnancy and there seems to be a general expectation that most fathers (but clearly not all) will attend the birth of their child. Four typical reactions have been identified by researchers: 'refusers', who regard pregnancy as 'women's business' and prefer to remain purely in the role of providers; 'observers', benevolent but detached with a traditional view of men's and women's responsibilities in relation to babies; 'sharers', almost 50% of the group, wanting to share the experience as fully as possible; 'identifiers', who would really have liked to have had the baby themselves (Richman and Goldthorpe, 1978; Jackson, 1984). Unfortunately the 'sharers' group expressed frustration that the warmth and closeness reported with mother and baby was often 'dissipated by the insensitive intrusion of medical staff and female relatives and by the demands of work.' (Jackson, 1987) Similarly another study of 100 first and second time fathers reported that they felt confused and alienated by the information addressed to them and excluded by the official agencies – clinics, preparation classes and procedures on the labour ward (Lewis and others, 1982)

## Influences on parenting

The increasing demands on parents today are many and varied. One is our **ever-developing knowledge of children's physical, intellectual, social and emotional development** and of the importance of growing up in a secure yet stimulating environment, especially during the early years of childhood. Research brings us a steady stream of new insights into the development, behaviour, feelings and capabilities of infants and young children causing us constantly to review our perceptions and our knowledge of the needs of children and the ways in which these might best be met. But there are still considerable gaps in our knowledge, many different ways of interpreting what we do know, and areas of conflicting information or a reversal of the perceived ways in which things were done in the past. One of the most dramatic examples of this is the physical safety advice on changing the sleeping position of babies which resulted in a drop of 50% in cot deaths in 1992 (FSID, 1993).

A growing **cross-cultural** literature from anthropology, sociology and psychology points to the immense variations in child-rearing practices and beliefs (see for example, Konner, 1991; Myers, 1992; Schieffelin and Ochs, 1991; Woodhead, 1990). Researchers point out that current theories of child development, and perceptions of children's needs – and thus advice for parents about appropriate child-rearing practices – do not always recognise the variations between cultures, societies and classes. Woodhead, for example, argues that alongside empirical claims about the needs of children, we should take care to examine personal and cultural values as well as those within the context within which the children are being brought up. Most patterns of caregiving described in the psychological literature are white, middleclass.

As the Commission for Racial Equality (CRE) points out, it is important when assessing children's development and parents' skills that only relevant norms and criteria are used, which:

> respect and value the diversity of childrearing patterns and family customs. Otherwise it is possible that parents with different childrearing traditions may be judged to be inadequate parents. Perceived lack of control for strict bedtimes, for example, may be a failure to acknowledge the importance placed by a family on being together in the evenings rather than being separated by defined bedtimes....While there may be some childrearing practices that might universally be regarded as unacceptable (for example, smacking), none should be assessed using criteria based on racial grounds. There is no single 'best' way to bring up a child, and there are as many differences in childrearing practices among white and among black families as there are between them. (CRE, in press)

There is also the growing awareness of the **crucial role that both parents play in their children's development.** This book is explicitly about parenting, a term which has often been criticised as really meaning mothering. Clearly many of the schemes we have found, ostensibly for parents, have indeed been directed mainly at mothers, or it has been only or primarily mothers who have chosen to use them. Traditionally, the rearing of children has been seen as women's business, performed by mothers not in paid employment, and many services are still only provided during working hours on weekdays making it very difficult for many working mothers as well as fathers to use them. Are there differences between mothers and fathers, mothering and fathering or is it acceptable to use the terms parents and parenting to encompass both?

Over the past decades a great deal has been written about motherhood from a variety of perspectives: developmental psychology, focusing on mothers' attitudes and interactions; child care manuals, telling women how to do it; research on the transition to motherhood; autobiographical writings giving personal experiences; feminist texts, exploring social structure and gender issues (Phoenix and others, 1991). The power of the mother and child 'madonna' image appears to be strong in most cultures and traditions, the concept of mothering appears to be one of the universals of humankind and most women do still become mothers. Whilst women may be having fewer children and participating more fully in the labour market, the 'myth' of exclusive mothering and of the centrality of mothering in a woman's life remains (Schaffer, 1990).

There has however been increased interest in the father/child relationship in recent years, sometimes springing from a concern over the increasing numbers of children being reared without a constant father figure. Although there is a growing body of literature on the role of fathers this has mainly focused on the experience of fatherhood at the time of the birth and male domesticity, accentuated by the ideology of the 'new man' who is involved in his children and their care as well as in the housework. A review of fatherhood research suggests that despite the wave of optimism 'the evidence for the existence of such a man is much less convincing' (Lewis and O'Brien, 1987). Not only is the evidence for the 'new man' or 'new father' hard to find but the paternal role is being limited by social, institutional and personal forces. While individual parents may be aware of the importance of the shared parental roles the opportunities are limited and pressures are brought by employment practices and child care services which assume the mother as primary carer and the influence of other family members.

No single study has set out to measure paternal involvement over many years. It is likely that our ambivalence over the father's role, while continuing to emphasise how important his role is, has changed little over the decades as this comment from a book in the 1950s highlights:

> As one reviews recent books and articles in the field of family life which make specific reference to the father's role, one finds that while some authors see today's fathers as further removed from the family, others quite to the contrary observe that he has found his way back to the

family and shares actively and creatively many activities with his wife
and children. (Dybwad, 1952)

In the 1970s, it was believed that a new family type was evolving,
described as the symmetrical family, with an equal sharing of
domestic and child care roles which was being seen in the professional
classes and expected to filter down the social scale (Young and
Willmott, 1973). However, as we saw earlier, parenthood tends to
accentuate the division of tasks and roles within a partnership. While
men appear to have become more involved around the time of childbirth they still tend to be seen primarily in the role of providers and
certainly most economic, welfare, social and employment policies and
practices are still geared towards the image of the father as the head of
the household and the mother as primarily responsible for child care,
even if she is also in full-time paid work. This maintains the image of
father as a figure with a distant 'work' location with child care and
housework seen as voluntary activities. This not only further
reinforces gender divisions between the couple and within the family
but influences family relationships:

> The ways in which fathers relate to children stems from their social
> position in the family. Their privileged status, authority, rewards and
> access to resources as men, relative to women, allows for a particular
> form of involvement. They play rather than carry out the more
> mundane tasks. They select what they do and the commitment they feel
> they are willing and able to make; mothers are left with the rest.
> (Pollock and Sutton, 1985)

There have been relatively few studies of families where fathers are the
main, or sole, child carers, or of the issues facing men with young
children. At a time when there has been an unprecedented movement
of women into the labour market, male unemployment has risen
dramatically (particularly in certain geographical areas) and the
majority of new jobs are being taken by women. Despite this move
towards equality in the workplace, it would appear that there has not
been a parallel move towards equality in the home. A study by
Brannen and Moss (1991) found that on average, full-time working
mothers spent 28 hours alone with their children each week, while
their partners managed only six hours. A recent study of 14,000
parents found that three quarters of mothers who worked and who had
a partner still did most of the housework (Katz, 1994).

But men have had reasons to encourage research and the debate on
fathering and fatherhood:

- the focus on mother/infant and mother/child relationships is

becoming so extreme and imbalanced that researchers are beginning to question whether fathers are relevant;
- concern over changes in childrearing and family structure high-lights how little is known about father/child relationships in the family;
- modern fathers do not want to be peripheral in the lives of their children;
- although full-time mothers spend more time with the children than working fathers there is a tendency to exaggerate the extent of actual interaction between mother and child;
- time spent with children is not linearly related to the amount of influence they have, evidenced by the daily separation of increasing numbers of working women;
- the quality of the interaction and adult behaviour is being seen as more important than the quantity of time (Lamb, 1981).

The debate about mothering and fathering is still ambivalent. Some equate parenting with child care which can be performed equally by either gender, whilst others are concerned with the different experiences of being parented by a man and by a woman. It is argued that men and women bring different qualities, styles and forms of interaction with a child and the father/child relationship should not be perceived as just an extension of maternal care (Sommer, 1993). It is not that men and women cannot undertake the tasks of parenting which (apart from breast feeding) are gender neutral but rather in what ways do children experience similar situations with their father or their mother. Some differences may arise whether from gender traditions, personality characteristics, own childhood upbringing, the bonding between child and parent or society's expectations. The importance of these differences should not be underestimated since the lack of fathering can also have a profound impact on the quality of mothering, particularly for boys (Miedzian, 1992), and the ability of mothers to feel confident in their role of parenting boys especially when there appears to be no socially sanctioned way for boys to show anxiety and seek help (Phillips, 1993). As Sommer points out:

> If the culture is saturated with an indifferent or clearly negative attitude to a close father-child relationship this will become part of the actors' own self-perceptions. This may in turn result in the relationship being felt to be of little importance or simply problematic even if the relationship actually works very well on a day to day basis. It is therefore of vital importance that traditional attitudes to fatherhood (and motherhood) are considered and discussed at several levels and not just 'privatised', ie left for discussion and negotiation between the sexes in the individual family. (p 166)

In reviewing British research on fatherhood, Jackson (1987) comments that there has been a tendency to aim for normality and that the gaps in research noted by McKee and O'Brien (1982) largely remain: 'Fathers of older children, fathers in communal and cohabiting units, black fathers, and grandfathers scarcely appear in the literature, nor do the growing numbers of unemployed fathers'. Missing from that list and one context in which the particular relationship of fathers and children have been observed is that of post-divorce fathering. Research following a group of 91 fathers, divorced in 1986, not living with their children post-divorce show the very real difficulties that can confront men who want to stay in touch with their children after separation. Some of the fathers had achieved successful adjustments but the researchers identified four closely related areas of profound loss expressed by them (Simpson and others, 1993):

- **loss of control,** in explicit areas of decision making such as education, schooling, health care; in the maintenance of order and structure within the family; in more subtle areas of passing on identity from parents to children of religion, manners, morals, values; an inability in terms of discipline to harmonise rules, boundaries, and sanctions;
- **loss of intimacy** and a sense of emotional distance, often linked to practical difficulties of contact being in a public place, or bed-sit, or home of a friend or relative; an artificiality where intimacy and closeness remained illusive; and where father and child had been suddenly and temporarily separated (because of the mother's unexpected death) getting to know your child again;
- **loss of routine,** the daily routine of child care and home making; the mutual familiarity and predictability of a relationship 'bonded' in the minutiae of daily interaction; just being around; involved in the routine of collecting from school or activities, spending quiet, ordinary and uneventful time with their children, time not premeditated or scheduled;
- **loss of role,** and of ambiguity; of only being fathers when they are with their children; of fatherhood becoming a conscious role; of being the one who is there to answer questions, help solve problems, give directions; of feeling dispensable.

It is likely that mothers separated from their children would experience the same sense of loss. There is a gender difference, as we noted earlier, with fathers finding it easier to maintain contact and relationships with their sons rather than their daughters. Fathers are three times more likely to have lost contact with children if they were all girls, or as the song from *Carousel* says 'you can have fun with a son, but you've got to be a father to a girl'. It seems that mothers rearing boys also find it harder to be a mother to a son (Phillips, 1993). And in step-relationships a reverse pattern has been found where same gender relationships may be seen as competing with the birth mother or father (Robinson and Smith, 1993). Interestingly an Australian study of the relationship 66 children had with their separated father and stepfather found the children tend to be involved with both or have little involvement with either (Funder and others, 1992).

The traditional role of men – that they earn the money and control the family finances – has become a major issue for many men in areas of high unemployment. This is confronted in a particular way in a stepfamily where some of the money for both the children and their mother will come from another man through child support. A man whose outlook and expectations are traditional may well feel his role as provider is undermined (Robinson and Smith, 1993) which is consistent with the sense of loss described in the study above.

Attention has been focused in the early 1990s by a highly publicised coalition of New Right political economists and ethical socialist sociologists on children growing up in families without fathers. They highlight the disadvantages of lone parenthood, cite fathers as a controlling influence and protective factor in deprived homes, express concern at the emergence of a new young male unable or unwilling to acknowledge the responsibilities of spousehood and fatherhood and claim that 'families without fathers produce egoists' (Dennis and Erdos, 1993). Firm parenting, as we note below, is a factor in limiting offending behaviour, but the level of violence and abuse within families is also a significant reason why some women chose to separate from their partners.

Clearly, there is a need for much more awareness of the qualities that men and women bring together and separately to the upbringing of children, both in terms of research and providing practical support and services, and in developing policies that enable mothers and fathers to share parenting and work responsibilities. As Phillips (1993) notes commenting on the importance of effective father role models:

> If men had applied themselves to fathering with the same diligence as women moved into the world of work we should be well on the way to producing a generation of young men and women with a rich reservoir of useful early memories to draw on for images of father love. (p 147)

High expectations on parents to bring up their children adequately put considerable demands on many parents. Stereotypes of good and bad parents have persisted throughout history. Many support programmes are aimed at mothers, as in reality they are generally the primary day to day carers of children, so mothers, in particular, have to contend not only with the role of super-woman and the emphasis on parents' responsibility for the way their children turn out but also the challenge to their perceived role and authority. The Newsoms (1976) summarised these tensions and demands when they pointed out how comparatively simple it was for parents to satisfy society's demands when the emphasis was upon hygiene and firmness, and when the parental ethic included the dictum that 'mother knows best'. It is much more difficult when parents are asked to recognise the child's emotional and egotistical needs as valid while still giving a moral framework of principles and, moreover, to present this in a democratic context which acknowledges that mother might not know best.

In this shift away from the more authoritarian view of the parent, there is a danger not only that parents are becoming undermined in their roles but that some have swung too far, and in focusing exclusively on the egotistical needs the children can be cast in the role of tyrants. One mother described her experience in a parent support group:

> I had to play what games he (sic) wanted, watch what he wanted on television, listen to what he wanted on the record player and, of course, he got to have very high expectations of me as entertainer. And I'd be sitting there feeling really bullied. (Sokolov and Hutton, 1988)

This tendency to see good parenting as giving way to what children want rather than to setting boundaries, or as another writer describes it as a battle between the child's struggle for independence and the parent's difficulty in letting go, seems only to result in guilt;

> Parents who have put their children's needs before their own needs in every way are terrified that they might not have done 'enough'. In some ways they are doing too much. (Jackson, 1993)

Too many parents, particularly fathers, are confused about their role, feel inadequate to deal with society's increasingly materialistic and individualistic expectations and have lost sight of what is good enough parenting – which includes setting clear and consistent boundaries for children.

# What do children need from parents?

Do we actually know what children need, in order that we can help the parents meet those needs. Many psychologists, educators, health professionals and others have described the basic needs of children which the 'good enough' parent seeks to meet. Cooper (1985) drawing on the work of the Bureau's founder, Mia Kellmer Pringle (1975) summarises these as follows:

a. **basic physical care** which includes warmth, shelter, adequate food and rest, grooming (hygiene) and protection from danger;

b. **affection** which includes

- physical contact, holding, stroking, cuddling and kissing, comforting,
- admiration, delight, tenderness,
- patience,
- time,
- making allowances for annoying behaviour,
- general companionship and approval;

c. **security** which involves

- continuity of care,
- the expectation of continuing in the stable family unit,
- a predictable environment,
- consistent patterns of care and daily routine,
- simple rules and consistent controls,
- a harmonious family group;

d. **stimulation of innate potential** by

- encouraging curiosity and exploratory behaviour,
- developing skills through responsiveness to questions and to play,
- promoting education opportunities;

e. **guidance and control** to teach adequate social behaviour which includes discipline within the child's understanding and capacity, and which requires patience and a model for the child to copy, for example, in honesty and concern and kindness for others;

f. **responsibility** for small things first, such as self-care, tidying play things or taking dishes to the kitchen, and gradually elaborating the decision making the child has to learn in order to function adequately, gaining experience through his mistakes as well as his successes, and receiving praise and encouragement to strive and do better;

g. **independence** to make his own decisions, first about small things, but increasingly about the various aspects of his life within the confines of the family and society's code. Parents use fine judgement in encouraging independence and in letting the child see and feel the outcome of his own poor judgement and mistakes, but within the compass of his capacity. Protection is needed, but over-protection is as bad as too early responsibility and independence. (p 60-61)

The quality of relationships that children experience are also crucial, between the child and each parent as well as with other key people in their lives. These are not always easy to define but as Pearce (1991) suggests, in setting out some of the positive and negative qualities below, it is also possible to see that these are not unique to parents and can be supplemented by others.

| Positive qualities | Negative qualities |
|---|---|
| warm and affectionate | cold and hostile |
| clear limit setting | inconsistent care |
| quick to recognise needs | unresponsive to needs |
| accepting of faults | rejecting |
| predictable and consistent | unpredictable |
| respecting the individual | disrespectful |
| recognition of good qualities | emphasis on bad qualities |

We could continue to expand such summaries by adding to them the 'building blocks of parenting' upon which Bavolek (1990) bases his nurturing programme for families who have abused or neglected children. His blocks include:

— **bonding and attachment,** the process of establishing an unconditional positive regard and acceptance of the child;
— **empathy,** the ability to see the world through another's eyes, and to consider the other as an equal, described by Bavolek as the single quality most critical to the overall growth and well-being of the child;
— **self-awareness,** for to be empathic to the needs of others, one needs to be clear about one's own needs;
— **touch,** gentle, calm, nurturing touch which communicates to the child a sense of trust, kindness and security;
— **discipline,** or setting clear limits for children;
— **unconditional love,** honesty and respect, for 'parenting is the process of helping children feel accepted by people without regard to their behaviour';
— **developmental knowledge,** knowing what to expect of children at their various stages of growth and development.

Children also need a sense of their own **identity and history.** For some this means being aware of their parentage and extended family because their parents have separated or because they are adopted. For many others, however, it is that while their children may be born in Britain their cultural, ethnic or religious roots may be different from the white Protestant or Roman Catholic traditions that predominate. Parents have the additional task of working out how to bring awareness of their particular identity and history whilst helping children to feel they belong to the community in which they live. Children, on the whole, like to feel they are the same as others, and that they are valued. Being black in a predominantly white country presents difficulties to many children. Research has shown that children as young as three or four distinguish between black and white and give different values to them (Milner, 1983). We have already noted the importance of being sensitive to cultural differences in child-rearing.

The development of separate schools, but more often Saturday schools, for a wide range of cultural and religious groups has highlighted the importance given by parents to maintaining both language and culture. Some of the tensions that may arise within families as the children reach adolescence and start to establish their own vision of who they are has been less acknowledged. For example, not all cultures see the teenage years as normally and necessarily a quest for independence leading to enhanced individual autonomy and the inevitable separation from the family group. Most Asian and Middle-Eastern families see such teenage years as the transition to adulthood which entails greater responsibility towards others in the household. For many parents this can be a painful moment when children sometimes feel they must choose between one culture or the other rather than celebrate the best of both.

Two other important aspects of responding to the needs of children should be highlighted. The first is to recognise that **parenting is a two-way process**. The way children turn out is often blamed on parents, but the impact that the child makes on the parent and the way that children themselves behave will affect how that child is brought up. An only child has a different experience of parents and family life than a child with one or more siblings. Each child is unique with their own personal qualities and idiosyncrasies. As any parent knows, children in the same family often behave very differently from each other and boys may behave differently from girls. Thus, whilst some specific behaviour in children can be linked to parenting styles, it is important to recognise that some children may present far greater challenges to their parents than others, and the emotional turmoil created may make it more difficult for a parent to act as rationally as they may wish. Child and family therapists are aware that an individual child may become a scapegoat when a family is in difficulties and may be seen to be the cause of their problems. The relationship between each parent and each child will also be different and needs to be acknowledged in any attempt to change parenting styles. As Schaffer (1977) describes in his book on mothering:

> Change cannot be imposed from outside; it can only start from within the relationship between parents and child and thus becomes a matter of *mutual* adjustment. The two modify each other continually; they grow with each other. Socialisation is a two-way, not a one-way business: like education, it is essentially a joint venture. (p 84)

The other issue is **time,** or as Haim Ginott (1965) put it 'don't just say something, stand there!' Finding adequate time to listen and talk to children, to do things together, to be there when needed, is one of the most difficult tasks for today's parents. As noted in chapter 1, one of the central issues of the 1990s is the struggle for both men and women to combine work and parenthood. A recent report reflects on the fact that the time the average American parent spends with their children has nearly halved in the last 25 years, although given the smaller family size today and less time spent on laborious household chores that can now largely be automated, this should be treated with caution. The author calls on governments and parents to reduce the 'parenting deficit' (Etzioni, 1993): for 'parenting cannot be carried out over the phone, however well meaning and loving the calls may be ... quality time takes place within quantity time'. Clearly for parents living away from their children both are important, the phone calls to maintain the relationship and the quality time to enrich it. This theme is echoed by Leach (1994) who argues for a realignment of work and parenting: 'the less time parents and children spend together, the fewer thoughts and activities they share, the more powerful secondary influences will be.'

## 'Good enough' or confident parenting

The term 'good enough' parenting, first coined by Donald Winnicott when he was writing about 'good enough' mothers, and more recently adopted by Bruno Bettelheim as the title of his book *A Good Enough Parent* (1987) recognises a central concept of this book – that although all parents want to do the best for their children, there is no single right way to bring up children, no rigid set of rules by which all 'good' parents should abide. As Bettelheim argues, parents should think for themselves and respond to their own child, helping him or her to develop into the person he or she wishes to be, rather than become a creation of the parents' making. This is sensible advice, but if we are arguing for the development of support and education for parents, then we need to be clear about what skills, knowledge and understanding are likely to be most helpful. We thus draw on research, much of it deriving from work with families where relationships have broken down or children have become very disruptive or broken the law, to paint some broad strokes in our picture of the 'good enough' parent.

We have already summarised the main needs of children that parents are responsible for meeting, and have earlier noted that defining needs has to be seen in the context of social and cultural differences between families – what kind of children do we as a society or we as individual parents want? But it is clear from research that the quality of relationships within families, and the style and nature of parenting, are far more important for children's healthy development than particular types or structures of families (Schaffer, 1990, Burghes, 1994). As the Commission on Social Justice point out:

> Instead of the current nostalgic obsession with family structures, we need to concentrate on family functioning. The issues at stake is good enough parenting, not how that is provided. As the research on marriage, cohabitation, divorce and lone parenting consistently shows, children thrive in any kind of family where there is consistent love and nurturance, support and discipline, and in no kind of family where those qualities are missing. (Hewitt and Leach, 1993)

Drawing on American research into how healthy families function (Lewis and others, 1976), and on a life time of family therapy, Robin Skynner and John Cleese in their best seller *Families and How to Survive Them* (1983) describe a number of characteristics of successful families: closeness and intimacy alongside self-sufficiency and self-confidence; clear parental authority and responsibility for making decisions while making sure the children were always consulted fully; straightforward direct, open communication and being honest with each other.

Other research is summarised by Gross (1989), who defines the outcomes of successful and unsuccessful parenting styles as follows:

- **over-protective** parents tend to have passive, submissive, dependent children;
- **permissive** parents tend to have aggressive, disobedient children;
- **authoritarian** parents tend not to internalise standards, and have low self-esteem;
- **authoritative** parents tend to have children who are compliant,

well-behaved, with a highly developed sense of right and wrong, who can resist temptation and accept blame.

A number of researchers in this country and the United States (Rutter, 1985; Wilson, 1987; Patterson, 1982; West and Farrington, 1982; Newson and Newson, 1974) have also identified factors which are – or may be – linked to unacceptable and sometimes criminal behaviour in children:

* lack of rules and clear boundaries;
* vague and confusing commands;
* inadequate supervision, with parents often not knowing where their children are;
* inconsistent discipline;
* empty threats (or bamboozlement as the Newsons describe it);
* conveying dislike for the child;
* ignoring good behaviour but punishing bad;
* lack of enjoyable shared experiences;
* conflict between parents;
* parents who are, or have been criminals;
* lack of adequate support systems for parents.

Other features which Bavolek (1990) describes from his work with parents who have abused or neglected their children include:

* inappropriate parental expectations of the child;
* inability of the parent to be empathetically aware of the child's needs;
* strong parental belief in the value of punishment;
* role reversal, with parents looking to the child for satisfaction of their own emotional needs.

Children build up their own sense of right and wrong within a social learning context, and they will do this by seeing how their parents react to their behaviour, what parents disapprove of, and how their parents behave in similar situations.

Bearing in mind the need to avoid a cookbook approach, the importance of the goals and values of parents, and the importance of being sensitive to the individual characteristics of children and to the cultural context, how then might the journey towards being a 'good enough' parent be described?

'Good enough' parents are confident, competent parents.

They are building up their *knowledge* about:

- human health and development, and particularly child development and what to expect at what stage;
- where to go for help;
- their rights;
- common ailments, and how to cope with accidents;
- the education system.

They are developing certain *skills or attributes*. Many of these are social skills, developed over a lifetime, which all adults need if they are to function adequately:

- they are authoritative, rather than over-protective, permissive or authoritarian;
- they offer their children love and acceptance, and are sensitive to their needs;
- they have confidence in their children's worth and abilities;
- they have appropriate expectations of their children;
- they find time to share experiences with their children – having meals together, playing games, going on outings;
- they are consistent, reliable and dependable, provided a stable and secure environment where rules are clear;
- they can set appropriate boundaries, provide adequate supervision and encourage their children to set their own boundaries;
- they can communicate openly and honestly, listening and reflecting;
- they can make decisions and accept responsibility for them;
- they can cope with stress and deal with conflict;
- they can see things from their children's point of view;
- they avoid harsh punishment, but reinforce good behaviour.

They are also developing practical skills, in managing the home and the family's finances, and combining work with family life.

They are developing *understanding and self-awareness*:

- of themselves as parents and of their needs;
- of their values and attitudes and how these impact on others;
- of how their upbringing affects their ability to be parents.

The importance of self-confidence and self-esteem is central to the various parenting courses and support schemes outlined in the chapters that follow. As Bettelheim (1987) observes:

to be a good enough parent one must be able to feel secure in one's own parenthood, and one's relation to one's child. So secure that while one is careful in what one does in relation to one's child, one is not over-anxious about it and does not feel guilty about not being a good enough parent. The security of the parent about *being* a parent will eventually become the source of the child's feeling secure about himself. (p 13)

The knowledge, skills and understanding we outline above are those to which the 'good enough' parent might aspire, but the social and economic pressures on parents outlined in chapter 1 are considerable, and no parent should be expected to provide the care and nurture required by a child without adequate levels of support. This book describes what this might look like in terms of preparation, education and support. But there is another crucial element of support without which 'good enough' parenting is very difficult: what Rutter (1974) describes as **permitting circumstances**, or necessary life opportunities and facilities, the 'bare necessities' of life.

The interaction between economic, social and educational deprivation is complex, but it is clear that many parents find it extremely difficult to bring up their children when basic personal and family needs, such as adequate income, whether through employment or benefits, and housing, day care and other support are not taken care of first.

Margaret Harrison points out from her experience of Home-Start that some parents may themselves need parenting before they can respond to the needs of their own children (Harrison, 1982). Parents who as children were brought up in care, or who experienced inadequate parenting, may have unrealistic expectations of an idyllic family life and it is 'an insensitive farce' to try to promote better verbal or physical contact with a child or the need for positive reinforcement before first working with some of the parents' personal and social problems.

Awareness of the negative impact of an accumulation of disadvantage, deprivation and disincentive is not new. As Rutter (1974) pointed out 20 years ago where permitting circumstances are lacking 'even the best parents may find it difficult' and despite our understanding of the issues 'most of our interventions, at any age, are quite inadequate because too little is done, it is done for too short a time, and sometimes because the wrong thing is done'(p18). As Rutter (1983, 1987) has also shown, there are protective factors that can enhance a child's resilience and reduce their vulnerability – a positive disposition, a supportive family milieu and an external support system – although as Rutter emphasises it is not the presence of these factors but the use made of them that is crucial.

While there have been many improvements for parents and children it is clear that significant numbers of children remain disadvantaged and that their parents are not receiving sufficient help and support. As the report from the Commission on Social Justice concludes:

> Poverty, unemployment, bad housing and restricted services do not necessarily produce inadequate parents any more than materially comfortable parents are always adequate. But poverty makes good parenting far more difficult, and under current policies, parents are the people who are most likely to be poor. (Hewitt and Leach, 1993)

Having looked at the social context within which parents are bringing up their children, and at the tasks and skills of parenting, we now turn to an examination of parent education.

# 3. Parent education

> Being a good parent is not simply a matter of having the right knowledge, or even the right skills. So much also depends on the personal characteristics of the child (and other children) and parents involved; their social and economic condition; their abilities to cope with stress; their relationships with one another; their sensibility to the aspirations and needs of others. Thus, even if there were an agreed body of knowledge about parenting to be transmitted (and there is not) and one could work on the assumption that knowledge always changes behaviour (which one cannot), it would still be necessary to bear in mind how much the inter-personal relationships and integrity of the parents affect their ability to be successful. So many previous well-meaning programmes aimed at changing behaviour for the benefit of health, have fallen short of their objectives that we urge that any programme of education for parenthood should be based on principles rather than prescriptions. (Committee on Child Health Services, the Court report, 1976)

## Historical

Advice to parents on how to bring up their children has been offered by those professing to have some superior knowledge and experience since time immemorial. All societies, from earliest days, have their rules about family life; and philosophers such as Plato, Aristotle, Aquinas, Locke and Hobbes made known their own views on the rights and responsibilities of parents and children. From Rousseau's 'back to nature' philosophy which idealised motherhood as 'the most enviable and delightful activity a woman could hope for' (1762) to the self-effacement of continual mothering implied by James and Joyce Robertson (1982), and the superwomen combining high powered jobs and bringing up children (Conran, 1979), a barrage of advice has issued from the pens of philosophers, doctors, psychologists, psychoanalysts and child care experts. Much of this advice has reflected not so much the needs of parents, as the social and cultural norms of society and the influence of successive groups of professionals.

The most enduring influences of the last two hundred years have been traced by the Newsons, from the religious and moral overtones of the eighteenth and nineteenth centuries when childrearing was 'clearly linked with the expectation of death rather than the hope of a balanced and integrated life'; through the 1920s and 1930s, dominated by the morality of aseptic rationalism, in which the 'evangelical concern to eradicate the Devil' is echoed by the advent of the hygienist movement, and the all-powerful Truby King; to the 1930s where the impact of psychoanalysis and nursery educators such as Susan Isaacs put the child and his (sic) needs firmly into the centre of the stage; and on the flexibility and individualism of many more recent writers (Newson and Newson, 1974). As a review of child care manuals from 1850 to the 1980s points out, 'while babies and mothers remain constants, advice on the former to the latter veers with the winds of social, philosophical and psychological change' and we should see the advice in the books we use today as a temporary crutch, not as eternal verity (Hardyment, 1983).

In the last ten years, new themes have emerged from the child care literature. In the wake of the UN Convention on the Rights of the Child, children's rights have become more prominent, particularly the right not to be smacked, a campaign spearheaded by EPOCH, the End Physical Punishment of Children Campaign (Newell, 1989; Cook and others, 1991). There has been a realisation that for too long the role of the father has been neglected in caring for and supporting children (Lamb, 1987; Lewis and O'Brien, 1987). A growing emphasis on understanding and responding to children's emotional development (Bettelheim, 1987; Brazelton, 1993), has led to a realisation that for many children, particularly black children, their self-esteem and self-image are inappropriately nurtured in what can too often be a racist society (see for example Milner, 1983; Maximé, 1991). The importance of understanding and responding to different child-rearing patterns has become more strongly emphasised (Konner, 1991; Myers, 1992). And as increasing numbers of mothers struggle to combine parenthood with work, there has been a flurry of advice from successful career women – Libby Purves, Paula Yates, Julie Walters, Shirley Conran – on how to combine such success with motherhood.

The theoretical exhortations in the literature were matched with a more practical approach during the late nineteenth and early twentieth centuries, when in an attempt to combat infant mortality and childhood ill-health the first health visitors were appointed and 'schools for mothers' were established, forerunners of a comprehensive system of maternity and child welfare. As an historian of the infant welfare movement wrote:

> Evidently the capacity to bring up a baby successfully through the first years of life was not an innate feminine characteristic, with which all women were endowed at birth...it was proved to be a skilled job requiring a technique which, like any other kind of technique has to be learned. (McCleary, 1933)

During the second half of this century the contributors to the debate and to the provision of parent education have been many and various, but these approaches, whether in schools, the health service or local communities have evolved separately, and we have not in the UK adopted a coherent policy. Stern's international survey in 1960 concluded that

> in Great Britain parent education has not yet been the subject of serious study. Yet practical measures are not altogether absent; but they have remained half-hearted, sporadic and, on the whole, ineffectual.

*The Needs of Parents* (Pugh and De'Ath, 1984) showed a considerable increase in provision in many areas but suggested that

> much remains to be done. Where interesting and relevant work is in progress it is all too often due to the energy and enthusiasm of an individual worker, rather than as the result of a policy decision to commit resources to preventive and educational work, and in many such instances the scheme stops if the worker moves on. (p 199)

On the international scene some 25 countries came together in 1964 to form the International Federation for Parent Education (IFPE), a voluntary non-profit making organisation working for the advancement of education for parenthood and family living throughout the world. Based in Sevres in France, the IFPE took its inspiration from the *école des parents* which had been active in France since 1929. Britain has never joined the IFPE and indeed attempts to set up a British Association for Parent Education in 1973 failed because of lack of support. Our only contact with the international body is through the Calderdale Association for Parents (see chapter 6).

The worldwide interest in family life and parent education is underpinned by the UN Convention on the Rights of the Child. A number of international and European organisations have become involved in work in this field over the last two decades, amongst them the International Union of Family Organisations, the International Federation for Child Welfare (IFCW) and the European Federation for Child Welfare (EFCW), the Committee of Family Organisations in the European Community (COFACE), the European Commission

Childcare Network, UNESCO and UNICEF (Myers, 1992), and international foundations and trusts such as the Bernard van Leer Foundation and the Aga Khan Foundation.

The largest international initiative is, of course, International Year of the Family in 1994. Although commanding substantial sums of money and staff in some countries, in the UK the small head office has had to rely on the voluntary cooperation of organisations who have their own busy agendas to work to. Nevertheless, within the three themes of family relationships, families in poverty and families and work, a number of projects, initiatives and conferences are being planned in an attempt to 'lift the pressure on families' and make Britain a more family friendly society.

Issues with which parent education in Britain has been concerned are not unique to Britain. There is widespread concern, for example, at the changing nature of social and family structures, at increasing rates of divorce and growing numbers of lone parent families, and at the considerable degree of both isolation and uncertainty. Although the United States in particular has pioneered a number of fairly structured parent education programmes, a general trend can be detected which rejects the didactic approach associated with the rapid rise of the child care expert, in favour of an approach which recognises parents' own skills and abilities. An international project on the educational role of the family (OECD/CERI, 1982), for example, reflecting work in Europe, North America, Australasia and Japan summarised a number of principles:

- a concern for quality and cohesiveness in family life;
- the effectiveness of programmes which help people discover their own parental capacities;
- parent education as following the individual life cycle;
- the need for non-intrusive preventive approaches;
- the importance of the setting in which parent education takes place;
- multi-dimensional approaches, using differing methods, such as the media, group work and so on;
- the need to retrain professionals working with parents.

The issues in developing countries are remarkably similar. In his introduction to Myers' (1992) fascinating account of child development programmes in Africa, Asia, India and South America, Bronfenbrenner summarises four key strategies in supporting parents and children:

- the programmes must be interactive and actively involve families;

- they must build on the values and customs of the culture in which children and families live;
- they must be multi-dimensional – physiological, cognitive, emotional, social;
- there must be stability and predictability in the lives of children, for the development process takes time to get going and must be supported over a long period of time.

The key is to focus on strengths, rather than deficiencies and defects. This reflects similar approaches adopted by the World Health Organisation in its work on health promotion.

In Britain, despite some developments in the 1970s and 1980s, and a renewed concern in some quarters during the early 1990s that parents are losing control of their children, there is still a conspicuous absence of a systematic approach to preparation, education and support for parents.

Many of the initiatives of the 1970s derived from the proposition put forward by Sir Keith (now Lord) Joseph, then Secretary of State for Social Services, that there existed within society a 'cycle of deprivation' whereby personal, emotional and social problems persisted from one generation to another. This led to a considerable body of research into aspects of transmitted deprivation and much discussion about the causes and nature of disadvantage (see Rutter and Madge, 1976). A series of consultations was set up jointly with the then Department of Education and Science, focusing on preparation for parenthood as a possible method of improving parents' attitudes to relationships with their children, thereby breaking, it was hoped, the cycle of deprivation (DHSS, 1974a and 1974b). Lord Joseph returned to this theme some twenty years later in a lecture he gave to the National Children's Home in 1991 (Joseph, 1991), and a debate he initiated in the House of Lords in June 1992, when a distinguished group of speakers debated 'the importance of the way parents bring up their children and the case for voluntary bodies to provide help and friendship where the parents so wish' (*Hansard* 24 June, 446 – 506).

Interestingly the debate raised many of the issues that we cover in this book. The importance of parenting, and acceptance that many skills can be taught; differences of opinion as to what is the most appropriate time and place to provide parent education – in schools (where it was recognised that the National Curriculum was squeezing out many lifeskills classes), antenatal classes, or the community; the role of the church and of the voluntary organisations. The impact of poverty and unemployment on parents' ability to bring up their children as they might wish was also raised as was the need for greater financial support, and particularly for better day care. The impact of parenting styles on children's behaviour was also debated, and the important central thrust of the Children Act. The inherent tensions between the responsibilities of parents, and government's responsibility to provide adequate support were evident throughout. Replying for the government, the Minister of State for Education agreed that government

> can create the conditions under which good parents and responsible citizenship can flourish, but we cannot, nor should we, relieve parents of their responsibilities....Government policy aims to ensure that young people are adequately prepared to undertake the duties and responsibilities of marriage and family life, and fully to understand that the responsibilities of parenthood are not to be taken lightly. (Hansard 24 June, col 498)

Not all who participated in the debate agreed that this policy was being successfully implemented.

The last ten years have seen fewer government reports or national research projects concerned with family life than in the previous decade, although as we saw in chapter 1, a considerable amount of legislation has had a direct impact on families. One of the few reports to refer specifically to parent education was the Elton report *Discipline in Schools* (1989) which tried to take an even handed approach to the problem by acknowledging the levels of family stress and poverty, but argued that this does not absolve parents from the responsibility of bringing up their children properly. The report recommends that the government and LEAs and schools should impress on parents the need to provide firm but affectionate guidance, a consistent example, and avoid permissive or harshly punitive response; and also recommends that the education system should provide

> systematic preparation for adult life, including parenthood. Pupils of both sexes should be introduced to the values and skills involved in good parenting, and schools should aim to identify and cultivate adult attitudes which form the basis of responsible parenthood. (p 137)

Education for parenthood is seen as a cross-curricular theme covered in personal and social education programmes. Many of the proposals in the 1994 DFE circulars on *Pupils with Problems* derive from the Elton report. We return to issues relating to school-based parent education in chapter 4. An evolving view of parents' rights and responsibilities as evidenced through legislation and the Parents' Charter were noted in chapter 1.

We have already noted the central thrust of the International Year of the Family in Britain, a thrust that will rely heavily on the numerous organisations which are already providing services for families, and are campaigning for better financial support, better day care, and the greater involvement of parents in their children's schooling. Many of these are noted in the pages that follow. A new initiative that was launched at the end of 1993, and which aims to raise the status of parenting across all political parties, is the All Party Parliamentary Group on Parenting, supported by Exploring Parenthood, and 'child' of the All Party Group for Children which has been supported by the National Children's Bureau since 1979. The Parents' Group sees IYF as the right time to raise the importance of good parenting and to support parents with new legislation.

The last decade has also seen a renewed interest in parenting and in the interests of parents from a number of quite different alliances and policy analysts. Two such examples focus on the education system and the criminal justice system. There has been a growing interest in improving links between home and school and in looking both at parents as their children's first educators, and at parents' rights in relation to the education system (see Wolfendale, 1992); and a parallel interest in adults as learners and in family education and adult literacy. And the publication of *Crime and the Family* (Utting and others, 1993) highlighted the role of parent education in improving childrearing and preventing delinquency. This report and a study by Knight and Osborn on family support and delinquency (Home Office, 1992) have increased the interest of police, probation officers and criminologists in the importance of preventive support for parents. Increasingly funding for new initiatives is coming from the Home Office and the Safer Cities campaign. All of these developments are picked up in the chapters that follow.

## The case for parent education

> There were times before I had my own children when I was already advising other people how to bring up theirs. I thought it was all really quite straightforward. These people who came to see me were in a mess. They weren't normal parents like we would be. And then we had children. And we were in a mess as well.

This paediatrician, quoted by Sokolov and Hutton (1988) in their book about Parent Network must speak for many hundreds of people who think parenting is easy until they try. Being a parent and bringing up children is probably the most important job that most people ever do, and yet it is one for which they receive virtually no preparation, no training and precious little support. Why do we continue to argue that whilst we may go to classes to learn French or how to use a computer, parenting is best learned 'on the job' or that it is 'caught' rather than taught. Is it because we find it so difficult to talk about relationships, or that we feel it is an admission of failure? Or do we have an inherent dislike of experts in the UK? Common sense, intuition and the model of childhood experiences of being parented are certainly cited as being the most widespread influence on parents. Yet, as we have seen, the world in which many of today's parents are bringing up their children is a very different one from that in which they grew up themselves; many parents come from small families and have little experience of caring for siblings; many live some way from their own extended family; and for many their own experiences of childhood simply serve as a reminder of how they would not wish to bring up their own children. As a paper prepared for the International Year of the Family (Einzig, 1994) points out, it is important to change the climate of opinion around parent education, and to eradicate the stigma attached to asking for help.

Whilst most parents manage very well most of the time, parenting can be a difficult and lonely job, and it can be argued that society has a responsibility both to help young people to develop some understanding of what is likely to be involved in bringing up children **before** they decide whether or not to become parents; and to provide parents with information, support and education as and when it is needed, and particularly at critical periods of the life-cycle, such as at the birth of a first child.

It is notoriously difficult to prove that preventive and educational intervention is cost effective, but we have brought together in the pages of this book such evidence as is available both of the difficulties facing many parents today and of the cost – human and financial – of family breakdown; and of the effectiveness of the schemes and projects that we cite.

Our overall definition of parent education is:

- **A range of educational and supportive measures which help parents and prospective parents to understand their own social, emotional, psychological and physical needs and those of their children and enhances the relationship between them; and which create a supportive network of services within local communities and help families to take advantage of them.**
- **It should be available to all parents and prospective parents.**

- It is a lifelong process and as such will have a different emphasis at different stages of the lifecycle.
- Its emphasis should be on individual's roles and relationships in the here and now, as well as on their future roles and relationships.
- The overall aim of parent education is to help parents develop self-awareness and self-confidence and improve their capacity to support and nurture their children.

How this is provided, and what skills and information are most appropriate and when, continues to be hotly debated. It has been argued that the private nature of the family as perceived by governments in Britain, where children are seen as the sole responsibility of their parents, is in contrast to the view of our European neighbours, who see children as an investment in the future in which society shares (Moss, 1992). Recent disagreements between Britain and her European partners over the Social Charter, and the earlier UK veto of a European directive to introduce leave for family reasons, are illustrative of this.

The dilemma is well summarised by Weikart (1980), speaking from the United States, a country with policies similar to our own:

> Society is concerned about the ways families are rearing children, and the situation appears to be rapidly approaching the juncture when the State will be assuming increased responsibility for children. Thus the stage is being set for massive conflict between the right of self-determination of families who desire children and of the responsibility they entail and the goals established by the State through family decisions for all children. Ultimately conflict will be between the state's need for a healthy and productive citizen and the family's right of self-determination.

This dilemma is at the heart of the debate about education and support for parents. On the one hand parent education can be seen as a means of social control, and of encouraging conformity to a particular type of socially acceptable or desirable behaviour, for example reinforcing role-stereotypes by preparing men to become breadwinners and women to be primarily home keepers and rearers of children; or focusing programmes on the role of parents in preparing their children to perform well and adjust quickly to the educational system. This view is taken by writers such as New and David (1985, p 79):

> The thrust of current family policy is to sidestep the causes of 'family inadequacy' which affect all families to a greater or lesser extent – the

isolation of mothers and the lack of public support for child care, exacerbated by poverty and racism

and Cannan (1992) in a recent critique of family centres, who argues that 'problem families' can be locked into deviance by poverty and a lack of family support:

Rather than being seen primarily as needing psychological help for parenting problems, mothers can be seen as needing practical services and as unemployed or seeking work or training. Daycare, providing opportunities for parents and enriching experiences for children, should not be cynically abandoned as an unrealistic objective. (p 123)

Critics of parent education programmes have drawn attention to the part played by professionals in fostering beliefs about the 'ideal' family and parenting, stressing child rearing as a private parental responsibility of mothers, and individualising and psychologising problems, rather than challenging structural issues of isolation and poverty and the plethora of advice from the experts (Allan, 1994).

On the other hand, and at the other end of the spectrum, parent education can be seen as a means to social change, whereby individuals are given encouragement and increased self-confidence to take greater control over their lives, to break out of traditional roles, and to question the status quo. Many of the projects and schemes in the pages that follow aim to provide this type of empowerment and support, but no programmes are neutral in their value position. It is important that those providing parent education are clear about their aims and objectives and the value position from which they start.

The essential issue is the need for a range of supportive services that enable parents to undertake the task of parenting with confidence and enjoyment.

# Principles for parent education

Each parent and each child is a unique individual; their life histories are unique, and so are their reactions to any particular situation and to each other in it. Furthermore, no set of circumstances is quite like any other set of circumstances. Most family tragedies, big and small, could be avoided if parents could free themselves of preconceived notions about how they or their children 'ought' to be or act. (Bettelheim, 1987 p 31)

The quotation from the Court report at the head of this chapter links the tasks and skills of parenting with the social and economic circumstances of families' lives; and Bettelheim reminds us of the uniqueness of individual parents and children. This suggests that any approaches to parent education should be based on principles rather than prescription; and the following principles have been derived from the various approaches described in the pages that follow:

- A child's development is dependent on the quality of the parent/ child relationship. Meeting children's needs must be the first concern of their parents, but there is no single right way of parenting, no blueprint for a perfect family, and it is important that diverse family patterns are acknowledged and respected.

- The ability to parent reflects each individual's level of self-confidence and self-worth. Work with parents must acknowledge, value and build on their own skills, experience and abilities, rather than induce dependency and guilt.

- Schemes and services planned in close cooperation with parents and based upon their own needs, are likely to be more acceptable to parents and more widely used.

- Parenting (usually) involves mothers and fathers and any approaches to parent education should therefore be relevant to boys as well as girls; men as well as women.

- All parents need help and support at some point in their lives but there are likely to be different needs at different stages and these can be met in different ways.

- Parenting is a continuous process. The development of a parent starts at birth and goes on through early childhood, schooldays, early relationships, committed partnerships, pregnancy, birth, parenthood and grandparenthood.

- Parenting is not simply a matter of childrearing: it is a constant interaction between parents and children, both of whom are continually developing.

- Because Britain is a multi-ethnic society, cultural diversities which are expressed through different childrearing patterns and views of family life, must be respected in any support for parents.

- If parenting is a sequential process, concerned with the development of the whole person, this has implications for all those working with young people and parents throughout the life cycle, who need to see their own involvement as part of a wider network of support.

- Bringing up children has to be seen in the wider context of

**adequate employment, financial provision (through equitable taxation and adequate benefits), housing and day care.**

How are these principles to be turned into practice? For as we noted in *The Needs of Parents*, 'whilst many professionals and para-professionals see parent education and support as a part – often a very small part – of their brief, for very few is it the main thrust of their work'.

# A lifecycle approach to parent education

Before going on to look at what is appropriate at different stages of the life cycle, we include a word on definitions. The term **parent education** as defined on page 66, we use as an overall term to encompass all approaches right through the life cycle. Work with young people before the conception of children we call **family life education** or **education about parenthood and family life**; work during pregnancy we call **preparation for parenthood**; and work with parents and their children we call **support for parents**, or when it is very specifically educational, **parent or parenting education**.

Ideally all of these approaches should be taken forward together, but with the exception of the 'Job for Life' project (Pugh and Poulton, 1987) that we describe in the Introduction, we have found no other 'lifecycle approach' to parent education.

## Education about parenthood and family life

Almost all the organisations which responded to our enquiry agreed that all young people, whether through schools, further education colleges, youth clubs or churches, should have access to a programme of family life education, or education about family life and parenthood. This could have a number of strands, perhaps the most important based on the notion that good parents are first and foremost confident, coping, caring adults and that young people need to be able to grow up in an environment in which they can love and be loved; respect and be respected; trust and be trusted; develop self-confidence and self-knowledge; establish good personal relationships both within the family and with their peers; and make balanced decisions about how they wish to lead their lives.

The second strand concerns the need to present young people with a more realistic and less romanticised picture of parenthood. A central theme of research studies on marriage and parenthood is of the discrepancy between the expectations of the sense of fulfilment that a wife or husband and children will bring with them, and the reality of an exhausting 24 hour a day commitment, amongst which one's own sense of identity seems to diminish (Mansfield and Collard, 1988; Clulow, 1982; Parr, 1993).

Thirdly, whatever courses are offered must be relevant to boys as well as girls, and must challenge traditional gender stereotypes about parenting as women's sole responsibility.

And finally, young people need access to sufficient knowledge of contraception so that they can make genuine choices as to whether and when to have children.

A recent study of preparation for parenthood amongst young people (Braun and Schonveld, 1992) summarised the aims as found in the literature as follows:

i. to create better parents so as to minimise child abuse
ii. to reduce unwanted pregnancies
iii. to improve the knowledge of future parents about child development and children's needs in order that they will then be able to meet those needs when they have children
iv. to improve the knowledge of future parents about pre-conceptual care so that they make appropriate health choices and decisions before planning a pregnancy;
v. to facilitate the personal development of young people by giving them opportunities to learn about themselves, their relationships and the influences, restraints and choices open to them in the future. (p 11)

The authors point out that the first four of these aims are about behavioural outcomes and cannot be achieved or evaluated, but that the fifth is educational and can be broken down into clear learning objectives:

Family life education aims to encourage the child's and young person's:

- self-awareness and self-knowledge
- self-confidence
- qualities of empathy and imagination
- communication skills
- understanding of the influences and constraints on their lives
- understanding of their relationships with family, friends and their wider network
- awareness of their own attitudes and values regarding race, gender and disability
- knowledge of the debates about the role of the family in modern Britain (p 12)

During the course of the project the young people were asked what skills they thought were relevant to them now and which might also be relevant should they become parents, and they listed:

- being responsible, seeing things through and honouring commitments
- handling difficult situations with young children (like temper tantrums)
- communication – listening, assertion
- handling conflict and managing stress
- developing patience
- developing mutually supportive and stable relationships

They also identified areas of knowledge and information, including how children develop, health risks in pregnancy, and sources of advice and help for parents.

An overview of what is currently available to young people is given in chapter 4. This points to the dwindling levels of advisory support for personal and social education, health education and sex education as local education authority funding is cut back and delegated to the schools, and the impact of the National Curriculum on what is, with the exception now of sex education, a 'non core' aspect of the curriculum.

## Preparation for parenthood

Once pregnancy has been confirmed, whether or not it was a voluntary choice to start a family, **preparation for parenthood** adopts a more practical and immediate importance. Although there is a considerable body of research on the effectiveness of preparation for parenthood and a growing awareness of the importance of embarking on pregnancy as fit and healthy as possible, a recent review of antenatal and postnatal education (Combes and Schonveld, 1992) identified many of the concerns that we noted ten years ago: the mismatch between the needs of parents and the provision available; the fact that many parents – particularly men, and women who are young, single, working class or from a minority ethnic group – miss out; that opportunities for providing education as part of routine health care are largely missed; that there is a narrow focus; and the educational quality is poor.

From the literature, Combes and Schonveld identify six key aims for antenatal and postnatal education:

- to influence positively the health behaviour of women during pregnancy, and as parents;

- to prepare women for labour and to enable parents to have an easier and more satisfying delivery;
- to help prepare parents for parenthood, and support them in their role as parents;
- to develop social support networks among parents;
- to promote the development of skilled, confident, informed parents;
- to contribute to reducing low birth weight babies, and perinatal and perinatal morbidity. (p 7)

However, the research on antenatal and postnatal education raises many of the issues about effectiveness and values noted above. For example, how far can parent education influence parenting, and what constitutes good parenting (Perkins and Morris, 1981); and how far should parent education be consumer led, meeting parents' needs and concerns and how far should health professionals direct its content (Taylor, 1985; Lindell, 1988)?

Preparation classes are now widely available and, as we show in chapter 5, offer information on physical changes during pregnancy and help with managing the process of labour and birth. However, the content of these classes is still found to be inadequate in many instances, and the research shows an overall tendency for health professionals to ignore or skim over social, emotional, and psychological aspects of pregnancy. Women are often seen simply as a vehicle for the baby rather than as a person in their own right, and fathers have few opportunities to discuss issues and anxieties (Combes and Schonveld, 1992). For women in disadvantaged circumstances, antenatal education is most effective when carried out on a one to one basis, when it is closely geared to the individual's circumstances, and when there is broader social support.

Research on the transition to parenthood (Clulow and others, 1982, Mansfield and Collard, 1988) illustrates the difficulty that many couples find in maintaining the quality of their relationship as their family of two becomes three. The importance of support at this time, and of building up a network of family, friends and health professionals is particularly valuable in coping with major life changes, as Parr's work illustrates (Parr, 1993). The effectiveness of postnatal groups has been poorly researched, although they are clearly effective for health professionals in terms of use of time. These issues are discussed in chapter 5.

## Support for parents and parenting education

The final and longest stage of the lifecycle begins with the birth of the first child. The needs of individual parents and their children will, as Bettelheim suggests, vary between parents and indeed between children, and will change too over the lifecycle, with some parents finding the early months most difficult, others the 'terrible twos' and yet others the rebellions of adolescence, or the pressures and anxieties of young adulthood. The evidence presented in chapter 6 suggests that at this stage a wide range of support is needed in every local community, offering information, advice, support and education as and when it is needed.

To categorise approaches to parent education and support, or to attempt to draw boundaries between them, is a difficult and often pointless exercise. Is an informal parent and toddler club offering a learning situation or mutual support? Is home visiting an interventionist strategy or an opportunity for education and support within the home? Chapter 6 is thus a long chapter, which for ease of reference has grouped together advice and information, homebased approaches, informal groups, groups with a parent education focus, home-school links, and support for specific groups of parents.

Writing ten years ago, we reported on the growth of parent effectiveness training and behaviour modification programmes in North America, Australia and Europe and commented that the approach in the UK, 'reflecting perhaps a national tendency to be wary of expert advice or to expect instant returns from a series of evening classes, is rather more tentative and informal' (Pugh and De'Ath, 1984, p 49). This is still to some extent true, and indeed a recent audit of family services (Exploring Parenthood, 1994) concluded that 'least is being provided in areas of family skills training and respite care'. However, the evidence in chapter 6 suggests that there are now a considerable number of courses and programmes which draw on these more structured approaches, and that hundreds of thousands of parents have participated in discussion groups, workshops and 'training sessions'.

Parent education has been defined as 'a systematic and conceptually based programme, intended to impart information, awareness or skills to the participants on aspects of parenting' (Fine, 1980). The aims have been defined as 'to effect change in parent role performance and upgrade child care practices of parents in the home' (Harman and Brim, 1980). Whilst the goals, format and materials in parent education differ widely, most programmes attempt to help parents achieve some of the following goals:

- develop greater self-awareness;
- use effective discipline methods;

- improve parent-child communication;
- make family life more enjoyable;
- provide useful information on child development.

These and other American commentaries reflect the influence of two main programmes, both of which have contributed to the thinking of British projects: Systematic Training for Effective Parenting (STEP), developed by Dinkmeyer and McKay (1982) drawing on the work of writers such as Adler (1930) and Dreikurs and Soltz (1964); and Parent Effectiveness Training (PET) developed by Gordon (1975) drawing on the work of Rogers (1951, 1961).

Although widely used in the United States, commentators remark on the lack of a theoretical framework and on the limited amount of research into methodology and effectiveness (Harman and Brim, 1980). A more recent review of 48 group parent education programmes concluded that the results were inconclusive, and that better research tools were needed (Dembo and others, 1985). This study also pointed out that too many programmes were based on parents' abilities as change agents to change their children's behaviour, and paid too little attention to the child's impact on the relationship. Critics point out that such programmes can raise in parents feelings of dependency, self-consciousness, guilt and anxiety with their stress on acquiring specific techniques and attaining high levels of perfection. One critique of PET for example, speaks of it demonstrating a 'degree of certitude which verges on moral fanaticism' (Doherty and Ryder, 1980). An evaluation of an Australian STEP programme, although finding a very positive response to the programme, did conclude that the value base of the programme

> reinforced disabling dominant beliefs and perpetuated social inequalities and disadvantage, especially for women. Programmes need to enable individuals to reflect on the contradictions emerging out of their day to day experiences as parents. (Allan, 1994)

Allan argues the need for parenting programmes to make clear their value base and to move away from gender-neutral assumptions and language.

It is also important to ask how responsive programmes are to different cultural norms and different goals of childrearing. As was pointed out in chapter 2, different cultural and religious customs and childrearing practices mean that families may have quite different approaches to such things as preparing and eating food, discipline, the views of children, the transition towards independence, verbal communication and the use of praise. Dembo and others (1985) argue that there is potential conflict between the needs and behaviour of many parents and the goals of parent education programmes. Many parent education programmes are based on white middle class norms, and are perhaps thus better suited to white middle class mothers who may have greater confidence in themselves as teachers, show less need to control children and a greater interest in playing with their children.

We have also pointed to the need to ensure that programmes are as appropriate to fathers as they are to mothers, and of the danger of reinforcing gender stereotypes that see parenting as the mother's responsibility, thereby excluding fathers. Dembo and others (1985) also comment that schemes that focus on the mother's role – as many do – and exclude fathers are less likely to be successful.

Chapter 6 reveals a considerable expansion in parenting education schemes in the UK, drawing eclectically on most of the American authors noted above, some using psychodynamic approaches, others developing empathetic communication, or increasing understanding of how children think and learn, or nurturing families, or developing skills in changing behaviour, or empowering and enabling. It is not therefore possible to say whether the criticisms above can be levelled at the two main 'open access' British programmes which draw to some extent on the American experience – Parent Link and the Veritas Basic Parenting Programme – because neither has been formally evaluated, and both have developed their own rather more informal style and approach. Small scale evaluations of Parent Link quoted in chapter 6 do not reflect any of these concerns. Both organisations appear to reflect the principles we noted above, and the literature of both organisations quotes many parents who have found the courses helpful, but it may be timely to mount a more thorough and objective evaluation.

Bearing in mind the eclectic nature of UK parent education programmes and courses, the main focus can be summarised as follows:

- a belief that 'good enough' parents are responsible, author-itative, assertive, positive, democratic and consistent;
- they are not autocratic, authoritarian or permissive;
- parents' strengths should be re-affirmed, building on confidence and self-esteem;
- parents need to know *what* needs to be done (knowledge), and *how* to do it (skills), but they also need to feel confident they *can do it* (attitudes, particularly self-esteem);
- experience and feelings are as important as knowledge;
- the importance of the relationship between two parents is emphasised, as is the impact of this relationship on the children;

- the impact of how parents were themselves parented is acknowledged;
- there is an emphasis on increasing understanding and enjoyment of children, and on parents' role as their children's first educators;
- skills include developing skills in handling children's behaviour: encouraging good behaviour, rather than focusing on bad behaviour, creating boundaries, being consistent, handling conflict, offering choices, improving communication skills, and listening reflectively;
- an approach which suggests strategies, rather than giving answers is most helpful.

Other American research which has begun to have a wider significance in the UK is the use of behaviourial principles, based on social learning theory, for work with families who are having difficulty in managing their children's behaviour. The work of Patterson (1982, 1990) and colleagues at the Oregon Social Learning Centre, for example, has over 25 years identified replicable ways of working with 'uncontrollable' children in highly dysfunctional families. Publications for parents have given guidance on encouraging good behaviour and using non-physical discipline. Through observing parents and children in their own homes, Patterson concluded that parents often had no idea of how to signal approval or disapproval, and that less skilled parents inadvertently reinforce children's antisocial behaviour and fail to punish transgressions. Children who got their way through aggressive disobedience became trapped in a downward spiral of coercion, reinforcing the interaction between inconsistent parenting and disruptive behaviour. Teaching parents to encourage pro-social behaviour was not sufficient – they must also be taught non-physical sanctions such as 'time out'. The success of Patterson, and of O'Dell and others (1977) and Forehand and McMahon (1981) has led to a number of the British initiatives cited in chapter 6, in which there is currently renewed interest inspired by initiatives to reduce levels of juvenile crime. Criminologists are increasingly coming to see the value of preventive work based on family support and parenting education: 'Good parenting protects against the acquisition of a criminal record' (Kolvin, 1990); and

> Problem children tend to grow into problem adults, and problem adults tend to reproduce problem children. Sooner or later serious efforts, firmly grounded on empirical research results, must be made to break this cycle. (Farrington and West 1990)

There is a long tradition of 'parent training' in this country in relation to children with learning difficulties and developmental delay, for example the Portage programme (Cameron, 1982) and work on involving parents in their children's reading (Topping and Wolfendale, 1985), both discussed in chapter 6. In more recent years the behavioural approaches used by psychologists to help parents manage difficult behaviour, drawing on the research noted above, have begun to be more broadly developed, and to be shared with health visitors (Stevenson, 1989) and teachers (Westmacott and Cameron, 1982) as well as parents. Training resources have also been developed (for example Douglas, 1988). Parent workshops are seen by some as making an important contribution to the bridge linking home to school. Hinton (1987) for example concludes from her report on parent workshops attached to primary and nursery schools that:

> By developing parents' ability to enlist the cooperation of their children we are not only alleviating parents' problems, and perhaps averting later ones, but laying the foundation stone for effective parental involvement in children's education. Some will argue that parent education in the field of behaviour management is not the responsibility nor the concern of schools. However this study illustrates how a multi-professional approach incorporating the interest and support of teachers can enhance the effectiveness of an intervention for the benefit of the child in school as well as at home.

The potential of behavioural approaches for health visitors in their work with parents is also discussed in chapter 6, although as Stevenson (1989) points out in a discussion paper, there are few studies evaluating outcomes, and those which are rigorous fail to identify significant and lasting effects. This is of concern across all behavioural programmes, but Topping (1986) in a study of 600 parent training programmes concludes that although there is always some attrition, there is little evidence of long term efficacy of other interventions either. He claims 'there is no longer any doubt about the durability of gains accruing from parent training programmes'.

Evaluation of the UK schemes discussed in chapter 6 is limited, though there have been some studies reported in recent years. Over a three-year period Jenner reports initial success in maintaining changes in parenting styles, in clarifying family roles in abusing families, and in developing trust (Jenner, 1992, Jenner and Gent, 1993). Bavolek's work with abusing families in the United States (1990) also found that original behaviours could be relearned, provided that intervention was based on helping adults and children develop a positive regard for themselves. Evaluation has shown that the re-abuse rate is as low as 7%, and this approach is now being used by the Parent-Infant Project (PIPPIN) and Oxford Family Skills Project. An ongoing study of parents with severe parenting difficulties in Scotland and London, involved in a programme using a range of approaches including psychotherapy and home videos to improve parent-child interaction, is showing considerable changes in positive interaction and child-centredness (Puckering and others, in press). An independent evaluation of Sutton's work compared three methods of parent training – individual, group and telephone support, and found that parents could be trained, that children did become more manageable, and that there was little difference between the three interventions in terms of their effectiveness (Sutton, 1992). The factors that appeared central to success were the availability of family or marital support; competence in using time out; and the use of training materials (as developed by the author). The work in Oregon (Patterson, 1982 ) proved particularly effective with children under 10, and has been found to be as effective with parents working in groups as in individual one-to-one situations.

In addition to the growth in these more structured approaches to parenting education, the informal work of countless adult and community education projects, churches, family centres, playgroups and groups attached to schools, continues to reach thousands of parents, although there is some evidence that cutbacks in local authority expenditure has led to the cutting of some parent support posts attached to nursery and primary schools. The emphasis in such work tends to be on the personal growth and development of parents, on increasing self-confidence and self-awareness, on improving communication skills, on increasing understanding of how children develop, of reducing isolation and on helping people gain greater control over their lives. The educational psychologist who started the Leeds HELP project, for example, describes the approach thus:

> All children need love, they need limits, and they need useful and interesting activities with happy and confident adults. But to cuddle and talk like this you need a sense of self-worth – what I call a candle warm heart. The candle snuffers are anger, guilt and depression. (Williams, 1993)

Schemes such as these tend to evolve from the groups and meeting places with which parents are already familiar, rather than by setting up classes in adult education institutes. Perhaps it is for these reasons that so many schemes have their roots in the strong community networks that have given us many voluntary and self-help organisations. The work of such schemes, and of the contribution made by the community education materials produced by the Open University, is summarised in chapter 6.

One of the issues to be addressed in relation to parenting education is the ability of schemes and courses to meet the needs of all parents, and not just highly motivated middle class women. Although it has been argued that working class women are not able to organise play-groups and other 'middle class' groups without assistance (Finch, 1983), there is evidence throughout the adult and community education literature that provided middle class values and methods are not imposed, groups run by and for working class parents can succeed very well (see Davis, 1988, and examples in chapter 6). There appears to be rather less success, however, in involving fathers in parent education courses, and only a limited number of schemes focus specifically on the needs of black parents. There are some notable exceptions, and these are described in chapter 6.

These are some of the many approaches which can be described as preparation, education and support for parents. Their labels conceal a wide variety of aims, objectives and methods of working and these will be taken up in the chapters that follow. None of the schemes would profess to present any definitive answers, but each goes some way towards increasing the understanding and pleasures and easing the isolation and burden of parenting. Some do, however, raise a number of questions. As one American commentator points out, parent education programmes can encourage parents to be excessively cerebral and self-conscious, and as a result they lack confidence and get bound up in what she describes as 'analysis paralysis' (Katz, 1982). Technique-based parent education may yield positive effects in the short term, but we must be sure that it does not induce failure and guilt in the long run. As the number of more specialist programmes and groups increase, it is important that the various approaches are monitored to ensure that confidence and skills are indeed improved and maintained.

There is also the issue of the underpinning values of parent education that we have already noted, and indeed of the relationship between parents and professionals. Many of the initiatives described in this book aspire towards the concept of partnership in working with parents, a concept which we have elsewhere described as 'a working relationship that is characterised by a shared sense of purpose, mutual respect and the willingness to negotiate' (Pugh and De'Ath, 1989). A number of studies, however, suggest that the views of parents – usually seen as mothers in the studies – and health professionals about bringing up children are not always in tune (McIntosh, 1987; Sefi, 1988; Mayall, 1990). This reminds us again of our underpinning principle that education and support for parents will only succeed if it starts from the concerns and interests of the parents involved, and acknowledges that the key is not only what parents know or do, but also how they feel about themselves and their children.

# Methods of parent education

Parent education covers the imparting of a wide range of information, skills, awareness and understanding. There are many different ways in which parents choose to seek help and guidance and a variety of ways in which parent education can be offered. The majority of parents are likely to get much of their information from family and friends, but beyond the family and community networks there are three main ways of reaching parents – through the mass media, through group work and through individual approaches. Table 3.1 shows what such approaches might include.

Table 3.1  Methods of parent education

| Mass media | Group work | Individual approaches |
|---|---|---|
| Books<br>Pamphlets and leaflets<br>Magazines and journals<br>Newspapers and<br>  general articles<br>TV and radio<br>Videos, audio cassettes,<br>  film<br>Talks and lectures | Drop-in centres<br>Informal self-help and<br>  parent and toddler<br>  groups<br>Playgroups, nurseries,<br>  family centres<br>Parents groups in<br>  schools and churches<br>Semi-structured parent<br>  education groups<br>Structured therapeutic<br>  groups | Informal network of<br>  family and friends<br>Information and advice<br>  services<br>Telephone help lines<br>Professional advice<br>  from health visitors,<br>  GPs, social workers,<br>  teachers etc<br>Home visiting schemes<br>Voluntary one-to-one<br>  schemes<br>Counselling<br>Family Therapy |

## Mass media

The principal features of this method of parent education are the potential breadth of the audience that can be reached and the fact that there is usually no direct contact between the educator and the audience. The number of books, articles, television, radio programmes and, more recently, videos, beamed at parents appears to be increasing substantially, although comparative information is not available. A recent BBC TV programme on child care (BBC, 1994) claimed that 300 child care manuals for parents are currently in print, with a further 30 due in the next six months. Television too has been expanding its output, and at the end of 1993, the BBC launched a specific initiative to draw together and expand its output on child development and parent education. Their recent publication *Fun and Learning with the BBC* lists a considerable number of television and radio programmes, books, videos and software for children under five and their parents. The daytime magazine programme *Family Affairs* follows two series of *The Parent Programme*, which went on the air with support from the National Children's Bureau following publication of *The Needs of Parents* in 1984. Carlton television is experimenting with a series of short one minute public service announcement-type films on parenting. In addition to those programmes geared specifically at parents, International Year of the Family has encouraged all four television channels to transmit a considerable number of programmes about children, families and parenting at peak viewing times, in current affairs slots (*Panorama, This Week, Dispatches*) as well as series such as *Living with the Enemy* (parents and teenage children), *Nanny Knows Best*, and *What Shall We Tell the Children* (sex education).

Pamphlets and leaflets too are widely available, particularly those issued by the Health Education Authority, the Scottish Health Education Group, Welsh Health Promotion Agency, British Medical Association and Health Visitors Association to all pregnant women. The HEA's *The Pregnancy Book* (1993) and *Birth to Five* (1992), for example, are given free to every first-time parent in England. One study of women's access to information during pregnancy found that for middle class women books, magazines and newspapers were the key information source for 80% of women, followed by husband or partner (75%). For women in social class V husbands and partners were more important, and books and written information less so (Ball, 1989).

Shortage of recent information on the media's attitude to parenting issues led the National Children's Bureau to commission Tim Kahn, a journalist, to monitor the national daily and weekly papers, the monthly magazines for men and women, the four parenting monthlies, and the religious and minority ethnic press for the month of February 1994 (Kahn, 1994c). A total of 985 articles were published in the 58 papers and magazines. The key points to arise from the survey are as follows:

• most articles were neutral in tone (neither blaming nor praising parents);

- one in five of the articles offered advice and information (particularly through the agony and advice columns);
- one in ten were for or about parents of disabled children. Over half of these were described as 'triumph over tragedy', where an individual or family successfully overcome their problems when the odds are stacked against them. Whilst inspiring, this did tend to exploit parents with disabled children and reinforce their separation from the main stream of life;
- very few articles were for or about men as fathers, and most of those that were published saw men/fathers as 'baddies' who do not do enough at home, abuse children, are delinquent or criminal;
- there was very little about parenting in the religious or ethnic press, and few articles for black parents;
- there was extensive exposure of parenting issues on television, particularly as part of the BBC International Year of the Family season;
- concern was expressed through a number of articles at the growing amount of computer pornography that children have access to;
- most parenting magazines are for parents of children under five, and there is a large gap in the market for magazines for parents of older children. (An attempt a few years ago to launch *Parenting Plus* for such parents was not successful).

Kahn concludes by noting that stereotypical attitudes are still perpetuated towards mothers and fathers and families with disabled children in particular, and that gay and lesbian family issues are mostly hidden, as indeed are the concerns of black families. On the basis of a number of mainstream current affairs programmes on parenting issues during this period, he also comments that

> television is the medium which can most profoundly affect attitudes towards parents and parenting. If the TV can be harnessed to support the idea that parents need and deserve support and education, then this could have a knock-on effect in the written media and to the rest of society.

As a means of reaching potential consumers, the mass media are clearly reaching large numbers of people, although there is no recent research to give up-to-date information on this aspect of parent education, apart from our small scale survey above. In *The Needs of Parents* we noted that parents have criticised the often contradictory nature of the material – particularly the literature distributed by the health services. When looking at clinic booklets as a help or hindrance to parent education, Perkins (1980) found that there were sometimes completely different approaches appearing in similar publications, and that little evidence was given to support the advice or to help mothers make decisions. The image of family life was far removed from the conflicts, contradictions and difficulties of the real world. Our impression today is that parenting books and television and radio programmes are now much more firmly grounded in the realities of everyday life, reflecting the cultural diversity of Britain and the challenges of parenthood that we outline in this book.

Books, of course, are unable to help with the emotional impact of individual children on their parents, and can simply induce further guilt, as Bettelheim (1987) points out when comparing reading a manual on putting together an appliance with a manual on child care.

> As we study assembly instructions, few of us are distressed that others may be able to proceed without needing such guidance. But as we read how best to deal with our child, we have the sinking feeling that other parents know and feel secure about these matters while we do not. Why do we have to read up on toilet training, or on eating idiosyncrasies, when others don't seem to have these problems ... (p 20).... The reality is that while there are experts on children and on child development in general, only a person who is intimately familiar with what goes on between a particular parent and a particular child can be an expert on them.(p 21)

Bettelheim also argues that we only seek advice from those who are likely to tell us what we would like to hear, 'in the hope that it will confirm our prior convictions'.

## Group work

Group discussion has become a popular method of parent education, and is particularly valuable for the opportunity it presents for drawing on the personal experiences of members of the group, and relating any educational input directly to those experiences. Groups vary considerably in their size and their composition; the frequency and context of their meetings; their purpose; the methods they use; and the nature of participation and leadership.

The following chapters include many examples of the range of groups listed above, from work in primary and secondary schools, through ante and post-natal groups, parent and toddler groups providing company and support, to more structured parent education groups using Open University or Veritas Basic Parenting materials, or run by Parent Link or Exploring Parenthood. The work described by Puckering and others (in press) and noted above and in chapter 6, found groups particularly valuable, and all the mothers ascribed the help they had received to other mothers and not the 'experts'. Studies of such groups show that in their various ways they are providing parents with opportunities to:

- have somewhere to meet;
- share their views and experiences with others;
- build up a network of friends and resources;
- learn new skills;
- develop greater self-confidence;
- develop empathy (described by Bavolek (1990) as 'the most desirable parenting trait');
- encourage parents to listen to and respond to the needs and concerns of others;
- increase their understanding and enjoyment of their children.

Groups are also a cost-effective way of working with several parents at once.

In looking at teaching methods for parent education in schools and colleges, a recent review (Braun and Schonveld, 1992) pointed to the need to use a wide range of resources and approaches according to the needs of the group. Some young people found TV and video most helpful; others preferred outside speakers who were not known to the students. The key was to start from the pupil's existing knowledge. There were also different views as to whether single sex or mixed groups worked best – perhaps a mixture of the two approaches offers the best solution.

A review of antenatal education (Combes and Schonveld, 1992) felt that most people saw the need to balance three main teaching methods at this stage: information giving, usually done by a talk from a health professional, often informally showing a video; group discussion; and practical skills sessions, such as breathing, relaxation and child care skills. Health visitors and midwives were reported to find lack of teaching skills the most difficult aspect of running classes. The same review looked at postnatal groups and found that parents regarded fairly informal groups as most useful, offering them a chance to meet other parents, but also with informal access to a health professional. In a follow-up training resource for health professionals (Braun and Schonveld, 1993) the authors point to some of the advantages of working in groups: a sharing of experiences that can bring relief and lessen the feeling of isolation; learning from others who are a bit further on; learning new strategies in a supportive environment; feeling valued; making new friendships; feeling safe to express fears and anxieties – and having fun.

The 'active' learning model, drawing on participants' own

experience and involvement, and offering opportunities to immediately put into practice what has been learned, has been found to be particularly effective for adult learners. A study for IBM, replicated by the Post Office, showed that 65% of staff who were given the chance to perform a new task, as opposed to simply being told about it, or told and shown it, could remember it three months later, where only 10% of those who had simply been told how to perform the task could remember (reported in Einzig, 1994).

Leading a group is, however, a skilled task as the many parent education materials noted earlier in this chapter make clear. The skills of the group leader, and his or her ability to 'match' the discussion to parents' concerns and interests, starting with parents' strengths, ideas and beliefs and valuing what parents bring to the group, appear to be critical to the success of parent education groups. As one review of parent education programmes summed up 'If parent educators attempt to proceed through material without regard for the needs, interests and ability of the participants, the possibility of negative reaction is likely to occur'. (Dembo and others, 1985)

Most of the parent education schemes described in the following pages offer parents a series of eight or ten or more discussion sessions, supported by discussion material, including sometimes audio and video material. The workshops run by Exploring Parenthood, deriving from a psychodynamic model, are often offered on a one-day introductory basis. The co-founder of Exploring Parenthood (Schmidt Neven, 1990) describes in some detail the group process – the structure and boundaries for the day, the skills of the facilitators, handling beginnings and endings, and positive and negative feelings, and the focus on the emotional milestones of development.

There is a continuing debate about the degree to which a structured group approach is appropriate. Groups which are too directive are not usually found to be helpful, and for many parents regular attendance is often a problem. The reading levels of materials used in discussion can also present problems: Topping (1986) cites studies which found that even assuming reading levels of age eight, some 25% of parents experienced difficulties. American studies report that drop out rates from courses tend to reflect whether or not the parents have been referred by others or are self-referred, the extent to which the pro-gramme meets their needs, and whether they feel it is having an effect (Harman and Brim, 1980; Dembo and others, 1985). There is at present little evidence from this country on the effectiveness or appropriateness of parenting programmes.

## Individual approaches

Individual contacts between parents and professionals vary considerably in the intensity of the contact, ranging from straightforward information to intensive counselling or therapy to help resolve a particularly acute personal problem. Parent education can happen everywhere that parents are, whether as part of a health check with a doctor or health visitor, or a discussion with a child's teacher, as well as the informal settings of home visits or casual encounters. The individual service offered by health visitors, doctors, psychologists, social workers, pre-school home visitors (such as those involved with Home-Start and Portage) and by those who offer counselling and family therapy, is the only way in which specific worries can be discussed personally, and as such is extremely valuable. But, with the exception of schemes using volunteers, it is also costly and time-consuming, and is limited by the individual experience and expertise of the professional concerned.

The telephone has become an important way of reaching people who might otherwise not seek information or guidance, and local and national phone-ins on radio and television have become popular in discussing current issues of child care. These can have a double value as parent education, in that they respond to the individual caller and also highlight the areas of concern which can be explored more fully through complete feature programmes aimed at a mass audience. Although many of the parents who call do not feel they have a 'problem' and would not consult a professional worker they do often express relief at being able to ask their question and learn from other people's experience or hear another point of view. We report on telephone services and information services for parents in chapter 6.

Choice of method will largely depend on whether the overall objective of the programme is to provide information to parents, to develop skills, to help with the development of understanding and identification of values, or to increase confidence and self-esteem. Different approaches also suit different parents, and are more appropriate at some stages of the life cycle than at others.

# Personnel in parent education

While in the United States parent education has developed into a separate educational profession, with degree courses available for family-life educators, in Britain there is no one group of professionals who could claim to have a monopoly on parent education. This report shows, as did our previous study, that programmes are being undertaken by – amongst others – health visitors, school nurses, midwives, doctors, educational and clinical psychologists, psychiatrists, psychotherapists, paediatricians, social workers, teachers, youth workers, playgroup leaders, adult and community educators, priests and other religious leaders, and by parents themselves. The Hampshire Job for Life project (Pugh and Poulton, 1987), which attempted to put into action the lifecycle approach of *The Needs of Parents*, described the approach as being a cross between community/adult education, and social work, and described the development officer as acting as

> a resource person, a catalyst and an enabler; an activist in supporting families to challenge the system where it was not meeting their needs and to use the networks available within the community; a group leader; a counsellor, working with individual families; an educator of parents and children; and a trainer of professionals and parent volunteers. (p 77)

A growing number of schemes – for example Parent Network/Parent Link, the Veritas Basic Parenting Programme, PIPPIN, Home-Start, community mothers and several of the self-help groups for parents with children with disabilities – use parents supported by some training to facilitate groups and to visit homes. This development has been particularly welcomed by those who feel that parenting is becoming too 'professionalised', and that facilitators should be part of the local community, sharing the experiences of the other group members, helping to create local networks, and not talking down to other parents. The point was well made by the Artemis Trust, pointing out that programmes that rely on professionals can disempower parents, whilst programmes that rely on self-help can easily be ineffectual. 'The para-professional plays a vital role in bridging the gap between parent and professional – but perhaps as importantly reduces the costs of the programme, compared with the intensive use of expensive (and scarce) professionals' (response to enquiry, 1993). There can, however, be a danger in exploiting parents if they are not provided with adequate payment for what can be a demanding and time consuming job.

The background and professional training of facilitators is perhaps less important than the skills required to work with parents. Facilitators need to:

- *be skilled in handling groups*:
- able to provide a supportive learning environment;

- clear about their aims and objectives, and the underpinning values of their work;
- able to develop strategies for handling sensitive issues and managing conflict;
- valuing what individuals bring to the group.

- *be skilled in communicating*:

- able to facilitate discussion;
- able to observe and listen.

- *have some counselling skills*:

- enabling participants to become more self-aware, and able to work on their own problems;
- able to avoid making judgements about people;
- be self-aware, conscious of their own values and behaviours; and able to handle their own emotions;

- *value what individuals bring to the group:*

- be open, honest and approachable;
- with sufficient expertise to feed into the group as appropriate.

How well does training equip the various professionals and volunteers for this task?

# Training

The methods of parent education outlined above suggest that the training of professionals working with young people and families should cover three main areas – relevant **knowledge** (of child and human development, family patterns, local resources); the development of **skills** in working with individuals and with groups in often very sensitive areas; and the ability to examine their **attitudes, values and feelings** in respect of family life, and a sensitivity of others point of view. It has not been possible within the limitations of this review to look in detail at the training of the many professionals who work with families, but it is still largely true to say, as we did in *The Needs of Parents* (p 60-61) that

> most professional training still tends to include little on family life or parenthood, and there is still no explicit training for specialists in parent education....While the training of education, medical and health care personnel in particular has focused on the acquisition of

knowledge, there is far less attention given to the development of group work skills or to awareness or sensitivity training.

There have also been criticisms that both teacher training and social work training include little on child development.

The training package *Brief Encounters* developed by One Plus One to support health professionals who are supporting couples whose marriages are in trouble is one example of new approaches being developed; this is being adapted for use with teachers, to explore the nature of 'teacher uncertainty' in dealing with sensitive material. Another ongoing project is training primary teachers to run groups for parents in schools in Barnet and Hertfordshire (Hartley-Brewer and Hills, 1994).

There has been perhaps more progress amongst voluntary organisations who are training parents to work with other parents under continuous supervision. Two examples here are Parent Network and Home-Start. Parent Network trains parents who have taken the basic 12 week Parent Link programme to become group coordinators. The training takes 96 hours over six weekends, with some written work between sessions, although the main emphasis is on experiential learning. Training covers personal development, group facilitation skills, group processes, and the content of the Parent Link course. PIPPIN facilitators receive a further 70 hours training, which is again largely experiential, including participating in small and large group activities, exercises, role plays, discussions, facilitation practices and self-, peer- and trainer-assessment (Parr, 1993).

Home-Start also trains volunteers, most of them mothers who have themselves once been visited. The courses are normally ten full-day sessions, including listening skills, child protection, welfare rights, the role of the social worker and health visitor, and the nature of anxiety and depression, child development and the ethics of home visiting. Further training, and ongoing supervision, are also provided.

Many of the other schemes and projects described in the following chapters also provide training for parents, and increasingly this is leading to accreditation for those parents who wish to take advantage of it, either under schemes such as the Liverpool Parent School Partnership scheme (see chapter 6), or for playgroup leaders, childminders and others within the developing system of National Vocational Qualifications.

# Evaluation and cost effectiveness

In 1984 we noted the paucity of research on the effectiveness of different approaches to working with parents, and little has changed in the last ten years. A review of American research concluded in 1985 that:

> much of the research in parent education is limited in the formulation of research questions, methodology, and measurement procedures. Many of the research issues raised over twenty years ago still have not been adequately addressed. A multidisciplinary approach using knowledge from allied fields (such as, parenting, family sociology, life span development) would contribute greatly to improvements in the quality of the research. (Dembo and others, 1985)

A more recent review of all the major parent support programmes aimed at 'disadvantaged families' in the United States concluded that

> parent support can produce meaningful short-term effects on discrete parenting behaviours; and on parents' efforts at coping, adaptation and personal development. But the modest long-term evidence that exists suggests that parent support may not set in motion causal processes leading to improved long-term child development outcomes for environmentally at-risk children....Programmes that combine parent support and direct developmental services to young children appear to hold the most promise of promoting improved long-term child development outcomes, while not neglecting parents' own developmental and support needs. (Center for Study of Social Policy, 1990)

In the UK there has been no cost benefit analysis of this type and the research has been even more limited. There has been no evaluation of the effectiveness of personal and social education or lifeskills work in schools; and a review of antenatal and postnatal education suggests research in this area is now a high priority; but acknowledges the different agendas in terms of outcomes – should success be measured in terms of birth outcomes, changes in behaviour, or consumer satisfaction? (Combes and Schonveld, 1992). They conclude that there is some research evidence to suggest that antenatal education can influence the knowledge, attitudes and health behaviours of pregnant women during pregnancy, but that the outcomes of postnatal education have been poorly researched.

As becomes evident in chapter 6, the growing number of parent education schemes have only had very limited and often fairly subjective evaluation, mostly relying on the self-reporting of parents. Such reports are on the whole enthusiastic, emphasising gains in parents' self-confidence and knowledge, enhanced skills, and changes in attitude and in practice. More rigorous research is however needed, as is noted in the recent Audit Commission report (1994) which comments on the somewhat haphazard development of social service departments' family centre work on parenting skills and notes that: 'Intensive intervention work such as specialist training in parenting skills and counselling should be evaluated'. There is no overall typology, no framework within which the different approaches can be assessed, although the Joseph Rowntree Foundation has recently funded the National Children's Bureau to begin to undertake such a 'mapping' exercise.

With regard to the costs of parent education, whilst it is possible to cost individual approaches, it is neither straightforward to cost a whole package (for parents' needs will be different), nor can the savings be easily identified in preventive terms. For whilst parent education and support can undoubtedly improve the physical and mental health of children, and can contribute to a reduction in maternal depression, to keeping families together and to cutting the costs of crime, the variables involved in proving such causal links would be many and complex.

However, if we look at the estimated costs of crime alone, Utting and others (1993) use Home Office data to project a figure of £18 billion a year in 1991 (equivalent to running the entire National Health Service), quite apart from the costs in human distress and wasted resources. Beside these figures, the cost of providing adequate education and support for parents seem minimal. As Utting argues,

> Each year vast sums are committed to researching the cause of different diseases and in support of experimental interventions designed to prevent them. If only comparable resources could be devoted to preventing the social cancer caused by crime, the savings in public health as well as wealth would surely more than justify the cost. (p 75)

The current costs of a child being 'looked after' by the local authority are on average £34,000 a year, with a place in a secure unit costing around £100,000 a year (Audit Commission, 1994). This report argues strongly for a coordinated approach to needs assessment, and a much higher commitment from local authorities to family support and preventative work.

Three possible ways of costing an effective package are suggested:

- The first is simply to note the cost of the individual elements, which can then be put against the costs noted above. Many elements of such a package would be provided by services already in place – in schools, churches and health clinics. For additional support, Newpin for example estimates it costs on average £2,200 to help a family in crisis; and Home-Start has averaged their costs at £182 per child, or £490 per family per year. For families wanting to join parenting groups, the costs to the family of a PIPPIN course are between £100 and £200 for a 17 week two hourly group, plus home visit and on-going self-help group. If this 'package' is bought by the health service, and provided through the GP and midwifery services, then it will be much cheaper for parents. A Parent Link course costs up to £100 per family, and the Family Caring Trust Veritas parenting course, run by parents for parents, costs about £8 per parent, including the cost of the book. The Open University has estimated that it has cost them only £2 per parent, setting the number of parents using their existing materials against the initial outlay of developing the materials.

- A second strategy would be to take the line that Titus Alexander, community education advisor for Waltham Forest, has argued:

  In this borough we spend £30,000 on each child's education over 11 years. Spending one per cent of that sum (£300) would enable us to offer every parent advice and support on helping their children learn at home as well as effective strategies for dealing with their children's difficult behaviour and emotional blocks to learning. Helping parents to become more effective as their child's first educator would, in the long term, make a huge difference in young people's educational achievement in this country. (Kahn, 1994a)

- A third and perhaps more promising approach would be to take the Hampshire Job for Life model (Pugh and Poulton, 1987) and argue, as Holtermann (in preparation) has done in a study for Barnardo's, for a network of parent education development officers to be set up on the basis of one worker to every community of 12,000 people (approximately the catchment area of one secondary school). The workers could be based either in the local authority or the health authority, and would work with the secondary school, five to six primary schools, GP's surgeries, parent and toddler groups, the youth service and so on, supporting ongoing work, and setting up new initiatives as necessary. At an annual cost of £35,000 per worker (£20,000 salary plus on-costs, travel, office support, payment for voluntary workers, teaching materials) this would cost in the order of £170 million a year throughout the UK, which is equivalent to little more than 0.5% of the education budget.

These are just three approaches, but it is clearly time for a more rigorous look at the costs – and savings – of a truly preventive approach to work with parents.

# Part II: Parent education in practice

# 4. Family life education: the role of schools and youth agencies

## Introduction

One of the main recommendations of *The Needs of Parents* (Pugh and De'Ath,1984) was that family life education should be part of a co-ordinated approach to personal, social and health education in primary and secondary schools, as well as in further education and in correctional settings. It was recommended that young people should be equipped with **skills** in understanding themselves and relating to others; with **opportunities** for developing self-confidence and for discussing values and attitudes; and with **knowledge** about human development. This, it was suggested, would help young people make balanced and informed decisions about the choices that affected their own lives. In addition, optional child development courses, accessible to both boys and girls, should be offered.

An important overall recommendation for family life education was that it should reflect the needs and interests of the young people to whom it was addressed, and should therefore be relevant to people of all ethnic groups and all social and class backgrounds. The need for adequate teacher training and support was recognised for the delivery of topics which might cover controversial and sensitive issues, as well as unfamiliar content and involve new methods of teaching.

Further recommendations were made about the role of further education settings, residential settings and the youth service in the provision of family life education.

In this chapter, then, we explore how schools and other youth settings are responding to this challenge during the 1990s. The chapter is divided into two main sections, covering first of all schools, and then settings outside and beyond school.

# Schools

## Why involve schools?

An important tenet of this book is that preparation for parenthood and family life education are life-long processes and must, therefore, begin during childhood. The most important and enduring influences on children, particularly during the early years, are their own parents and close family. Nevertheless, outside experiences, such as day nursery, playgroup, nursery school or childminder are undoubtedly of importance too. Once a child reaches statutory school age the power of factors outside the family increases and, despite the fact that little more than 15% of a child's waking hours are spent actually in school up to the age of 16, schools do have an important role to play for social, educational and pragmatic reasons.

This section explores the contribution that primary and secondary schools, and other agencies, can make to the development of their pupils as family members and future parents, particularly in the light of the extensive changes which have taken place in the education field during the last ten years. *The Needs of Parents* traced the gradual emergence of family life education from the early days of mothercraft teaching to a point where more schools were beginning to take a more coherent approach to the social and emotional development of pupils, although the extent of provision was found to be patchy. The authors reported that there was then little sign of a policy on family life education at either national government or local authority level. Such family life education as did exist tended to be implicit in much of what a school was doing and in a quiet way pervaded the whole curriculum. We need to ask whether things are any different today?

The same publication also noted that where family life education was the main aim of a course, this tended to be an optional child care and child development course, often with rather low status within the school and taken almost entirely by girls, often less academic girls, and most of the teachers were women. There was thus a danger that a subject intended to improve family relations might actually be reinforcing traditional gender roles and stereotypes. How have things changed in the 1990s?

Lack of adequate initial and in-service training opportunities was highlighted in 1984 as one of the important factors working against the successful development of skills required to teach a subject which was inherently controversial and where the personal view of the teacher might conflict with those of the school, the children or their parents. Are teachers any better supported today?

## Parenthood education in the school curriculum

In discussing the role of schools in education for parenthood it is important to note that this topic, like sex education, has often been a politicised issue and, indeed, continues to be so. Its place in the curriculum has tended to be dependent on political concern or pressure, whether eugenic concerns during the 1930s over differential birthrates, anxiety in the 1970s about the 'cycle of deprivation', feminist concerns during the late 1970s and 80s about equality of opportunity, or current worries about the breakdown of the family, juvenile crime and 'moral decline'.

## What can schools hope to achieve?

It has proved difficult to provide a comprehensive picture of parenthood education in schools in 1994. Since the introduction of Local Management of Schools and grant-maintained status, and a consequential reduction in the influence of Local Education Authorities (LEAs), it is impossible to obtain an overview of what is currently happening since this information is not systematically collected. In addition, changes brought about by the introduction of the National Curriculum (NC) following the Education Reform Act of 1988 (ERA) have led to a gradual decline in opportunities for secondary school pupils to study recognised examination courses on child development, and to increasing concern about where and when it is appropriate to prepare young people for family responsibilities. This has been accentuated by the fact that during the last ten years there has been a marked increase in the number of young people staying on at school after 16 (some 60% of 16 to 18-year-olds – 37% of whom were in schools – participated in education in 1990/91, compared with 52% in 1980/81), so that schools now have contact with far more young people who are on the brink of adulthood and independence. On the other hand, as we noted in chapter 1, parents are tending to have their first child at an older age, so that for many parents schooldays are more remote from the time when information and knowledge about parenthood is likely to be needed and put into practice.

Beginning with the White Paper *Better Schools* (Department of Education and Science, 1985), there has been a long series of consultation documents, working groups and proposals over the last ten years, leading to some very significant legislative changes, the most relevant in the context of family life education being the implementation of the National Curriculum in autumn 1989. Every maintained school is now obliged by law to provide a broad and balanced curriculum consisting of religious education and a basic curriculum of ten subjects:

- core curriculum: English, Mathematics, Science;
- foundation subjects: Technology, History, Geography, Modern Languages, Art, Music, Physical Education.

This broad and balanced curriculum must:

- promote the spiritual, moral, cultural, mental and physical development of pupils at the school and of society;
- prepare pupils for the opportunities, responsibilities and experiences of adult life.

(Education Reform Act 1988 Section 10)

In order to provide the necessary breadth, the National Curriculum can then be augmented by:

- additional subjects beyond the ten subjects of the National Curriculum;
- an accepted range of cross-curricular elements;
- extra-curricular activities.

It is this second area of cross-curricular elements, or themes, which was originally intended to offer a wide choice of opportunities through which to develop the teaching of child development and family life education. Five important themes were identified by the NCC:

- economic and industrial understanding;
- careers education and guidance;
- environmental education;
- education for citizenship;
- health education.

It is primarily in the last two elements, **education for citizenship** and **health education,** that the NCC suggested that topics related to parenting and family responsibilities would be covered. For example, it was proposed that courses on **citizenship** should have eight essential components, the first three covering the broad areas of the nature of community, roles and relationships in a pluralist society, and the duties, responsibilities and rights of being a citizen. The remaining five components were intended to explore specific, every-day contexts for citizenship in the present and future lives of pupils:

- the family;
- democracy in action;
- the citizen and the law;
- work, employment and leisure;
- public services.

In the component which deals with **the family** it was suggested that areas of study might include:

- the importance of the family for physical and spiritual well-being, parenthood and child development, the fulfilment of emotional and physical needs;
- family life-cycles, patterns of marriage and family structure and how these change;
- challenges facing family units, for example, separation, divorce, domestic problems, single (sic) parent families;
- relationships and responsibilities, for example, in the home and legal and moral responsibilities of parents and children;
- images of the family and marriage in the media.

The second cross-curricular theme incorporating elements of family life education was **health education**. Indeed, family life education has been described by the NCC as 'an essential component of health education'. *Curriculum Guidance 5 : Health Education* (National Curriculum Council, 1990) identifies the components of a framework for health education and outlines areas of study for each Key Stage. These study areas are intended to lead children through an awareness of different types of family and an understanding of the roles of individuals within the family (Key Stage 1); on to some understanding of relationships (Key Stage 2); and some knowledge of what is involved in planning and maintaining a family (Key Stage 3); thence to Key Stage 4, when pupils should:

- understand the importance of feeling positive about oneself and others; be able to express feelings confidently;
- be aware of the part that family life can play in happy and fulfilling relationships;
- be aware of problems which can occur in family life, for example, domestic violence, abuse, bereavement, substance use, unemployment, illness; be aware of the effects of such problems; recognise that some individuals have special needs;
- know about the technology available to help in the reproductive process and be able to discuss the ethical, moral and legal issues involved;
- know in detail and be able to put into practice child care skills;

- understand that the roles of different members of the family may alter over time;
- know how to use the helping agencies, for example, clinics, hospitals, dentists.

It would appear, then, that by using the curriculum guidance for the implementation of the cross-curricular themes (especially health and citizenship) the education service would be in a position to implement a coordinated approach to personal, social and health education. The components described above would be able to provide young people with at least some of the skills, opportunities and knowledge which the authors of *The Needs of Parents* felt were essential.

## What has happened to family life education under the National Curriculum?

Although, as already noted, it is difficult to obtain a comprehensive picture of family life education in schools, there are some indicators worth examining. First of all, the curriculum itself is still in a period of transition. Schools are still experiencing serious difficulties implementing the ten subjects of the basic curriculum, and the additional pressures of teacher appraisal and pupil testing have meant that time and space have been under severe pressure. Furthermore, the five cross-curricular themes were the last parts of the curriculum to be introduced and so their implementation is naturally less advanced. Even more recently the government's acceptance of almost all the proposals of the Dearing review (Dearing, 1994) has meant that further adjustments need to be made. This review, set up because of teachers' serious concerns about over-crowding of the curriculum, will lead to a somewhat slimmed down National Curriculum, with 20% of the timetable (the equivalent of approximately one day per week) available for more flexible planning. To what extent this increased flexibility will enable the reintroduction of some of the squeezed out topics is at present not clear. Dearing also advised that 2.5% of the timetable (approximately one period per week) should be reserved for sex education, along with careers education.

However, there is anecdotal evidence and some research which suggests that the cross-curricular themes may be being abandoned, or at least being given low priority. It would seem that most schools are not teaching the themes in the way envisaged by the NCC, many are choosing to preserve a personal and social education (PSE) slot in the curriculum where certain aspects may appear, whilst others have been unable to address them at all. Rowe and Whitty (1993) asked a sample of one in four secondary schools in England and Wales whether they had made any changes in cross-curricular policy and practice since the NCC guidance was issued. Eighty two% claimed to have changed their approach by 1992, although more detailed enquiries revealed different patterns for the different themes. Health education was one of the themes which was least permeated through other subjects, and was also more likely to have its own curriculum slot or be part of a PSE programme. This study also showed that 70% of schools had written policies for health education, while only one third had written policies for other newer themes, including citizenship. Health education was also more likely to have a designated coordinator, backed by an allowance although, as already noted, it was one of the least permeated themes and therefore presumably required less whole-school planning. Advisory teachers for health education have been playing an important role, being involved in the development of health education policies in 49% of schools, although paradoxically, central government funding for these posts (Grants for Education Support and Training) was discontinued in April 1993.

The Rowe and Whitty study looked at eight schools in detail, and found that there was increasing pressure to submerge the themes into the core and other foundation subjects. They found that the newer themes were 'difficult to identify at classroom level'. The researchers found that the themes had 'a rather shadowy presence' in most of the schools they visited, and concluded that 'it is difficult to see how they will recover from their present position when so much emphasis is placed on the subject orders.'

A survey of 544 schools carried out for the Health Education Authority (1993) confirms some of Rowe and Whitty's findings:

In 1989 (HEA/MORI 1989) the findings... were generally positive: seven out of ten secondary schools had a written policy for health education or PSE and most of the rest were planning to formulate one; 61% of primary schools and 76% of secondary schools had a sex education policy; just over half... of primary schools and 80% of secondary schools had a designated health education co-ordinator.

By 1992 the picture was less positive. Although there was a great deal of commitment and good will towards health education in schools, the general pattern was one of increasing marginalisation. Unsurprisingly, schools were giving top priority to implementing the National Curriculum, to the detriment of health education. The two-thirds of schools who had appointed a health education co-ordinator were not able to give them sufficient non-contact time to carry out their work, and this severely limited their impact. This was combined with a lack of resources for in-service training or new teaching materials, and

> reduced support from LEA advisory teachers (many of whose posts had already disappeared). The quality of health education was found to be variable, depending largely on the commitment and teaching styles of individual members of staff. However, some findings were encouraging: over two-thirds of schools in the survey had developed a written policy on sex education... and between one-half and two-thirds of schools now have a written health education policy.... (p 5)

The HEA felt that, although it was clear that some of the ground gained since the early 1980s was in danger of being lost, the targets set out in *The Health of the Nation* (Department of Health, 1992), for example a large reduction in the numbers of teenage pregnancies, could not be achieved without school-based health education. Indeed, they emphasise that schools have a major part to play in helping to meet many of the objectives and targets.

> The cultivation of healthy alliances between health and education authorities, schools and youth organisations is of paramount importance if the full potential of young people is to be realised. (p 5)

Cross-curricular teaching, of which health education is one theme, has also been affected by cuts to in-service training (INSET) budgets, and by the disappearance of expert advice and support from LEA personnel, so that the development of staff skills to enable cross-curricular teaching and planning are largely unsupported. Furthermore, it would appear that there has been lack of support for the cross-curricular themes from the Department for Education (DFE), and the minimal reference to them in the revised framework for school inspection (the guidance for the new OFSTED inspectorate) means that schools will be under no compulsion to teach these subject areas from either school inspectors or from the pressures of the Standard Assessment Tests (SATs) league tables. This, incidentally (as pointed out by Rowe and Whitty), contrasts with the situation in Northern Ireland, where the inspectorate makes it clear that curriculum organisation will not be considered good where 'although there has been discussion about the introduction of the educational themes ... the themes make little impact at classroom level.'

A further factor influencing, and perhaps squeezing out, the implementation of the original NCC plans is the rise of a moral agenda in education, as exemplified by numerous statements by government ministers. There is now increased emphasis on religious education, along with a move away from multicultural education and equal opportunities. Recent NCC guidance (1993) on spiritual and moral development makes no reference to the cross-curricular themes, and sex education (apart from that included in National Curriculum

Science) is now separated into discrete lessons, from which parents are entitled to withdraw pupils.

Before leaving the area of the National Curriculum, it is worth noting the effects this has had on a subject which was, until recently, an important way in which pupils gained at least some of the knowledge and skills related to parenthood – child development. The foundation subject Technology is now intended to incorporate some aspects of the old home economics and craft, design and technology (CDT). The amalgamation of these specialist subjects has not been straightforward. While it was readily accepted by teachers that textiles could make a valuable contribution to pupils' understanding of technology, the relevance of child development was not regarded as a potential contributor to technology at any Key Stage. Consequently, the survival of child development as an optional examination subject at Key Stage 4 now looks unlikely. In fact, there has already been a marked decline in the number of schools offering courses in child development leading to GCSE or alternative qualifications. One of the reasons for this in 1993 was that schools were still waiting for national guidelines on the future curriculum for Key Stage 4 and the uncertainty had made them cautious about providing courses which might not attract support in the new arrangements. Child development as an examinable subject (that is, Home Economics: Child Development) is now offered by a minority of examination boards (Southern and Northern) and is thought by some to be a challenging course. Because of this, the National Association for Maternal and Child Welfare (NAMCW) is experiencing a continued take-up for its child care courses, which are viewed as more suitable for less academic pupils. More than 200 schools nationally run NAMCW courses, although there are indications that with the implementation of Key Stage 4 there will be a drop in numbers over the next two years.

A further complication in the child care course scenario in schools has arisen from the introduction of General National Vocational Qualifications (GNVQs). However, there is at present very little child care in the Health and Social Care module of the GNVQ, and this is, in any case, considered by some to be inappropriate preparation for working in the child care field.

Despite the continued popularity of child development studies as an optional subject in years 10 and 11, albeit mainly taken by girls, many schools have eliminated it from their list of courses. Its lack of recognition as an aspect of technology in the National Curriculum has denied teachers of the old home economics opportunities to promote separate courses in child development. They must now look towards making a contribution to cross-curricular work. It seems likely that the future of child development in the secondary school curriculum will depend upon the determination of teachers committed to the subject and their influence on school governors, head teachers and examination boards. It is to be hoped that this influence will extend to making such courses more attractive to boys, since this would be likely to have a knock-on effect in increasing the number of men working in the child care field, and on the perceived status of child care and parenting, as opposed to mothering, more generally.

## The role of sex education in family life education

Although the implementation of the National Curriculum is still going through a transitional stage, it would appear from the above description that during the reorganisation and reprioritisation of the curriculum, there has been a distinct marginalisation of areas such as parenthood education, equal opportunities initiatives, health education, home economics and other non-academic subject areas. For a number of reasons sex education is one of the few areas that has survived this reorganisation, although not as part of the cross-curricular health education theme as originally envisaged by the NCC. A late amendment to the Education Act (Department for Education, 1993) now makes sex education a separate, yet compulsory, component of the secondary school curriculum. However, it is a lesson from which parents may withdraw their children where the content is over and beyond that required by National Curriculum Science. In primary schools, governing bodies may choose whether or not to offer sex education, over and above that already required by the National Curriculum Science Key Stages 1 and 2.

What then are the links between sex education and family life education? Should sex education retain a narrow approach to the avoidance of parenthood, rather than preparation for it, in view of the fact that the number of teenage pregnancies still has a long way to fall in order to meet lower government targets, and that there is concern about the social consequences of lone/teenage parenthood and worries about parenting skills? Can sex education be totally divorced from the discussion about relationships, feelings, emotions, family, social context and gender roles?

Section 46 of the 1986 Education Act calls upon LEAs, governing bodies and teachers to:

take such steps as are reasonably practical to secure that where sex education is given...it is given in such a manner as to encourage...pupils to have due regard to moral considerations and the value of family life.

Recent draft guidance from the DFE (*Circular X/94, Education Act 1993: Sex Education in Schools*) on sex education in schools again draws attention to the moral framework in which this subject should be taught. In addition to providing knowledge about the processes of human reproduction and the nature of sexuality and relationships, it 'should lead to the acquisition of skills and attitudes which prepare pupils to manage their relationships in a morally responsible and healthy manner.' The clear moral framework implies consideration of 'the importance of self-restraint, dignity, respect for themselves and others, and sensitivity towards the needs and views of others.' The Sex Education Forum, which represents more than 30 agencies involved in the field of sex education and is based at the National Children's Bureau, suggests in its response to this draft guidance that a distinction needs to be made between a **moral** approach and a **moralistic** one, concluding that:

sex education that includes an exploration of values, relationships and feelings is not only more effective than education that is solely biologically based, it also addresses the concerns expressed by young people about the sex education they receive.

As we have consistently noted in this book, such an approach is also essential to the preparation of young people for eventual family responsibilities.

Recent research by the Sex Education Forum (Thomson and Scott, 1992) showed that there was **inconsistency** between LEAs in terms of numbers of school sex education policies, LEA monitoring of sex education, levels of school governor training in sex education and in terms of the degree of leadership given to schools by LEAs. The study also identified widespread **confusion** concerning the place of sex education in the National Curriculum, the role of a school policy for sex education, and in relation to the different roles and responsibilities of local and national government, school governing bodies, teachers and parents concerning the provision of school sex education. Widespread **anxiety** was found at all levels concerning the teaching of sex education, so much so that the impression was given that the anxieties of those significant adults involved in the provision of sex education was overriding responses to the needs of the young people receiving the education. The Sex Education Forum has now summarised its agreed framework for school sex education in a leaflet (Sex Education Forum, 1992).

## Conclusion

Among the organisations contacted during the preparation for this book, there was considerable support for the view that family life education should have an **official place** in the core curriculum. However, it would seem that in 1994, as in 1984, schools which wish to develop a pastoral curriculum which includes family life education will have to do so independently, with little encouragement or support from the DFE, LEAs or OFSTED. There are, however, indications that OFSTED inspectors will inspect pupils' spiritual and moral development, and consultations about how this will be carried out are currently under way. This could, perhaps, be a way forward for ensuring that schools include some element of family life education in this area of their work.

## Approaches to family life education in schools

We now consider some of the ways in which family life education is being approached in schools, first noting the findings of a small scale study by O'Connor (1990) which set out to establish the priority given to education for parenthood courses as part of school curricula. O'Connor asked 20 teachers attending professional updating courses at Roehampton Institute about the status of parenthood education courses in their schools. The findings indicated that such courses were 'a low status, neglected area of school curricula', and that where they were run as separate child care courses they tended to be seen as 'the province of less academic girls'. Whilst arguing for a central role for parenthood education in school curricula, O'Connor felt that it was 'sensible to avoid being prescriptive about where such courses should occur, or how they were labelled', adding that 'any such courses should aim to explore students' own perceptions and attitudes about parenting and child care'. The author's experience of teaching expectant and actual parents of both sexes on a project for unemployed school leavers reinforced her views on this. Apart from the need to understand how their bodies work, how to keep them healthy and how to avoid pregnancy, pupils also need to understand themselves and make some sense of their own family experiences, and to learn ways of relating to other people in a variety of relationships.

Prout (1988) has also emphasised that teenagers are more knowledgeable than is often assumed and that their understanding might be a major classroom resource. In a study carried out for the Health Education Council (Prendergast and Prout, 1986) it was suggested that some of the assumptions often made about teenagers' knowledge and awareness were 'at best exaggerated and often unwarranted'. Are teenagers really unaware of the reality and demands of small children? Do they accept the romantic images portrayed by advertising? Are they really unaware of the developmental needs of babies and young children, and of the importance of health care in the pre- and post-natal period? This study indicated that, in general, young people were surprisingly knowledgeable and understanding about the implications of parenthood, before receiving any formal education in this area, highlighting the need to set the content of new learning available to them at an appropriate level.

In a study carried out for the Gulbenkian Foundation the Community Education Development Centre (1992) explored the question of whether young people **thought** they received preparation for parenthood in the school setting. Overall, young people felt that what they learned was 'patchy and inadequate'. The authors concluded:

> Firstly, and not surprisingly, that any discussion about parenthood raises painful and sensitive issues for many young people;
>
> Secondly, that young people had very mixed feelings about whether preparation for parenthood had any relevance for them, and that young men particularly found it hard to be positive about its relevance or value;
>
> Last, but not least, that there are some issues about which young people would welcome discussion, and which are all relevant to preparation for parenthood but which do not have a direct focus on parenting, such as communication skills and exploring relationships. (p 26)

The researchers, while acknowledging that young people already know a lot about parenting, suggest that this knowledge is individual, not shared, and much of it is 'unconscious'. They identified what they saw as two important omissions from the list of skills and knowledge which young people felt were relevant to parenthood:

- that becoming a parent is a matter of choice;
- that gender stereotypes are restrictive for young women and for young men – so they need to be examined and debated.

The authors of the CEDC study provide a useful summary of their views on the role of schools in preparing young people for parenthood:

> Schools can provide all young people with the experience of being valued and respected, and with structured opportunities to reflect on their own life experiences and to recognise how these have affected them.

Preparation for parenthood in its widest sense will therefore be best understood as family life education, cross-agency, cross-curriculum, learner-centred, and based in the reality of young people's experience.

It will explore political and sociological aspects of parenting and family life as well as looking at the emotional and psychological perspectives and valuing the diversity of lifestyles. It will aim to enhance young people's self-esteem, confidence and autonomy and have a strong skills base encouraging assertiveness, communication and the building of relationships, negotiation over conflicts and the handling of disruptive events and transitions.

It may be unrealistic to think that we can radically influence the behaviour of future parents. We would need to know more about the complex interaction of knowledge, understanding and future behaviour. It must also not be forgotten that there are significant sources of influence on young people other than school or youth clubs. The most we can do in direct work is to give young people opportunities to see family life and parenting in a wider context, and to equip them with the skills and confidence to make decisions and choices about their own lives now and in the future. (p 28)

The CEDC has now been commissioned to pilot a project in some West Midlands primary and secondary schools that will test out different models of education for family life and parenting. Amongst the broad aims of the project are to ensure that children will be prepared for choices and decisions they will need to make about family life as adults, and to improve their self-esteem through the development and use of personal and social skills which will be relevant within school and beyond. The project will examine the curriculum of schools, the availability of support, information and facilities for children and parents, and relationships between families and schools. As part of this project, which is to be monitored, some schools will develop particular interventions to suit their own circumstances. Such interventions include a support group for Bangladeshi parents, a cross-school and cross-curricular PSE initiative and a collaborative project with parents (fathers in particular).

The foregoing sections have revealed that a number of factors are now working together to make it difficult for schools to give adequate attention to the provision of family life education, whether through the routes of PSE, child development or as elements of subjects such as sociology and psychology. Although the Dearing review (1994) reduced the pressure somewhat, and allowed schools more flexibility over some aspects of the timetable, there is still enormous pressure on teachers to fulfil all that is legally required of them. The cross-curricular themes, where there are definite options to include elements of family life education, are continuing to be squeezed out. Sex education has survived the reorganisatiion and, in fact, been given higher prominence, and it is here that schools can build in some of the broader themes around relationships, as illustrated by the example on page 115. Before moving on to describe some practice models in primary and secondary schools, we consider what can happen at the pre-school stage.

## Pre-school

While few would suggest that children under the age of five years should receive anything approaching formal teaching in family life education, any pre-school experience – be it playgroup, day nursery, nursery school or childminder – does provide an environment outside that of the child's own family where children can be valued and helped to gain self-esteem and self-confidence, as well as learning to value and care for others and to take responsibility for their own choices and decisions. All of these are lifeskills which cannot be learned too early, and will be put to use throughout childhood and adult life, including during parenthood. Projects and themes, such as 'Myself' or 'People who help us' or 'Where we live' provide vehicles for helping children to be aware of themselves as well as of others and of the differences between people. Group sessions can be used to encourage children to listen to others and value their contributions and to take turns. Free play sessions, and more formal ones too, can allow children to make choices about activities, to contribute to the daily routine and then to begin to understand that making choices carries with it responsibilities for the outcomes of such choices. Such approaches to work with the very youngest children – those under three – have been described by Goldschmied and Jackson (1993).

The High/Scope approach (Hohmann and others, 1979) is one example of the kind of curriculum widely used in nursery schools and day nurseries, in which children are encouraged to make decisions and choices for themselves, and to plan and review their activities. Schweinhart and others (1993) show that, not only does a high quality cognitive curriculum lead eventually to a more responsible attitude to adult life, and therefore to parenting, but is also extremely cost-effective overall. Resources provided at the pre-school stage permit large savings later on.

A similar approach is described by Whalley (1994) whose work in a family centre in Corby, Northamptonshire focuses on the need to promote children's self-esteem and self-confidence. The centre's curriculum document includes the following principles:

> Children should feel strong
> Children should feel in control
> Children should feel able to question
> Children should feel able to choose (p.26)

The staff of this centre, who have written their own assertiveness programme for under fives, feel that children should be allowed to plan their play activities, to be offered a variety of first-hand experiences, and to be in charge of their own learning. Whalley suggests, however, that this approach may be under threat because of the practice of baseline assessment of four-year-olds and teaching to attainment targets, leaving less room for children to develop self-confidence at their own pace.

## Primary schools

Pring (in Lang (ed), 1988) suggests that it is self-evident that personal and social education (and hence, preparation for adulthood, including parenthood and family life) should be at the centre of what teachers are planning and doing in primary schools. Indeed, most teachers would claim that they are doing just that. He warns, though, that therein lies the problem, for what is seen to be so self-evidently true rarely receives the critical examination and scrutiny it requires. Pring calls for a systematic reflection upon the values which should be promoted in each school, or in each classroom, together with a detailed analysis of what is defensible as personal development. He spells out his own views of what it is that characterises a person:

- the development of the powers of the mind – to think, to reflect, to engage critically with received assumptions;
- the capacity to recognise others as persons deserving of respect;
- the capacity to act deliberately, and take responsibility for such actions;
- consciousness of one's own value and dignity.

From this Pring argues that every aspect of curriculum planning should be accompanied by a consideration of the impact of all aspects of the curriculum on these qualities which go to make up the mature, adult person.

The topic-based approach is, as at the pre-school stage, much used in primary schools, so that projects on 'Self', 'Growing' or 'My family' can all be used to extend children's knowledge, understanding and respect for different cultures and ways of living. The involvement of parents and other family members will extend the value of such activities. Visits from parents or teachers (both mothers and fathers) with babies and toddlers can be used to enhance children's awareness of the needs of babies and young children. In a specialised version of the familiar group time activities, some schools have developed 'circle time' as an opportunity to build up children's self-esteem, encourage the sharing of thoughts and feelings, to listen to one another and to recognise that each has something to offer (see for example Mosley, 1993).

A further example of family life education in primary schools, developed as a direct outcome of the publication of *The Needs of Parents* in 1984, was the introduction of a pilot programme of **Lifeskills** sessions into the curriculum of a community primary school as part of the 'Job for Life' project in Hampshire (Pugh and Poulton, 1987). The Lifeskills sessions, led by one of the authors, were attended by 10 and 11-year-olds over a period of two years. The aims of the group were:

- to encourage children to think about what is important to them;
- to enable children to develop skills in sharing their ideas and listen to each other's point of view;
- to explore their attitudes to their own parents, siblings and grandparents;
- to explore their attitudes to babies and young children;
- to enable children to explore their own impending physical, emotional and sexual development.

Evaluation of this work found that it increased children's self-confidence, self-respect and understanding of themselves, their ability to negotiate, and to talk to their parents, and helped them to cope with stress, all of which must be qualities of value to people who may become parents.

## Secondary schools

As already noted, with the implementation of the National Curriculum still in some state of turmoil, aspects of family life education may be scattered throughout a wide variety of timetabled subject areas: English, history and art, as well as PSE, health education, biology/science/human biology, sex education, religious education, citizenship or child development courses. Many of the Core Curriculum subjects cover aspects of relationships and families, and it might therefore appear at first sight that a considerable amount is going on in this area. The problem is that, although there is evidence of good practice, it is often uncoordinated and its relevance to family life education not explicit.

Child development courses, where still available, provide an opportunity for young people to have practical experience in caring for young children in placements with playgroups and nurseries or with childminders. However, the restriction on the amount of time available (PSE for 14-year-olds may be allocated just one hour per fortnight) tends to mean that topics covered within this slot are likely to be of more immediate and current interest to pupils – drugs, sex, alcohol and careers education. The Deputy Head of Harlington Upper School, a comprehensive in Bedfordshire, says she does not have a unit called 'parenting' in PSE. 'The practicality of squeezing anything more into a programme that is already bulging would be absolutely impossible' (*Guardian*, 11.1.94).

The implementation of the National Curriculum has made considerable demands on schools and prompted many changes in the organisation and teaching styles of most departments. Whilst aspects of family life education may find expression in a wide variety of timetabled subjects, more often than not it is the programme for PSE which provides the main framework within which a range of relevant issues may be explored. Science and religious education departments, too, play an important role in pupils' acquisition of relevant factual information and the exploration of social and moral issues. Work experience, which usually occurs in Year 10, and child development courses, where they are still offered, are highly valued by older pupils because they provide them with opportunities to take more responsibility for themselves and for others. Perhaps more important is the fact that pupils say that for the duration of their placements they are treated more as adults and this boosts their self-confidence.

The gradual loss of child development courses is a matter for concern. The long-term effects of the assimilation of home economics into technology in the National Curriculum have yet to be seen. The exclusion of child development from the National Curriculum has already created a noticeable gap in the range of optional courses available to pupils at Key Stage 4. As we have noted, the time allocated for PSE is limited and demands for the inclusion of more intensive courses on education for family responsibilities, in an already crowded curriculum, seem unlikely to succeed.

*An example of a PSE course including sex education and family life education was supplied by a teacher at Walton le Dale High School Lancashire. The programme runs through from Year 7 to Year 11 (ages 11 to 16), one hour per week during half the school year, although it may be possible to extend this to the whole year following the Dearing review recommendations.*

*Year 7:*    *The beginnings of sex education, using the TV programme 'Living and Growing'. Topics include friendship groups, physical changes in our bodies, being aware of our bodies, and the idea of respect and responsibility for each other. All this is in the context of healthy lifestyles.*

*Year 8:*    *Social development, friendships and so on.*

*Year 9:*    *Being yourself: drugs, HIV/AIDS, relationships.*

*Year 10: Relationships: attitudes, values, morals, sensitivity to other people's feelings.*

*These sessions often have the support and involvement of a local health visitor and AIDS counsellor from a local hospital. A teenage mother comes into the classroom to talk about what it is really like to be pregnant and a parent. Also use input from the National Childbirth Trust mothers, and fathers, to cover what is involved in preparing for parenthood. This school also uses a Liverpool drama group (First Bite Theatre Group) who perform to all 150 Year 10 pupils and follow up with a one-hour workshop.*

*Year 11: a look at the wider issues, lifestyles, relationships.*

*Another interesting example of work with High School pupils in Years 5 and 6 (nine and ten-year-olds) is supplied by Drumchapel High School in Strathclyde. Students meet in the Drumchapel Family Learning Centre, which offers a range of activities for the local community, for five periods a week for half the school year. The course does not look at parenting as such, but rather asks students to look at, think about and discuss a range of topics which relate to children and their care, such as:*

- *the purpose and effectiveness of local resources in meeting the needs of children and their carers in areas such as housing, health services, employment, leisure amenities and transport;*
- *children's development – meeting children's physical and emotional needs and the importance of stimulation and play.*

*The course involves outside speakers and a week's work experience in one of the local nurseries, including the one at the Centre.*

## People and resources

The primary human resource for family life education in schools is, of course, the hard-pressed teacher. Health visitors and school nurses, a disappearing breed in some areas, also play a leading role when possible. Organisations such as RELATE (formerly the Marriage Guidance Council) and the National Childbirth Trust (NCT) can provide volunteers to go into schools at all levels. The Education and Training arm of RELATE, for example, despite funding constraints, have a structured programme of courses which they run in schools, amounting to over 7,000 hours per year and constituting about half of the organisation's total training service. These courses are usually aimed at children aged 14 plus, and focus on relationships, sexuality and assertiveness. One example is the course entitled *Room To Be Me* run by Brighton RELATE and aimed at helping young people to express their needs more effectively. An evaluation of this course by the University of Sussex (Freeman and Hemmings, 1994) reports its success in changing the views of young people, in particular in promoting their self-esteem and viewing their teachers as people who will listen to their concerns. Other branches of NCT have developed a training programme involving schools, such as the one in Farnham, Surrey where mothers were asked to contribute to Year 6 (ten to 11-year-olds) sex education studies, looking at 'growth and change' during the mother's pregnancy and the baby up to one-year-old.

The NCT, through its education groups, promotes birth education for pre-school and primary age children through its *Birds, Bees and Babies* workshops in pre-school groups and schools. Groups also visit secondary schools and colleges where students gain invaluable experience of parenthood at close quarters, talking to real parents and observing real children. This is 'a far cry from learning about child development and pregnancy just from a book' states the NCT Annual Report 1992. Students on child care courses are also placed in the homes of NCT members in order to gain direct experience of family life. The Brook Advisory Centres are also now taking an active role in schools, with advice to teachers, parents and school governors about sex education and related topics.

Teenage parents themselves can provide a very vivid and meaningful view to their own peer group in their old schools, of what it is really like to be a parent. One example is a Bristol project, the Barton Hill and Easton Young Mothers' Group, who have now produced a video and booklet to try to counteract the glossy image of motherhood and babies portrayed in the media, and give young people a more realistic account of life as a young parent (Teenage Parenthood Network, 1992).

In some areas, for example in parts of Nottinghamshire, Classroom Support Service workers are available to primary school teachers in the field of PSE and broadly based family life education.

The organisation Schools Outreach (pioneered in the 1950s) employs a small number of pastoral care workers, currently working in about 20 schools, both directly with pupils and as support for teachers. The topics covered by these workers include some elements of preparation for parenthood such as relationship building and 'parentcraft'.

There are numerous resource packs for sex education and family life education on the market, and some examples of those likely to be helpful in the area of family life education are listed in Appendix 2.

## Training and support for teachers

Family life education draws upon a wide range of curriculum subjects. Its effectiveness very much depends upon the teacher's skill in restructuring classroom discussion which permits pupils to explore attitudes, values and beliefs. Teachers need to be well trained to do this and to feel confident to deal with sensitive and controversial issues. Unfortunately not all teachers who are involved in the teaching of programmes which focus more specifically on family life matters, for example in PSE, have sufficient confidence to engage pupils in discussion. Instead they may rely too heavily on written work, usually in the form of worksheets. In consequence, for many pupils the lessons become boring and fail to promote learning with understanding. Indeed, it would appear that there has been little or no evaluation of PSE in schools, so that this is an important area for monitoring and research in the future.

Against this background the provision of appropriate INSET is extremely important. In some respects the devolvement of budgets to schools means that schools have more control over the type of in-service courses they choose to support. It means, however, that in order to identify more accurately the needs of staff, schools should have well-thought-out strategies for monitoring and evaluating teaching and learning.

The availability of in-service courses which are tailor-made to meet the individual requirements of schools has important implications for the provision of INSET. LEA advisory services are rapidly diminishing in size, leaving some schools with little support for specialist subject teachers and even less for those involved in cross-curricular work. The education policy makers will need to take note of the possible long-term effect of this trend.

Initial teacher training, which is becoming increasingly school-based, may not automatically equip teachers with the skills required to deal successfully with teaching cross-curricular issues such as health education (Wiliams, 1985). Access to appropriate in-service training therefore becomes even more important.

# Outside and beyond school

The first part of this chapter described the current complexities resulting from recent changes to the school curriculum, which have been followed by less emphasis being placed nationally on the role of schools in family life education. Overall, the opportunities for children to take part in such courses are, therefore, even more 'hit and miss' than they were during the 80s.

The peer group is still a powerful influence during the teenage years as young people seek to define their own identity. Relationships or friendships formed both in and out of school may lead to cohabitation, marriage or parenthood, and may introduce young people to a set of values and attitudes very different from those of their families. Economic, social, moral and legal changes have eroded many of the past sanctions related to sexual experimentation, as well as many of the opportunities and expectations for future careers or life plans. Yet the pursuit of personal and sexual fulfilment is, more than ever, promulgated by the media. And, as we noted in chapter 1, the current generation of young people is faced with a significantly different situation to that experienced by their parents in terms of unemployment, poverty, housing and family structure.

## The youth service and informal education

Despite the fact that there have been major changes in the structure and role of the youth service since the late 1980s, the precise nature and content of the work is determined at local level, or within individual voluntary organisations and is still, therefore, very variable and uncoordinated. While the service remains locally determined, many youth service organisations are now basing their curriculum on a Statement of Purpose agreed at a government-sponsored national conference in 1991 (National Youth Agency, 1991):

The purpose of youth work is to redress all forms of inequality and to ensure equality of opportunity for all young people to fulfil their potential as empowered individuals and members of groups and communities and to support young people during the transition to adulthood.

The government-funded National Youth Agency, reconstituted in 1991, describes the youth service in England as 'part of the education system, offering young people planned programmes of personal and social education. It provides opportunities for young people to pursue activities and interests not as ends in themselves, but as part of a wider developmental process, in which they learn about themselves and the society they live in.' An ideal setting it would seem for family life education.

The search for clarity in defining the objectives of the Youth Service began in the 1970s with a series of government reports and reviews. The Thompson report *Experience and Participation* (Thompson, 1982) acted as a catalyst for further review and reassessment at local level. *Taking Shape* (Smith, 1989) documented the results of these reviews, with a survey focusing on organisation and delivery, curriculum issues, and priority groups for young people. In terms of organisation the greatest concerns were training, staff development and partnership with the voluntary sector. In relation to curriculum issues the priorities were the participation of young people, and antisexist and antiracist work. Girls and young women were seen as a priority group by 80% of the survey returns although, ironically, at about the same time the National Girls Work Unit was being abolished, pointing up just how far apart policy and practice can sometimes be.

Thompson's report had paved the way for new patterns in the Youth Service, leading to the establishment of a Youth Service Unit at the Department for Education, the appointment of a National Advisory Council for the Youth Service, a review of the National Youth Bureau (leading to its eventual rebirth as the National Youth Agency), and the establishment of a Council for Education and Training in Youth and Community Work to undertake accreditation and endorsement of training. Most recently the three Ministerial Conferences of 1990, 1991 and 1992 have continued the work of developing the youth service into a more coherent education service, with greater common purpose and clearer indicators of what it seeks to achieve. In the 1990s there is considerably more centralised direction of policy by government for a service which still depends on local resources for its delivery, thus the service is vulnerable, having no real statutory base. Smith (1988) argues that, as a result of this,

Youth Service delivery is distinctly 'hit and miss' compared with other major schemes such as Intermediate Treatment (IT) and Youth Training. Although the service is open to all young people within the age range 11 to 25 (with priority given to 13 to 19-year-olds), this open access can sometimes lead to some groups of young people being excluded. Some provision is therefore targeted at, for example, young women, young black people, young people with disabilities, young gay men and young lesbians. The commitment to be open to all then has to be balanced against the need to focus increasingly limited resources on young people most in need of the service.

Although many youth clubs are for mixed groups, there is an increasing tendency for youth work to be specifically with boys and young men, or with girls and young women. Both, however, may be under threat from cuts to provision. With young men there are examples of programmes focusing on sexism, sexuality and masculinity and the tensions and contradictions involved in being young and male, for example, Cousins, 1986; Davidson, 1988; Lloyd, 1985, 1986; Youth Work Advisory Group, Scotland, 1987. Work with young women focuses on a variety of topics including sexuality, assertiveness, sexism, the position of women in society as described, for example, in Carpenter and Yeung, 1986 and Youth Clubs UK, 1987.

Although youth work offers opportunities which are educative and empowering, there are probably still few explicit social education programmes within the youth service, although there are many which incorporate the key areas of adolescent development:

- adjusting to puberty and sexuality, including responsibilities connected with sexual activity;
- developing a widening range of social skills and competence;
- relating to peer group and family;
- developing emotional maturity, independence, self-knowledge, self-esteem and examining values and norms of behaviour;
- achieving intellectual potential;
- increasing awareness of adolescent and adult needs and development;
- considering the relationships between work, home and family;
- being with young children and discovering what is involved in being a parent;
- using leisure time, unemployment and enforced leisure constructively and competently.

Whatever its form, and there are many variations, the youth service is concerned with creating opportunities in which different programmes, projects and groups can be provided for young people. One of the purposes of such groups is to examine and discuss issues related to being a person – as an adult, worker, parent and citizen. Such programmes may be more acceptable to some young people outside the confines of the school curriculum and, usually, the school premises. This context of informal settings and natural groups which young people have chosen to attend is conducive to both individual and group approaches. In response to research which showed that young people wanted quality information available in accessible environments, the National Youth Agency set up its Information Shop Initiative in 1991 in Bradford. There are now 12 such shops, with other projects making use of the NYA's classification system for youth information (White, 1994).

There has been considerable growth over the last ten years, since *The Needs of Parents* was written, in the involvement of the churches in work with young people, in youth clubs and other settings. However, there is evidence of concern at the falling numbers of young people attending church and being involved in associated youth activities (Brierley, 1993). In addition, the changes in local government funding arrangements means that youth clubs generally, including some of those run by the churches and faith communities, now have to enter into contracts to provide services for local councils. The Church of England, with its own financial problems, is experiencing pressures of its own, with diocesan youth officer posts under severe strain.

Other faith communities – Jews, Muslims, Buddhists and Hindus – also provide for their young people as demonstrated, for example, by the work of the Jewish Marriage Council, and the weekly discussions (study circles) for young Muslims in which discussion is promoted about relationships, choice of marriage partners, families and upbringing of children.

In the more structured settings and context of the uniformed organisations there is an assumption that their general method and approach is designed to encourage reliability and responsibility. There are opportunities for learning in small groups and experiencing the need for care and consideration for others, which is seen as important training for family life. Individual organisations, such as Cubs and Scouts, Brownies and Guides, Woodcraft Folk and the Duke of Edinburgh Award, provide specific opportunities in the form of work for 'badges', some of which are relevant to the field of family life education.

A similar age group is now catered for in the 1,000 or so **out-of-school clubs** which have developed during recent years with support and funding from the government via the Training and Education Councils (TECs). Pressure for such provision has come from both parents and employers and, although not yet adequate to meet the demand for such services, these clubs can form part of the network of support for parents who are in employment, and provide opportunities for confidence-building work with children.

## Other educational opportunities

A large number of colleges in the UK offer a variety of full-time, part-time and day release courses. In the past some of these courses (such as YOP and YTS) have provided opportunities for training in life and social skills for trainees. The present Youth Training scheme is now part of the government's policy for young people, supposedly guaranteeing a place for each school leaver. Although it includes vocational training as well as workplace learning and experience, there is much less opportunity for the inclusion of social and life skills than was the case with the earlier schemes, with the emphasis being given to job-related skills.

The increasing number of community schools and colleges opening their doors to adults as well as to young people could lead to useful opportunities for shared discussion in courses related to family life education, although there is little evidence so far to indicate that this is happening widely. Sections 12 and 13 of the Further and Higher Education Act 1992 grants all schools the power to provide further education, but at present there are a number of issues to be worked through, such as schools' concerns about the security of children during the school day, and traditional adult education providers' concerns about competition. As we said in *The Needs of Parents*, bringing young people into contact with 'practitioners' of family life and parenthood provides an excellent grounding in parenting skills for prospective mothers and fathers, as well as training young people for jobs in day and residential nurseries and preparing them for careers in a wide variety of social, community and health agencies.

There are obviously many informal settings where workers other than youth and community workers and further education lecturers create opportunities for individual counselling and advice or informal discussion groups. Two such examples are work with young people leaving care, undertaken by both statutory and voluntary organisations; and intermediate treatment. During the middle to late 1980s Intermediate Treatment (IT) developed as an intensive programme for young offenders as a direct alternative to custody. The group work focus of previous years was phased out in favour of individual programmes for young people, including elements such as counselling, exercises designed to increase resistance to peer group pressure, community service and social skills programmes. IT as a form of preventive work for young people at risk was largely discredited in the 1980s, so authorities who still wished to pursue this approach organised their provision separately from court-based programmes and called it 'diversion' or 'youth support'. However, social services departments which needed to make cuts to their budgets in the late 1980s and early 1990s usually pruned the preventative work first. It is unlikely that the programmes that remain currently provide extensive opportunities for family life education.

There seems to be little evidence that opportunities are taken in residential care settings to explicitly prepare young people for the responsibilities of parenthood. However, work with young people 'ceasing to be looked after' by the local authority (in the terminology of the Children Act 1989) or leaving care, such as that carried out by the six after care projects managed by the Royal Philanthropic Society in the south-east of England, is very much aimed at enhancing young people's self esteem and self-confidence, in preparation for independent living (Smith, 1994). Combating feelings of isolation and coping with and sustaining relationships are also foci for the work of these projects. Indeed, the need for such support for this vulnerable group of young people has been demonstrated in recent studies, for example, Garnett (1992) and Biehal and others (1992). These studies highlighted the high proportion of young women leaving care who become young mothers and raise concerns about the lack of support services these people receive. These concerns are shared by the National Children's Bureau's Children's Residential Care Unit (Phil Youdan, personal communication April 1994) who perceives the need for young people in care to be able to relate to an adult who has overall 'ambitions for that child' in helping to prepare him or her for adulthood.

We make reference to programmes of work on parenting and family life with young men in Young Offender Institutions and with fathers in prisons in chapter 6.

## Summary

There is still little evidence of a coordinated approach to family life education in schools and other youth settings. To a large extent the provision of family life education in schools has been the victim of a series of legislative changes, leading to expansion of a core curriculum, allowing less time for broader subjects related to education of the whole person. It has proved difficult to obtain a comprehensive picture of what is actually going on in schools, following the introduction of local management of schools and reduction in the role of local education authorities. Furthermore, it would appear that whatever is going on in schools in the area of family life education is very dependent on the interest of individual teachers with the support of heads and governors. It seems likely that training and support for teachers in this area is still inadequate, as it was ten years ago.

There would appear to be support for personal and social education in schools from the Department of Health, because of the need to meet Health of the Nation targets, and it may be through this route that increased emphasis and resources can be found. Sex education has survived the reorganisation and perhaps provides one of the ways in to provision of some elements of family life education in schools.

The Youth Service, whilst providing educational opportunities which are participative and empowering, is not a major provider of family life education, and its role is unclear, despite recent moves towards a more common purpose, and opportunities for family life education in other settings appear to be limited.

# 5. Becoming a parent: the transition to parenthood

## Introduction

In 1984 *The Needs of Parents* recommended that for people in the period of transition to parenthood a range of support should be provided, right through from pre-conception, during pregnancy, birth and during the postnatal period. Such support should be available to fathers as well as mothers and should be relevant to people's needs – especially the young and parents from minority ethnic families. Antenatal services should provide information not just about the birth process, but about fatherhood and motherhood too and about the social and emotional changes/challenges of parenthood. Such services should be accessible and provided in line with research findings about prospective parents' wishes. One of the most important recommendations was about the need for continuity between the antenatal and postnatal stage, and for local support networks to be set up for new parents. This chapter, then, seeks to explore the facilities and opportunities that currently exist to help people plan their parenthood; the care and support that is available before conception; antenatal care and antenatal classes; choices in childbirth; care and support in the postnatal period; special needs and provision for certain groups; and resources available.

*Life Will Never Be The Same Again* proclaims the title of a review of antenatal and postnatal health education (Combes and Schonveld, 1992). Indeed, the transition from being a couple to becoming parents with children is widely recognised as presenting parents with the need for complex psychological and social adjustments. Le Masters (1957) has referred to this period as a 'crisis' for the men and women concerned. More recently Cowan (1987) has drawn a number of conclusions from a review of research, some of which are relevant to the subject of this chapter:

- 'new parents' are at high risk of depression;

- conflict or distress in the family while a child is young is accompanied by less optimal parent-child relationships and slower progress in the child's cognitive and social development up until and beyond starting school;
- difficulties in parenting may be predicted from the level of stress and distress couples experienced during pregnancy;
- limited amounts of professional intervention with couples during the first year of parenthood which focuses on the partner-parent relationship had a significant impact on reducing the separation rate of couples, improving the quality of parenting and their child's adjustment and development.

In *The Needs of Parents* we reported that, following the Court Report (Committee on Child Health Services, 1976), research studies indicated that in coping with birth and the transition to parenthood it is not so much what you know that is important but how the experience is managed (Clulow and others, 1982 and Draper and others, 1981). A supportive network of friends, family and professionals which will provide continuity of care and advice from early pregnancy to the early months of parenthood may well be of more value than a series of classes in coping with a major life-change. Almost a decade later, in assessing the effectiveness of antenatal support and education, Combes and Schonveld (1992) conclude that there is a long way to go in making full use of educational opportunities during pregnancy, and immediately after birth.

## Planning parenthood

The idea of being able to plan when and where to become a parent assumes certain conditions – choice, rationality and means. Certainly for many the potential for choice is greater than it was ten years ago. Contraceptive and family planning advice is widely available and is generally socially acceptable. Despite this, however, for many, whether for legal, social, religious or medical reasons, the choice may be theoretical rather than real. There is still a common expectation, sometimes exacerbated by pressure from friends and families, that married and cohabiting couples will have children. Nevertheless, some couples do choose not to have children and, as noted in chapter 1, the arrival of the first child at an older average age of the mother indicates that more people are consciously planning when to enter parenthood. Figures from the Family Planning Association, however, (Factsheet 3C, 1992) suggest that one-third of births are still unplanned. Add to this the estimate of the number of terminations, and it would seem that up to one half of all conceptions are unplanned.

Even when pregnancies are planned, that is, a conscious decision is taken to have a child, it is still necessary to think through and recognise the full implications of what it will mean to be a parent, and the objectivity of this task is made considerably more difficult by the romantic presentation of parenthood, especially motherhood, in the media. In their study of couples becoming parents (Mansfield and others, forthcoming) the authors demonstrate the complex way in which the arrival of children alters the level of interdependence in all partnerships and how in particular partnerships this leads to an erosion of the relationship between father and mother. Cowan and Cowan (1992) report that couples who are in their thirties when their first child is born experience a larger decline in marital satisfaction than younger couples – they tend to have been married longer before becoming parents and find the integration of a baby into their lives presents a greater challenge to them as a couple. However, on the positive side, compared with younger mothers and fathers, they maintain higher levels of self-esteem throughout the period from pregnancy to two years after the birth.

## Care and support before conception

The importance of preparation for both pregnancy and childbirth in terms of the mother's general state of health has long been recognised (Ministry of Health, 1932). However, despite numerous studies and reports which have documented the links between poor health care and nutrition and the increased risks to both mother and baby, the National Health Service (NHS) does not widely provide clinics or centres to give health or nutritional counselling to couples before conception. Smoking, though, has been the subject of much campaigning and advice in recent years and there is now a clear message that prospective mothers, and fathers, who smoke should take steps to curtail the habit before and during pregnancy.

*The Health of the Nation* (Department of Health, 1992) provides a focus to reassess how health education can contribute to the improvement in health of children and parents and recognises 'the importance of sustaining and building on progress which has been made already in...maternal and child health'. Health promotion at this key stage (that is, before conception) aims to encourage and support parents to adopt and sustain healthy life practices, thereby reducing the risk factors believed to be harmful to the good health of the family. It also aims to encourage prospective and new parents to use the health services available to them and make decisions individually and collectively to improve their health status and environment.

Despite the general lack of pre-conceptual advice, some groups have been providing information, advice and services to parents and those professionals who are interested in developing better pre-conceptual care, for example, the Foundation for Education and Research in Child-bearing, which has consistently promoted the need to recognise that low birth-weight and disability are associated with maternal nutrition (Wynn and Wynn, 1981). The Maternity Alliance has produced a leaflet for women, and also one for men on preconception health.

An example of a series of experimental evening health education sessions is described by Gillies and Chaudry (1984). These sessions, in Surrey District Health Authority, were offered to couples interested in having a baby in the future and also to those in the early stages of pregnancy. The response to the classes was enthusiastic, and a follow-up questionnaire indicated that, as a result of attending, those not already pregnant intended to make changes in their life-style to reduce smoking and alcohol intake, ensure sensible eating patterns and maintain regular exercise, when planning pregnancy. One woman said she would discontinue oral contraception earlier than she had planned to, after having had the facts presented to her.

An increasing number of general practitioners (GPs) and health visitors now run well woman clinics, an ideal venue for counselling sessions on pre-conception issues. The impact of GP fund-holding has, however, meant that such provision may be patchy, and indeed absent in some areas. Family planning clinics provide similar opportunities to promote healthy lifestyles and nutritional counselling.

Genetic counselling is increasingly available to those couples who have reason to suspect that a child might be born with a disability and genetic testing is becoming available for a wider range of conditions. Indeed, there is current debate around the ethical issues raised by such an approach which could lead eventually to the birth of the 'designer baby'.

## Looking forward to becoming a parent

As already indicated, and as Mansfield and Collard (1988) found, expecting a child is a major transition in the lives of couples. During the change to parenthood, these authors found that becoming a mother had a great impact on women's sense of self, and this began during pregnancy. The physical changes of pregnancy, and the anticipation of other changes, such as giving up work or organising child care, helped them to recognise change. Husbands found this much more difficult: they often expressed a sense of watching change in their partners, rather than being involved themselves. This was confirmed in the Combes and Schonveld (1992) study which included interviews with fathers, some of whom felt that they were not really fathers until their baby was born, although they saw their partners as 'mothers already'. Generally, they felt that they were just waiting, and there was not much they could do until after the birth. Some fathers mentioned preparing financially and budgeting for the time when they would only have one salary; and some first-time fathers saw fatherhood as a challenge and an exciting opportunity.

# Antenatal care and support

The NHS provides two services for pregnant women:

- antenatal care through hospital and GP-based clinics, primarily concerned with the physical health of both mother and foetus; and
- antenatal classes which provide information and advice to women (and to a limited extent, to their partners).

Antenatal **care** is primarily a screening process concerned with monitoring the expectant mother physically for the job of labour and childbirth. Antenatal **classes** have an educational role and are designed to prepare the mother (and sometimes the father) through information, instruction and discussion. Generally speaking, professionals tend to hold to this distinction, although parents them-selves may not perceive it in this way.

Voluntary organisations, such as The National Childbirth Trust (NCT), provide more parent-run and parent-centred groups with a greater emphasis on peer education and mutual support after birth, and, in many instances, these innovative and supportive services fill the gaps in existing statutory provision.

An earlier enquiry into maternity care (Department of Health and Social Security, 1980) addressed the issue of mortality and how to make birth safer. In contrast the recent Health Committee chaired by Nicholas Winterton MP, took as its starting point how the NHS provides care for healthy women giving birth to normal, healthy children. The report (House of Commons Health Committee, 1992) concluded that women wanted continuity of care and carer throughout pregnancy and childbirth and during the postnatal period, and that most women had little choice about where their baby was born. In fact, an NCT survey in 1992 indicated that women were likely to receive care from up to 20 different professionals during this period. The Committee made a series of recommendations about how maternity care should be changed to make it more effective and satisfying for all:

- women should receive care from a small number of individuals whom they can really get to know;
- women should be able to make choices about their care as equal partners with midwives and doctors;
- parents should be offered reliable written information about the range of options available;
- women should feel in control of what happens to them.

It appears (NCT Annual Report, 1992) that many health regions, health districts and provider units have responded to the Winterton Report without waiting for further government deliberations: more clinics are providing written information; new schemes for midwifery-led care are being set up; more hospitals are providing birthing pools to extend the range of birth options.

Following publication of the Winterton Report, the government set up an Expert Maternity Group to review policy on care during childbirth, including the place of birth. This Group held a conference in March 1993, one of the outcomes of which was a consensus statement drawing attention to aspects of the provision of choice for women. One extract from this statement highlights the need for improved consistency of maternity services:

> It is evident that some groups of women are offered less choice than others. Women from black and minority ethnic communities, disabled women, travellers and those in poor or no housing, find that choice and access which is sometimes available to others is frequently not available to them.

So what can antenatal care and support offer during this transition period, for prospective mothers and fathers, and for special groups such as young parents, minority ethnic groups and adoptive parents? Combes and Schonveld's review (1992) seeks to answer three questions:

- What needs do parents have for education?
- How are these needs being met? Are they being met appropriately and effectively?
- Is parent education equally accessible and appropriate to all?

The main findings of their study revealed serious deficiencies:

- needs and provision are mismatched;
- certain parents are missing out;
- education in care settings is underestimated;
- men are missing out;
- there is a narrow focus;
- aims are unclear;
- educational quality is poor;
- management support is lacking.

We shall return to consider some of these points in more detail later in this chapter.

The Health Education Authority (HEA) has recently (1989-1993) undertaken a major family and child health initiative whose strategic objective is to contribute to improvement in the health of pregnant women and their partners, children under five and parents with children under 16. The key objectives of this programme, which includes two new publications aimed at parents (the *New Pregnancy Book* and *Birth to Five*), a parent education project and a family education project, are:

- to improve knowledge amongst pregnant women, partners and parents with children under five about key health education priorities;
- to increase parent and family skills, confidence and ability to make health decisions.

Guidance for purchasers and providers of parent education is given in another HEA publication (Rowe and Mahoney, 1993). This manual is intended to enable the purchasers and main NHS providers of parent education to respond effectively to the demands of consumers. The publication covers the roles of purchasers, providers, health promotion departments and the training needs of professionals, together with the attainment of quality standards and targets. It includes a model specification (p 27-28) for parent education intended as a statement of purchasing intentions, and to inform contract negotiations with individual providers (health professionals and managers). This model specification is reproduced on the following pages.

# Model specification for parent education

## Summary

This specification sets out the Health Authority's requirements for parent education. The Health Authority expects each provider to ensure that women and their partners are offered high-quality information and education throughout pregnancy, labour and the early months of parenting.

### Objectives

- To ensure that parent-focused education programmes are developed with and for the consumers.
- To incorporate parent education into all contacts across all agencies with women and their partners, including confirmation of pregnancy, antenatal visits and post-natally.
- To provide women and their partners with high-quality consistent information about pregnancy, labour and postnatally that is culturally and ethnically sensitive.
- To ensure that parent education will be carried out by skilled and appropriately trained health visitors.

### Services to be provided

- Parent education in the care setting.
- Encouragement of women and their partners to be active participants in their care plan and to feel able to ask questions whenever they wish.
- Full explanations to be given to parents, and informed consent obtained for all investigations and tests carried out during the antenatal and postnatal periods.
- Explanation of recognition of onset of labour, together with provision of names and telephone numbers for contacting services.
- Provision of advice and support on smoking, alcohol, diet and medication to all women as early as possible.

### Coordination of parent education

- To nominate an appropriately qualified senior member of staff to work as parent education coordinator for maternity services and links into health visiting and GP services.
- To review the training needs for all staff providing parent education and ensure that their knowledge and skills are maintained.
- To identify those staff with specialist training in group work skills, participative teaching skills and smoking cessation counselling: to provide the purchasers with an account of the numbers to be trained at contract monitoring meetings.

### Parent education classes

- To offer a range of parent education classes that are based on consumer need and that consider access, timing, location and frequency for the women and partners who are attending.

- To review the needs locally for parent education to target individuals and identify groups with differing needs in terms of service provision or referral, for example:
  - teenage parents;
  - black and minority ethnic parents;
  - disabled women and their partners;
  - women who are HIV positive and their partners;
  - drug-using parents;
  - adoptive parents.
- To ensure that classes are offered that provide the maximum opportunity to include health advice and support at appropriate times during the pregnancy and postnatally.
- To offer staff resources to community organisations who work with parents.
- To ensure that classes for parent education are evaluated by those parents with an agreed protocol.

## Provision of information

- To provide all first-time parents with a copy of the HEA's *Pregnancy Book* and *Birth to Five* (HEA, 1993 and 1992), free of charge.
- To provide parents with written information about the availability and location of local parent education classes, clinics and postnatal clinics.
- To provide information appropriate for women and their partners whose first language is not English.
- To provide explanation and ready access to information in the antental and postnatal clinic waiting areas that can refer parents to, for example;
  - local community organisations;
  - leisure classes;
  - crying baby services;
  - local health visiting services;
  - GP surgeries;
  - postnatal support groups;
  - breastfeeding counselling.
- To provide information about the names and roles of the different professionals involved in their care.

## Management coordination

- To carry out a review of the current practice of parent education on an annual basis and provide purchasers with an overview and action plan for any changes to be implemented.
- To ensure that the maternity and health visiting services provide consistent, accurate and timely advice on:
  - diet;
  - infant feeding;
  - child development;
  - smoking;
  - immunisation;
  - sexual health.

Childbirth at home is still a rare event, with only one per cent home confinements in 1990 (Department of Health, 1991), although there is some evidence that it may be on the increase again in recent years (one community midwife repeatedly clocks up about 30 per year in her west London patch) (*The Independent*, 11.8.93). Modern antenatal care, with its emphasis on elaborate techniques and expensive equipment such as ultrasound scanning for diagnosis and treatment of potential problems has increased the 'medicalisation' of birth and pregnancy. In *The Needs of Parents* we concluded that 'the social and emotional aspects such as reassurance, relief from anxiety and the need for information and discussion tend to have been sacrificed to the sophisticated technology.' Eight years later Combes and Schonveld (1992) still find it necessary to write:

> Studies consistently report that significant numbers of mothers feel unable to ask questions of staff, learn very little from their experiences of [antenatal] care, and tend to have their emotional, social and psychological needs disregarded through a focus on medical aspects of antenatal care and baby management aspects of postnatal care.

Recognising this, the Parent-Infant Project (PIPPIN) began in 1989 a four-year action research project in collaboration with Parent Network. The aim of this project was the development of an innovative education and support programme which could support expectant and new parents by encouraging the development of nurturing family and parent-infant relationships (Parr, 1993). PIPPIN, intended as a complement to medical and health aspects covered by NHS antenatal and postnatal classes, aims to help parents understand the emotional aspects of pregnancy, the birth process and the effects of a new baby on men, women and other family members; promote the learning of communication, listening and problem-solving skills for new parenthood and family life; and help parents develop sensitivity and trust between themselves and their baby, in order to respond confidently to his or her needs. The programme is based mainly on small group sessions, in three phases: during early to mid-pregnancy, during late pregnancy and in the first month after birth, and when the baby is between one and four months old. A fourth phase takes the form of a home visit as soon as possible after birth. The scheme is still in its pilot phase, having (up to May 1993) involved just over 100 couples (50 in the intervention group and 56 in a control group) in nine group programmes, and is being evaluated as part of a PhD study (Parr, 1993). As expected from the evaluator's experience of earlier antenatal group work, one or two couples from each group did not complete the course, leaving after the first or second session. On following up these couples, it was found that there were existing problems within their relationships which might have benefited from other forms of intervention. The parents who did complete the course expressed high levels of satisfaction with the content and focus of the intervention, and a follow-up after six months found that the intervention group parents were better adjusted in terms of a number of measures such as their confidence as parents, the parent/infant relationship, parental anxiety, coping mechanisms and the couple relationship. These couples were also found to be more open and honest in expressing dissatisfaction with the challenges of new parenthood, as compared with the control group who tended to bottle up their resentments. The evaluator reports that analysis of the group process shows that the intervention appears to have achieved its benefits through equal attention to group dynamics and the choice of topics. An indicator of the popularity of this approach is that two years after the completion of the study, all the intervention groups are still continuing to meet on their own, and fathers are still actively involved. The research programme under Parent Network is now complete, but is being replicated by PIPPIN (now an independent charity) in other parts of the country, and further long-term research is planned with support from the Artemis Trust.

## Antenatal clinic attendance

The take-up of antenatal care has repeatedly been reported as being very high, with a large majority of women attending most or all of their clinic appointments. This contrasts with the relatively low take-up rates reported for antenatal classes (see following section), so that for a significant proportion of women (the majority in some areas) attendance at clinics provides the main opportunity for the health service to respond to educational needs. It can be argued that this group of women, who do not attend classes for a variety of reasons, are the very ones who are in greatest need of education in the antenatal care setting (Combes and Schonveld, 1992).

Most women confirm their pregnancy at the surgery of their general practitioner, who is therefore in an ideal position to give information and advice in the very early stages of pregnancy, and to refer women to antenatal clinics. There is evidence (see, for example, McCabe and others, 1984; Madeley and others, 1989; McKnight and Merrett, 1987) that opportunities are missed at this stage, and that even where advice is given it is generally concentrated on medical topics, rather than on the emotional and social aspects of pregnancy.

The antenatal clinic 'booking visit' is perceived by many professionals as crucial in assessing the needs of pregnant women and
planning their future care. It is therefore important that this should
take place as early as possible in pregnancy. Studies (for example
Chisholm, 1989) have found that a high proportion did not, in fact
attend their first clinic early, sometimes due to late referral by GPs.

## Antenatal classes

Antenatal classes provide the main formal educational opportunity
for groups of pregnant women. Usually, however, they are only on
offer from 26-28 weeks into the pregnancy, and generally run over a
set number of six to eight meetings. Classes may be run by midwives
or health visitors, alone or jointly, and sometimes with input from
obstetric physiotherapists. The detailed content of the classes varies
widely, but there will always be an emphasis on relaxation and
breathing techniques.

Quite separately from and outside the NHS, classes are offered on a
fee-paying basis by the NCT. These classes cover much of the same
subject matter, but tend to put more emphasis on sharing experiences
in the group, encouraging prospective parents to make an informed
choice about birth, and techniques for pain reduction. NCT is working on ways of extending its work to include young women, single
parents and minority ethnic groups (NCT, 1991).

Studies on attendance rates at NHS antenatal classes tend to
produce a confusing picture, with different definitions of attendance
being used. But parents themselves seem to have three main reasons
for the generally low rates of attendance (Combes and Schonveld,
1992):

- they are not invited or did not know about them;
- they do not see the need to attend;
- they face practical difficulties in attending.

The Combes and Schonveld review cites three important studies
which try to elucidate more about these reasons for non-attendance
(McKnight and Merrett, 1986; Taylor, 1985; McIntosh, 1988).
Obviously if people do not know about a service they will not use it.
Telling prospective parents verbally at an early clinic visit may be
insufficient – they need information in writing and reminders as the
time approaches for attendance (as the Newcastle scheme referred to
below showed). With regard to the need to attend, their own study
indicated that 'for working class women, and particularly those who

are single, going to classes is equated with not being able to cope.' The practical difficulties in getting to the classes are a very real problem for many women: lack of transport, inconvenient timing, lack of child care and work are all factors which need to be addressed if attendance rates are to improve.

Combes and Schonveld (1992) note that the provision of quality care can influence the uptake and success of antenatal classes, and vice versa. Few evaluations of the effectiveness of ideas intended to increase attandance rates at classes have been undertaken. One of the few which has been evaluated is the Newcastle Community Midwifery Project (Evans, 1991) which showed a dramatic increase in class attendance for a particularly disadvantaged group of women. The success of this project appeared to be due to the enhanced home-based community midwifery service to pregnant women. The midwives had time to actively recruit for the classes by reminding people when they saw them and putting reminder notes through their doors. The evaluation also showed that the classes were more informal, and focused on the particular needs of the group.

Parents' and professionals' views about classes have been reviewed by Combes and Schonveld. Although overall at least two-thirds of class attenders rated them as 'helpful' or 'very helpful', parents did have a number of criticisms about class content and approach:

- lack of teaching about child care;
- understanding about parenting is badly covered;
- unrealistic expectations not dispelled;
- lack of advice on how to avoid negative feelings and experiences;
- unrealistic preparation for labour;
- failure to recognise individual's circumstances.

(p 31)

Of particular relevance to the theme of this book is parents' dissatisfaction with the ability of classes to transmit some understanding about the parental role and adjustment to parenthood. Dissatisfaction was highest in relation to some of the social and emotional aspects of parenting, such as effects on social life and becoming a family (Cox, 1985).

Combes and Schonveld's own small research study indicated that most women who attended antenatal classes were positive about the experience, but wanted more time to talk about individual concerns. It was felt, especially by first-time mothers, that very little time had been given to considering what happens after the birth and how to cope with being a parent. Some felt that the focus was too much on the baby and not enough on the feelings and experiences of the mother.

# Childbirth: choices and options

Numerous surveys and reports have documented the disparity between the services which the NHS offers and the actual needs and wishes of women. What is more disturbing is that so many women describe their labour as a bad experience. This dissatisfaction, aroused by the increasing 'medicalisation' of pregnancy and childbirth, has become an important issue and has often been portrayed as a conflict of power and goals. Health professionals, in the pursuit of greater safety for mother and baby, have centralised services and introduced a 'high technology' screening and monitoring service. The report of the Expert Maternity Group which was set up following the work of the Select Committee, *Changing Childbirth* (Department of Health, 1993), now proposes changes which aim to enable women to choose how their pregnancies and births are managed. It remains to be seen how far the recommendations of this report are implemented. Many of these recommendations are those for which we called ten years ago, and still support, for example, 'antenatal care...should ensure that the woman and her partner feel supported and fully informed throughout the pregnancy, and are prepared for the birth and the care of their baby.' (p. 77). With regard to the birth itself, the report says that women should be able to choose where they would like their baby to be born, and should have the name of a midwife who she can contact for advice. Furthermore, within five years the report recommends 75% of women should be cared for in labour by a midwife whom they have come to know during pregnancy. Maternity services should be based on an understanding of local health, social and cultural needs, and be planned with the active involvement of users, the report continues. The report concludes with a number of indicators of success within five years, including that, overall, providers of maternity services should be able to demonstrate a significant shift towards a more community-oriented service.

In fact, an NCT survey of 1,271 members in 1992 showed that many women were unaware of the choices they had for childbirth. Fifty six per cent said they were offered no choice about where they could have their baby, and who might be responsible for their care, and an overwhelming majority (94%) said they were given no written information about alternative places of birth and who could provide the care. A further point revealed by this survey was parents' dissatisfaction with the lack of continuity of carer during the birth, and, for 80% of those having a first baby, being looked after by midwives (and perhaps doctors) who they had not met before.

The Maternity Alliance has published a birthplan teaching aid called *Your Baby, Your Choice* which is intended for use in an antenatal group, and incorporates individual birth plans to help women understand the choices available to them.

# Postnatal care and support

Once the baby is born it is important that there is continuity of care, with consistent practical help and guidance, whether at home or in the hospital. Shared-Care Domino Schemes, in which care is provided by general practitioners and their teams, including community mid-wives, and health visitors, assists continuity. However, there are sometimes difficulties because of shortages of community midwives and, since they tend to work from maternity units rather than being members of primary health care teams, there can be problems with team working.

Another way of developing continuity is through encouraging health visitors to visit all mothers and new babies some ten days after the birth. In fact, there is no statutory visit by health visitors, but by local agreement health visitors generally replace midwives after 10-14 days, so that how well the two professions communicate is often locally defined. There are some concerns that skill mix, reductions in health visitors, policy changes caused by NHS reorganisation and the recommendations of the recent Audit Commission report (1994) will mean that health visitors may not visit as often as previously, so that postnatal depression and parenting difficulties are more likely to be missed. There are, however, examples of health visitors and midwives working together to help create new parent groups and networks between new mothers. One such group is described by McConville (1989), a health visitor who felt that the postnatal period was crucial in establishing relationships within the family. This group, at the wish of parents involved, was not limited to 'first timers', since they felt that the sharing of knowledge and experience was important. It is difficult to assess exactly how widespread such schemes are, but one example is the Newborn Early Support Team (NEST) group initiated at a community school in Hampshire as part of the 'Job for Life' project (Pugh and Poulton, 1987).

A further example of postnatal groups is described by Lloyd (1983), in which she undertook a small investigation of mothers' reactions to three types of postnatal group: formal (with a health visitor as leader and a formal programme); semi-formal (with a leader but a less structured format); and informal (with no leader and no prescribed organisation). In general mothers in this small sample in this Essex town seemed to prefer an informal group and considered that the social aspects – meeting other mothers and making friends – were more important than health education and advice on baby care. The author's conclusions draw attention to the importance of planning and of setting aims and objectives, with group participation in this process, rather than 'simply regarding the postnatal group as a good thing in itself.'

As part of a study of the health and social support needs of families with a baby aged under one year, 20 families on Merseyside with a baby born in the same month in 1988 were interviewed at home when the baby was seven to nine-months-old. Most interviewees felt that postnatal groups would provide valuable support (Curtice, 1989). By the time of the interview parents were in a position to reflect on the preparation they felt they had received for parenthood and to evaluate this against life at home with the new baby. To these parents the idea of postnatal groups seemed an appropriate response to a number of the difficulties which parents felt they had in meeting their needs for support: their need to learn specific skills; to obtain emotional support; and to have a testing board for working out ways of dealing with complex parenting problems.

A particular type of health visitor support to first-time parents is provided by the implementation of the Child Development Programme, resulting from the work of the Early Childhood Development Unit at the University of Bristol, which focuses on first-time parents. In this scheme, designated health visitors give a structural programme of monthly visits to first-time parents before handing them over to 'family visitors'. The programme embodies a system of partnership and empowerment of parents, highlighting child development and the skills required for child care. The Child Development Programme, begun in 1980, is now a widespread initiative offering support to parents in the rearing, nutrition, health and all-round development of their children. It is carried out mainly in areas of social and economic disadvantage and by 1992 had spread to 25 health authorities and one health board, across England, Wales and Northern Ireland, with some 15,000-20,000 new families annually involved in the programme (Barker and others, 1988; 1992).

A modification of this method of providing postnatal support, the Community Mothers Programme, appears to have had a measurably beneficial effect on families in Dublin and the surrounding area (Community Mothers Programme, Annual Report 1992). This scheme is a support programme for first and second-time parents with infants in the birth-one age span in areas of social and economic disadvantage. It aims to give power to parents, developing their latent skills and restoring confidence and self-esteem, so that they tackle their own problems in their own way. Experienced mothers with similar demographic and life histories to their 'clients' are recruited as community mothers in these areas to give support and encouragement to parents in the rearing of their children. They emphasise health care, nutritional improvement and overall development. The community mothers are trained, monitored and guided by family development nurses (the equivalent of health visitors in England), each unit consisting of one nurse working in partnership with 15-20 community mothers, and dealing with about 150 first and second time parents per year. In 1992 there were ten nurses and 150 community mothers visiting 1,000 parents in the home each year. A behavioural approach is used in which parents are encouraged to undertake agreed tasks. There have been various spin-offs from this project: parent-child groups, antenatal visiting, support for breast feeding mothers and initiatives with the travelling community. An evaluation of this scheme in Ireland (Johnson, Howell and Molloy, 1993) concluded that where first-time mothers received the support of experienced community mothers on a monthly basis for a year, children were more likely to have received all of their primary immunisations and to be read to daily; to play more cognitive games; and were exposed to more nursery rhymes. They were less likely to begin cow's milk before 26 weeks or to receive an inappropriate diet. Mothers, too, also had a better diet than those who had not received the extra support, and were also less likely to feel tired or depressed; had more positive feelings; and were less likely to display negative feelings. Although this type of support was originally subject to some doubts and criticisms, the Health Visitors' Association now concedes that community mothers supplement the skills of the family development nurses (*The Independent*, 20.7.1993).

Similar schemes using community mothers in Essex and Nottingham are described by Jackson (1992), the Nottingham scheme providing particularly relevant support for Asian mothers for whom English is not their first language. The scheme now employs 25 community mothers from Sikh, Muslim and Hindu communities who between them speak all the Asian dialects, and reach 90% of the target group in the city. Other examples can be found in the Medway Health District and on the Isle of Sheppey.

Parents of newborn babies in the majority of health authorities, as part of postnatal support, are now likely to be given their own parent-held Child Health Record, in which will be recorded details of clinic attendances, immunisations and so on, together with parents' own contributions about their child's health up to the age of five. The standard format developed by the British Paediatric Association (1990) is the one most commonly in use, although some modified local versions have been developed. When used properly (that is, by **all** health professionals) the child health record can prove empowering and confidence-building for parents and encourages partnership with health professionals. The key to the successful use of child health records is adequate preparation and training of all health professionals in their introduction and use.

## Postnatal depression

Isolation, loneliness and lack of adult company have been thought to increase depression after childbirth and to undermine self-confidence. Typically such depression falls into three types: the transient, common fourth-day baby blues, post-natal depression and puerperal psychosis. The first is liable to affect four out of five of all women, with weepiness as the outstanding feature, and support, reassurance and the understanding of partner, relatives and friends in the familiar circumstances of home are often seen as the best remedy. Post-natal depression, developing in or after the third week, is also alarmingly frequent. Health visitors increasingly have a role in the diagnosis of and treatment of postnatal depression. See, for example, Briscoe (1989), Holden and others, (1989) and Cullinan (1991).

A number of voluntary groups are beginning to respond to this widespread problem: the Association for Postnatal Illness, for example, and local groups, such as that set up in Oakworth, West Yorkshire in 1988, offer one-to-one counselling, a small library of books, magazine articles and videos on postnatal depression and related issues and a monthly group meeting. The Maternity Alliance has published a postnatal pack, comprising *New Lives* and *New Lives Together* (available for the cost of postage only). The first is intended to be used by new mothers, with their partners, friends and families during the period of adjustment to the arrival of a new baby. It covers physical changes, changes in lifestyle and in relationships with other people. The second is designed to help new parents in a group share and compare the information they have about themselves and their own birth and new parenthood experiences. Indeed, the more that can be done to build parents' confidence during this crucial postnatal period, the better it is likely to be for their ongoing development as self-confident parents.

# Special areas and needs

Throughout this book we have assumed that different families will need various forms of advice and support at different times for a variety of reasons. The period of pregnancy and childbirth is a particularly vulnerable time for all parents, and when events do not turn out as expected there is an additional need for support. The fear of losing a planned child is a very real one for many couples, particularly if this should happen more than once. It is estimated that as many as one in six pregnancies end in a miscarriage. The Miscarriage Association has a newsletter and local support groups to help members cope with loss and provide support and advice for future pregnancies. The Stillbirth and Neonatal Death Association fulfils a similar support function to parents who suffer an even more stressful experience when their child dies at birth or during the neonatal period. Statistics for 1992 (OPCS, 1993) indicate that over 8,000 babies were lost through stillbirth (after the 28th week of pregnancy) or neonatal death (up to 28 days after birth).

Other organisations have been formed to educate and support parents who feel that they are in some way different from the norm, for example, those needing a Caesarian delivery or suffering toxaemia. Often these are self-help groups providing support from members' own experiences.

## Special care babies

Each year 80,000 babies (10-15% of all those born in the UK) need some kind of special or intensive care. The organisation National Information for Parents of Premature: Education, Resources and Support (NIPPERS) was set up to support families with premature or sick newborns. As its leaflet says, 'The birth of a baby who requires special care is a traumatic experience. No matter how individual and supportive the hospital is, parents always seem to have worries and unanswered questions'. They aim to provide information on prematurity and sick newborns, leaflets on medical conditions and treatment, audiovisual materials; to encourage the setting up of both hospital and community parent-to-parent support networks; to foster communication, cooperation and sharing experiences between parents and professionals through workshops, conference, support schemes and a newsletter. The organisation Action for Sick Children (formerly the National Association for the Welfare of Children in Hospital) takes the view that, wherever possible, sick newborn babies should be cared for with their mothers and only admitted to special care baby units when care cannot be provided in other ways (1987 policy paper).

Baby Life Support Systems (BLISS) was founded in 1979 primarily to raise money to provide resources for poorly equipped special care baby units. BLISSLINK, a parent support network started in 1984, developed from the original organisation and exists to ensure that all parents and families of special care babies have access to the support they need. This can be by means of local befrienders, parent support groups, leaflets, newsletters, and so on.

CONI (Care of the Next Infant), a parent support scheme for parents who have had a 'cot death' and are concerned for any subsequent pregnancy, is offered to health authorities by the Foundation for the Study of Infant Deaths.

We refer in chapter 6 to the work of many other specialist groups, such as MENCAP, the Spastics Society and the Down's Syndrome Association, which have an important role to play in supporting parents during the perinatal period.

## Teenage expectant mothers

Teenage expectant mothers may have specific needs which may not be met by mainstream antenatal education and preparation for parenthood, just as they may have needs for particular services once they are parents to which we make reference in chapter 6. Pregnancy for teenagers may be unplanned, happening at a time when they are still adolescents, there may be variable support, and perhaps negative attitudes, from partners, friends and family, and all this may well be in the context of social and economic disadvantage.

An innovative project in Nottingham, 45 Cope Street, opened in 1987, is an example of a service which decided to concentrate most of its efforts on support for pregnant teenagers expecting their first child, offering group support, home visiting and, after the birth, a new parents support group. The staff described their approach as follows (Perkins, 1988):

> For effective learning it is important that people should define their own health needs, i.e. they learn because they want to learn, feeling confident and are involved in the process of learning. In our groups the topics are always chosen and often prepared by members of the group themselves. We aim for a relaxed, informal and supportive atmosphere. We always aim to involve members of the group in the organisation, planning and evaluation of group sessions. We also give time for socialising and individual consultation. We often had a practical

activity, e.g. craft work, cooking, collage making, taking blood pressures, using a foetal heart monitor. By focusing on an activity freer
discussion between individuals can take place and new practical skills
can be acquired. (p 6)

Billingham (1989), in describing how the project works in partnership
with parents, suggests that developing parenting skills has little to do
with teaching hygiene, nutrition, home safety, play, child management, and so on, but 'a lot to do with increasing self-confidence,
improving material conditions and providing the opportunities to
learn.' She concludes: 'A woman who has a sense of self worth is better
able to meet her child's needs and to provide appropriate child care.'

## Minority ethnic groups

Several studies report very low levels of attendance at antenatal classes
by women from minority ethnic groups (Adams, 1982; Jain, 1985;
Newham Parents Forum, 1988 – all cited in Combes and Schonveld,
1992). Asian women gave the following reasons for not attending:

- lack of knowledge about classes and likely benefit;
- the need to look after children at home;
- language barriers;
- a reluctance to go out at night, or being accompanied.

The Asian Mother and Baby Campaign, a government-funded
three-year initiative aimed at Asian mothers and their families, was
launched in 1984 and involved 16 health districts (Rocheron and
Dickinson, 1990). Its stated aims were to encourage early diagnosis of
pregnancy and uptake of maternity services; to improve communication between mothers and health professionals; to help health
professionals gain the cooperation of Asian families; to help Asian
families to become more aware of services; and to ensure that the
services provided are accessible and acceptable. The campaign had
two main features: a programme of publicity and health promotion,
and the employment by the district health authorities (DHAs) of
linkworkers – Asian women who were fluent in English and at least
one Asian language, who could help to overcome cultural and
linguistic barriers. The campaign and its evaluation (Rocheron and
others, 1989) suffered from politicisation because of conflict about the
ideological orientation of the scheme and issues of control. The
evaluation indicated that the publicity element of the campaign had
only very limited success, mainly because the 'Asian' population had
tended to be treated as a homogenous group with more or less the same

needs for information. The evaluation also criticised the concept and management of the scheme, in that it generally failed to consult seriously with Asian community leaders about the scheme, and because of its lack of specific objectives. Despite these shortcomings, however, the authors of the evaluation conclude that 'undeniably, the...campaign had a positive impact, through the linkwork schemes, on the quality of service offered to individual women...'. The main impact was on improving communication and giving of support and advice, together with other improvements such as the provision of longer dressing gowns, facilities for private prayers, more appropriate hospital food, greater guidance about hospital procedures which allowed a better choice, health education leaflets about local services in relevant languages, and Asian women-only parentcraft classes in more suitable community settings. One obvious way to take this type of work forward is by the recruitment of more Asian health visitors and other health professionals. However, this strategy has not proved very successful, partly because of the culture in some Asian communities who prefer women to become doctors rather than nurses.

Another example of the introduction of a service specifically for a group of women from a minority ethnic community – in this case Bengali women – is described by a health visitor from Tameside (Munro, 1988). The women showed no interest in joining an existing parentcraft group, but responded with enthusiasm to a group specially for them. The topics covered conception and pregnancy and then moved on to subjects related to baby care, safety, hygiene and family planning. It appeared that, as a result of attendance at these classes, women were generally booking earlier for antenatal care; bottle hygiene had improved; and the women were more confident and more ready to think for themselves.

## Multiple births

The birth of twins, or of more than two babies, can present a particular challenge and the Twins and Multiple Births Association is a parent support group for families with twins and multiple births. The Multiple Births Foundation is a voluntary organisation which prepares, educates and supports parents expecting multiple births from the time, usually in early pregnancy, that the diagnosis of a multiple pregnancy is made. That support can continue throughout childhood and adolescence. Twins Clinics, to enable parents to obtain professional advice or talk to a paediatrician, have been established at hospitals in London, Birmingham and York. In addition, in London and Birmingham there are regular prenatal evening meetings for families expecting twins or more.

## Adoptive parents

Although a minority, and a decreasing group over the last 20 years (there are approximately 7,000 adoptions per year, almost half of which are adoptions into stepfamilies), there are still a few couples adopting a baby for the first time and becoming 'instant parents'. In contrast to biological parents, who know they have nine months in which to prepare, mentally and physically, adopters often have no idea how long the wait will be. Even once they have the baby, adopters have a sense of being 'on probation' until the adoption order is passed and the child is legally their own, and this can isolate them from other new parents and possibly from professional help.

Although in some locations adopters are invited to join part of an antenatal group, this is clearly difficult for infertile couples who may have been trying for years to conceive a child. Stewart and Ring (1991) describe a parenthood class in Bristol specifically for adopting couples. They conclude that the needs of this small group of parents should be considered and may extend beyond providing just a parent-craft course, to cover topics specifically associated with the adoption process. They challenge professionals to look at the service adoptive parents currently receive and to ensure that there is appropriate liaison between social services departments and health workers. It is probably unrealistic, however, since only some 900 babies are adopted annually, to suggest that such a specialised service could become universal.

## Summary

Becoming a parent is a far more complex process than just the arrival of a baby. There may be fundamental changes in relationships between parents, both practically and emotionally. There may be economic changes, caused by the mother or father giving up work, returning to work and paying for day care and, of course, the cost of supporting the child. During the pre-conceptual phase there is still relatively little support and advice for prospective parents. Once pregnant, support through clinics and classes is aimed mainly at mothers, so that fathers may have particular difficulties in preparing for the change in lifestyle to come.

Despite the publication of government reports, such as that of the Expert Maternity Group, and HEA initiatives, recent studies indicate that parents' needs for education during the antenatal period are still not being efficiently met: needs and provision are often mismatched; certain parents are missing out (for example, fathers, and young women, lone women and women from minority ethnic groups); the focus tends to be narrow, giving too little time to social and emotional aspects of parenting. Parents are not given sufficient information, either about antenatal care or birth, and continuity of care both before and after the birth is the preferred option of many women. Also, opportunities for education input during clinic attendances were missed.

Postnatal care takes on a particular importance, in view of parents' dissatisfaction with their antenatal care and education and the levels of postnatal depression. Such care, and support from other parents, particularly through informal support groups, is particularly relevant and crucial **after** changes in the family have taken place: two have become three, relationships may have altered and a whole set of new skills and responses have to be quickly learned. This may, indeed, be a more appropriate time to introduce practical parenting skills, and discussions around the reality of having a baby, rather than during antenatal classes.

Particular support and services exist for especially vulnerable parents, such as those who have suffered loss, whose babies die, or those born prematurely. Teenage parents and parents from some minority ethnic groups, for whom mainstream support may not be relevant, have particular needs to be met in the perinatal period, although care must be taken not to treat all as one homogeneous group.

The hope for the future is that the slow process of change and improvement in antenatal and postnatal services, based on what parents want and need, will continue, given the impetus of and targets set by the Department of Health's *Changing Childbirth* report.

# 6. Support for parents

## Introduction

As already noted in chapter 1, the preamble of the UN Convention on the Rights of the Child recognises that the family '...as the fundamental group of society and the natural environment for growth and well-being of all its members and particularly children, should be afforded the necessary protection and assistance so that it can fully assume its responsibilities within the community.' Furthermore, several Articles of the Convention set out measures to provide **support for children and for those who are responsible for their care**. It is this support – its variety, extent, availability and efficacy – which is the focus of this chapter.

In 1984 *The Needs of Parents* recommended that a range of services and schemes should be available in each local area which met the overall aims of parent education and support. In particular, we felt that such services should be flexible enough to meet the varying needs of parents at different stages in their parenting 'career'. Thus, for parents of young children, information and support should enable parents to have control over their own lives, to retain their individuality as adults, to develop increased self-confidence and to acquire increased parenting skills. Parents of older children should be enabled to understand their adolescent children and be enabled to participate in educational and employment decisions. In order to achieve these aims, we emphasised the need for professionals to support parents who themselves wished to lead groups and become involved in support services, and for priority to be given to work with vulnerable families. The important role of self-help groups, community groups and voluntary organisations was highlighted, but only as a supplement to services provided by statutory agencies. The importance of schools working in closer partnership with parents and with the wider community was emphasised. In the light of these recommendations made in the mid-1980s, we describe in this chapter some examples of the support and education services being provided for parents during the 1990s.

For even the most fully prepared new parent the first few weeks – or months – of life with a new baby are seldom easy. Feelings of isolation and of vulnerability in the face of the high expectations that society places on parents, suggests that society itself has a responsibility to ensure that parents are afforded access to help, advice and support in bringing up their children, not just to combat particular moments of severe crisis, but also to deal with the everyday practicalities of being a parent. The emphasis on universal availability of support for **all** families is a vital point. Families do not necessarily fall into one of the two pigeonholes often created for them – either that they are coping adequately and are felt to need no assistance at all, or that they fall below an accepted level of providing 'good enough parenting' and become the focus of intervention. As already noted, the skills of parenthood do not necessarily come naturally and most parents, even those who manage well on their own for most of the time, would welcome some support part of the time, without feeling that they run the risk of becoming stigmatised or being labelled failures by asking for or using support. In addition, at particular points of crisis the majority of parents are likely to need to seek additional help and guidance in their parenting role. Exploring Parenthood (1994), believes that support for parents, in the form of early intervention and prevention, is the most effective way of reducing problems within the family, and has carried out an audit of parent support services potentially available throughout Britain, particularly those provided by the voluntary sector. This survey confirms that parent support services are not easily accessible and available to **all** parents: rather they tend to be focused around specific areas of need, or are located within specific geographical areas and thereby targeted at local groups in the community. Furthermore, the audit concludes that 'few services are available for parents who wish to develop better parenting skills in an atmosphere which does not pre-judge some failure.' A follow up magazine survey of 14,000 parents found that two thirds would have liked education and advice on bringing up children (Katz, 1994).

The focus of this chapter, then, is the range of support, sources of information and education available to parents. We identify projects which work with parents and families and are specifically concerned with the quality of relationships within the family and with parenting skills. We have chosen to group the material into seven main sections:

- advice and information;
- home-based support;
- group-based support;
- more structured parent education groups;
- home-school liaison;
- support with a particular emphasis;
- support for people in a particular parenting relationship.

Within this structure we have also made use of the idea of a *continuum of support*, particularly within the second, third and fourth sections covering home-based and group-based support and education, since although we have drawn attention to the need for support services to be available on a universal basis for **all** parents, there are families who may be more vulnerable than others, especially when their children are very young. Poor housing and poverty are just two of the underlying factors which may have a negative effect on parents' abilities to care for their children; and there will be particular times of stress in many parents' lives when, for a short time, extra support may be welcomed. Problems might be presented, for example, by a difficult pregnancy and birth; a high degree of post-natal depression; a lone mother with several young children; very young parents whose own developmental needs have not yet been met; parents who have grown up in care with inadequate models of parenting; or ill health or unemployment. All of these may need extra help and advice, or support of a particular kind.

The special area of links between home and school, important for all parents, is described in the fifth section.

Following this, we turn to the needs of a number of particular groups of parents, or people who have a special parenting relationship, who have their own specific needs in addition to the more general ones felt by all parents, and for whom a whole range of specialised schemes, organisations and projects have grown up. These are each given separate consideration in the last two sections.

# Advice and information

The provision of advice and information to parents is an example of an area in which there has been considerable growth since 1984. Indeed, an essential part of any programme of parent support is to ensure that parents know about its existence, in order to give them access to information and resources, and thus to some basis on which to make decisions and have a greater sense of control over their lives. Many of the agencies and organisations outlined in this chapter see the provision of information and, where appropriate, advice, as part and parcel of their work. It is, nevertheless, worth emphasising the need to make information about services and resources widely available in an accessible way (including translation into relevant languages) and in accessible places, such as post offices, supermarkets and launderettes as well as the more obvious clinics, doctors' surgeries, schools and libraries. The variety of services provided by different local authority departments, and increasing numbers of voluntary groups, is confusing for parents. The Children Act 1989 put a duty on local authorities to publish information about the services for children under eight which they themselves, and others, provide. The additional corporate duty to carry out a review every three years of services for under eights in their area, and publish the results, should also vastly improve the quantity and quality of information available to parents.

A number of local groups and agencies have produced handbooks or directories of services for young children and their families. The Voluntary Liaison Council for Under Fives (VOLCUF) and the National Children's Bureau have joined forces to publish a directory of national organisations concerned with the under eights and their families, with services listed under broad subject areas, such as family support and substitute care (VOLCUF and National Children's Bureau, 1992). In recent years a number of computerised children's information services have been set up, such as the Children's Information Service in Sheffield (evaluated by Smith and van der Eyken, 1990) and Childcare Links in Brighton (Childcare Links, 1990), allowing parents access to a 'one-stop information database' which holds up-to-date details of a wide variety of services for families with children. Some 40 such services and developing services are linked together through membership of the network organisation Choices in Childcare (see Choices in Childcare, 1994). With the rapid development of information technology, it is likely that in the future there will be far more networking and sharing of such information on a regional, or even UK-wide scale.

In recent years, in recognition of employees' domestic as well as work-based needs, a number of employers and businesses have developed work-based advice and information services for their employees. One such example is 'Check-it-Out', operated by IKEA, the Swedish owned furniture retailer with large retail outlets in London and other major cities. In conjunction with Exploring Parenthood, and with funding from the Joseph Rowntree Foundation, IKEA has looked at issues affecting families with young children. The advice and counselling service which developed from this project is available to all employees and covers general family matters, parenting and child care. The service is run by a team of independent advisors trained in child development, parent education, counselling, child care and personnel. An audit towards the end of the pilot period (Burnell and Goodchild, forthcoming) indicates that the scheme has had a high level of take-up and has been used by 20% of the staff. Another example of employer involvement is the Midland Bank subsidised child care scheme, with a network of child care managers who help to arrange placements and discuss any anxieties with parents. The scheme provides day care places for some 1,000 children, and demand is high, especially for parents of babies and young children, enabling parents to return to work. The quality of care provided in the 112 day nurseries in the scheme has been evaluated by Smith and Vernon (in preparation).

As already noted, almost all the organisations and projects contacted in preparation for this book saw themselves as providers of advice and information in some form or another. For example, the Family Rights Group (FRG) through its advice and advocacy service advises about 800 parents a year; Parents Against Injustice (PAIN) offers confidential advice, counselling and support to parents, children, family members and others when a child is allegedly thought to be at risk or to have been abused.

## Telephone helplines

Parents are frequently faced with acute problems which will not wait until the next visit from the health visitor, or until the doctor's surgery is open. The growing number of telephone helplines go some way to filling this gap and provide immediate help and support or, at the very least, a listening ear. In fact, the opportunity to talk and express feelings, with a sympathetic response from the listener, may be all a parent needs to start to feel better about a predicament and more able to cope with it. Other callers, however, may require advice on how to deal with a particular situation; some may want information which they can follow up, or 'signposting' to a further source of help; some may require in-depth counselling. Not all helplines can offer such a range of services – much will depend on the subject being dealt with and the training and qualifications of helpline staff. Helpline workers are often selected because they have first-hand experience of the type of problems the callers present. For example, The Twins and Multiple Births Association (TAMBA) Twinline staff are all parents of multiple-birth children. Some helplines are linked to a network of local support groups, so that a caller to one central number can be referred to their nearest group. Broadcasting Support Services has published a useful guide to standards of service for helpline providers (Telephone Helplines: Guidelines for Good Practice).

Parentline (OPUS) is a nationwide network whose helplines are staffed by paid and voluntary counsellors, dealing with callers' problems in bringing up children. Parentline carried out an evaluation (1993) of their helpline service, which showed that the majority of parents using the service felt that their expectations had been met. The evaluation indicated, however, that there was a need to target a wider cross-section of the community and areas experiencing particular disadvantage or difficulty, and to recruit more volunteer helpers from minority ethnic groups. Exploring Parenthood advertises a parents' advice line which 'offers counselling to parents whatever the difficulty.' National Children's Home Careline can deal with a number of family and marital problems. Other more specialist subject areas are covered by CRY-SIS (persistently crying and/or sleepless babies and toddlers); Cot Death Helpline (a 24-hour helpline offering advice, information and support for bereaved parents, and for other parents worried about cot death (6,174 in 1991/92)); Epilepsy Helpline (care and support for families with epileptics); Grandparents Federation Advice Line; STEPFAMILY telephone counselling service (family/stepfamily issues, access, money, new baby, re-marriage, and so on); TAMBA Twinline (problems of bringing up twins and multiple-birth children); NSPCC Child Protection Helpline (for callers who know or suspect that a child is being ill-treated or neglected). The Family Planning Association (FPA) runs a national helpline, staffed by professionals, and has recently introduced a dedicated 'parent helpline' to assist parents in dealing with the sex education and sexuality of their children as part of a three-year project aimed at improving the effectiveness of parents as sex educators of their children.

An example of a more local helpline service, run in conjunction with a self-help group for parents, is Parents in Crisis with projects based in Perth and Dundee. They claim to be able to help parents who have a variety of problems and concerns, such as problems in school, aggressive or unruly behaviour, solvent/alcohol/drug abuse, gambling, communication problems, involvement in petty crime, and so on. Parents' Helpline has been operating in Brighton since 1978, having been formed by a group of concerned parents following the Maria Colwell tragedy. These founders acknowledged that 'parent-hood could create very stressful moments and that a telephone call made in confidence and anonymity to a sympathetic listener could help ease the tension with beneficial effect to both parent and child' (Parents' Helpline leaflet).

Helplines have particular advantages for users, over and above other forms of advice: the caller is in charge; the conversation is confidential; the conversation can proceed at the caller's own pace; somebody is listening; callers can be helped to explore the options open to them. On the other hand, problems have started to arise since the introduction of itemised telephone bills, allowing other members of the family or household to discover that contact has taken place.

# Home-based and individual support

For most new parents the first sources of strength and support are their own families and friends and neighbours. Changing patterns of family life and employment (for example, more women, including grandmothers – a traditional source of support – now working), however, mean that families and friends are often widely dispersed. As we noted in the introduction to this chapter, if the needs of individual families are to be met, a broad spectrum of services is required in any one area, to complement – or in some cases replace – family networks, and to enable parents to be able to 'plug in' at whichever point they feel is relevant.

Peer group support is illustrated by the work of the Meet-A-Mum Association (MAMA) which aims to provide 'a network of care' to mothers and mothers-to-be (and in some instances to fathers or to both parents), partly by means of its 70 nationwide support groups, but also by attempting to put enquirers in touch with other parents in the area. In common with some other organisations, MAMA holds the view that 'current antenatal education is woefully inadequate, focusing as it does on the delivery of the baby and scarcely touching on the realities of life after birth.' (Bryony Hallam, National Organiser, response to enquiry, May 1993).

The Foundation for the Study of Infant Deaths is another, if somewhat specialist, organisation which promotes contact between parents so that a family bereaved by a cot death can be put in touch with another who has been briefed by the Foundation as a 'befriender'. In 1991/92 the Foundation ran 19 Befriender Preparation Days and had a total of 529 Befrienders around the UK. We also refer later in this chapter to a number of parent-parent support schemes for parents whose children have special needs.

Although not generally perceived as part of the peer support network, the National Childminding Association (NCMA) has evidence from parents that childminders do have an important, and developing, role in preparing and supporting parents, particularly those who are trying to combine their parenting roles with their working lives. Childminders are almost invariably parents themselves, and can draw both on their experience of parenting their own children, and on that gained during the job of looking after other people's children.

Moving on to the role of the statutory services, and in particular the role of health visitors, the Health Visitors Association emphasises that 'a recognition has to emerge that parenting does not 'just happen' in all cases and the support by people like health visitors is invaluable' (Margaret Buttigieg, response to enquiry, May 1993). Indeed, health visitors are uniquely placed to be available to support individual families in their own homes and in child health clinics, with a knowledge not only of child health and development, but also of local resources and of other new parents experiencing similar problems with whom contact might be made. The health visitor is also in a good position, either alone or as part of a team, to undertake regular health and developmental assessment of all mothers and babies in order to identify any problems as early as possible. Health visitors though, have had an increasing burden of work placed on them over the years, and the extent to which they are able to give attention to the needs of parents may depend very much on the priority put on such work by individuals. A further worrying indicator of cuts in health visiting comes from a recent survey of 70 of the 196 NHS trusts carried out by the Health Visitors Association (1993) which claims that in this sample health visitor staffing has been cut by up to a third, and 30% of students qualifying in 1993 have not been offered jobs. The changes imposed by the National Health Service trends towards the creation of fund-holding general practitioners and health trusts have also had an impact on the role of health visitors. The role of GPs and health visitors in clinics and surgeries continues however, to be important in offering support and advice and indeed, more specialist support is provided through child psychiatrists, educational and clinical psychologists, child psychotherapists and so on. There is however, some concern (Steve Flood, Young Minds personal communication, February 1994) that many child and family consultative services and child guidance clinics which are well placed to offer such help, are closing, despite increasing referrals (Kurtz and others, 1994).

## Home visiting schemes

The number of people, both professionals and volunteers, who visit families in their own homes would appear to have increased considerably over the last ten years. Reference has already been made to the role of health visitors, but other professionals such as day nursery and family centre staff also visit homes prior to admission, as do some teachers before children start nursery school or infant school. Some LEAs (for example, Birmingham, Cleveland, Humberside, Coventry, Leicestershire, Knowsley and Strathclyde) employ a considerable number of home-school liaison teachers who form part of the authorities' overall home-school links programme referred to in the section on home-school liaison. Trained volunteers have a similar home-visiting role in a number of the schemes mentioned below.

There is sometimes a thin dividing line between home visiting schemes intended to provide general family support, and those intervention programmes designed as part of a strategy for supporting the development of young children, particularly those such as the Portage programme designed to help children with special needs. Indeed, Powell (1990) posed the following questions: 'Who is the client in home visiting programs – the parent or the child? What if their interests are incompatible?...Is the home visitor to function as a friend, teacher or social worker? Is the relationship between home visitor and parent to be a collaborative partnership or a conventional professional-client relationship?' The schemes referred to here fall into the former rather than the latter category, with parents as the main focus of support.

Home visiting schemes, such as Home-Start, embody the concept of peer support already referred to, using volunteers, all parents, some of whom have themselves been visited in the past, to offer regular support, friendship and practical help to young families under stress in their own homes helping to prevent family crisis and breakdown. Home-Start emerged in 1973 in response to a need created by the discrepancy between the expectations of families with young children and the realities they encounter. Although Home-Start volunteers may be perceived as 'just another mum' by the families they visit, they are carefully recruited, trained and prepared for the work they undertake with families. By 1994 there were 140 Home-Start schemes in the UK (together with others in Germany, Cyprus, Gibraltar, Republic of Ireland, Australia, Canada and Israel) providing support for approximately 20,500 children and 7,500 families annually. Margaret Harrison, who pioneered this method of support, says (response to enquiry, June 1993) that the 3,500 Home-Start volunteers

are privileged to be with families, sharing those very human qualities for which one can neither legislate nor train – human qualities such as caring, optimism, generosity, encouragement, joy, kindness, touch and laughter.

What many parents need is someone to whom they can relate and who really cares about them and this is what Home-Start aims to provide. Whilst offering support to the parents, the volunteer is also offering a positive stimulus to the children, and in encouraging parents' strengths and emotional well-being is working towards the point where parents feel able to widen their network of relationships and use community support and services effectively. Holman's definition of the 'resourceful friend' (1983) could equally well apply to the Home-Start volunteer, who because of the non-statutory nature of the work and absence of professional status, can offer to 'be with' rather than 'do things to' the family with whom she works. For those who are concerned with cost-effectiveness, this is an extremely economical form of family support – the average annual cost of supporting a family in 1992/93 was just £490. In areas such as the London Borough of Hackney, whose population includes a wide range of minority ethnic groups and cultures, the Home-Start scheme ensures that its volunteers reflect the local population. In 1993 there were 24 volunteers in this scheme: 13 African-Caribbean, 1 Asian, 5 Caucasian, 1 Mixed parentage, 2 Nigerian and 2 Turkish. The work of Home-Start was evaluated by van der Eyken in 1982, finding that this particular form of community care was extremely effective with families where the direct involvement of statutory services was either inappropriate, or where services were inadequate to meet the real needs of families. More recent references to the work of Home-Start can be found in Shinman (1987), Gibbons and Thorpe (1989) and Bagilhole (1994). A further study of five Home-Start projects in Wakefield is currently under way at the University of Leeds Department of Adult and Continuing Education (Wallace, forthcoming).

Home-Link is a similar home visiting scheme for families with young children based in Edinburgh. As with Home-Start, volunteers are trained and supported in their work, although not all are parents themselves. Visitors may come across problems such as lack of money and poverty, as well as more specific need for advice about child rearing. One volunteer worker feels that 'the knowledge that someone cares might help to prevent frustrations building up to an unbearable level' (Highmore and McCann, 1989).

Another example of home visiting is the well established Family Aide Scheme operated in East Leeds by Family Service Units (FSU). This scheme provides structured practical support to families in their own homes, the aim being to pass on parenting skills, develop routines and improve parent/child relationships. Another FSU scheme in Liverpool goes further than this, providing a package of support which offers families practical support in the home with parenting and also counselling in relationship difficulties (response to enquiry, November 1993).

The Radford Shared Care Project in Nottingham employs shared care workers to visit families' homes (Fleming and Ward, 1992). A particular feature of this scheme was to offer families culturally appropriate support and advice, with black women and women with black children being offered support from shared care workers of the same ethnicity. Most families valued this approach. From many points of view, the evaluation indicated, this project succeeded in its aim of helping parents look after their children to adequate standards, although the evaluators felt that insufficient attention had perhaps been given to addressing **why** the women had difficulties in being good parents:

> Whatever its achievements and good intentions, in practice, the project points the finger of fault at the women. It is the women who are expected to change and to learn. It is the women who are blamed, rather than the problems being seen as products of their circumstances. (p 37)

Parents & Co is a project run by Elfrida Rathbone in the London Borough of Camden, providing a variety of support for families with children under five. One of the project's major services for parents who are concerned about the development or behaviour of a child, or who are under considerable stress due to illness, disability or depression, is home visiting. Home visitors go to homes usually once a week for two to three hours, over a period of a year or so, helping to work out ways of tackling concerns about a child, or stresses that are affecting a parent's relationship with a child. Home visitors can then introduce parents to other Rathbone services, such as the six parent support groups in the Borough and the creches and summer play-schemes.

Many of the schemes referred to in this and the previous section involve the use of volunteer parents themselves (usually mothers, and usually with some element of training) in the support of other parents. A recent paper by Cox (1993) reviewing the nature and effectiveness of the voluntary befriending schemes Home-Start and NEWPIN is therefore of interest. Cox finds that most befriending schemes have been shown to have some positive effects. However, the benefits are largely in improving the confidence, self-esteem and coping skills of mothers. Effects in changing the quality of parent-child relationships are much more limited. Cox argues that, whilst befriending schemes do play an important part in mental health promotion, there needs to be adequate professional liaison and support available to both organisers and volunteers, and adequate access to professional services for those mothers and children needing different or supplementary interventions.

## Sponsored childminding/day fostering

A growing form of support for families, both parents and children, has been in community childminding schemes in which families are linked with local childminders (often specially recruited and trained) who offer them both practical and emotional support as, for example, in the scheme run by South Glamorgan social services department. Two other schemes, both run by Barnardo's, are the Sandwell Under Fives Project and the Hackney Sharing Care project. The services offered to referred families by the Sandwell project include:

- day care for children under five;
- specific activities with young children to encourage both their physical and emotional development;
- monitoring children's development;
- support and advice to parents.

Evaluation of the Hackney project (Caesar, Smith and Berridge, 1993) indicated that the sharing care method was effective, and much valued by parents, who gained support and education for themselves as well as care and education for their children, from a carefully recruited and trained group of individual home-based workers.

# Group-based support

In this section describing group-based support we move along the continuum of support again, starting with those types of support to which all parents can have open access, towards those which provide higher levels of support, and can generally only be accessed by referral of some kind.

## Informal community groups

Loneliness, depression and isolation are key themes in studies of mothers with very young children (see for example, Cummings and Davies, 1994) and the availability of informal groups which provide an opportunity for meeting with other parents and exchanging experiences is an important part of the network of services for parents. Out of such contacts can come friendships which continue beyond and outside the life of the group. We have already referred to the work of the Meet-A-Mum-Association (MAMA) as an example of linking new mothers with other new mothers in their immediate area. There are also numerous examples (as described in chapter 5) of health visitors running post-natal support groups from which links and friendships may develop.

The self-help group approach, through which parents can provide mutual support for one another, is widespread. The Parents in Crisis groups in Perth and Dundee are examples of this type of support. Parents in a local area meet on a monthly basis to 'discuss their problems, share experiences and reassure one another'.

> Because we are all parents worrying about our children we can address issues which may be quite difficult to discuss with friends – or even partners – because they are not trying to cope with the problem on a day-to-day basis. (Parents in Crisis leaflet)

The Leeds Early Education Support Agency (EESA) is an example of a form of parental group support set up by the education department in 1987 and now running groups for parents and their under fives all over the city. The scheme employs nine full-time workers and is engaged with over 300 families with pre-school children. Parents refer themselves (and each other) and each group is open to anyone who has the care of an under five. Parents take an active part in running the groups – deciding on activities, trips out or courses, and so on. One parent user commented: 'My child has settled so well in school and it's all down to the work we did with EESA' (EESA leaflet, 1993).

Thanet Early Years Project (core funded by Kent County Council Social Services Department) is typical of many such projects across the country. It provides a range of services to young children and their parents from five playcentres in Ramsgate and Margate. Its core activities are:

- structured play sessions for children aged two and a half to five, where the all-round development of each child is monitored. Parents are encouraged to become involved in all aspects of the playgroup;
- First Steps: for parents with children birth to three years who can benefit from the support of the discussion group led by a health visitor;
- a less formal parent and child group, open to all parents;

- health visitor baby clinic: welcoming clinics on neutral ground where parents can stay for a whole afternoon;
- language development group: twice weekly sessions for referred children;
- rising fives groups;
- rising threes groups.

The First Steps groups are of particular interest in relation to parent support. They aim to:

- raise parents' self-esteem and confidence;
- teach parents some assertiveness techniques;
- encourage parenting skills;
- enable children who are understimulated to reach their potential development status.

Work with parents is done in an informal group setting in which members are encouraged to build up mutual trust and support. An environment that is non-threatening and safe allows parents the opportunity to discuss personal and child rearing issues. Problem solving is high on the agenda, and is encouraged by a facilitator who is usually a health visitor. Work is done to enable members to gain insights about themselves and their children, which lead to changing attitudes towards themselves, children and family life.

An evaluation of these groups (Canterbury and Thanet Community Healthcare, 1991) found that friendships had been established which continued outside the life of the group; parents were finding it easier to look after their children; parents were saying that they felt more confident and had gained some assertiveness skills which affected the way they dealt with people in authority roles, such as GPs and social workers; parents said that they recognised and dealt more effectively with day-to-day problems, and had begun to enjoy and value their children.

A multi-agency approach to support for parents is illustrated by a scheme in Peterborough, where projects for parents and young children have been set up with resources from social services, education, the city council and the health authority. These schemes originated from needs expressed by parents themselves and the extremely limited facilities available in the area. The projects operate from community centres or school bases, and offer complementary provision to that offered by playgroups, since they cater for parents with children under three as well as over threes. The aims of the projects go beyond the provision of play experiences for children, offering a meeting place for voluntary and statutory organisations to work with young children and their families, and also opportunities for parents to develop and learn, both with and without their children. Parents are encouraged to take over responsibility for running the groups, knowing that there is still a support network in the background if needed, thus fulfilling one of the recommendations we made in 1984 (Westwood and Ravensthorpe Family Project, Annual Report 1992/93).

## Parent and toddler groups

The UK does not have the statutorily provided network of 'Open Pre-schools' available in countries such as Sweden for parents and their very young children, but parent and toddler groups and drop-in centres, run by a whole variety of organisations, offer support of a similar kind and allow parents to escape from the isolation and alleviate the stress experienced by so many. This type of support is continuing to expand and, while health visitors, schools and community workers have a crucial part to play in the establishment of informal groups, the majority of such groups are run by parents on their own or in association with voluntary organisations such as the Pre-school Playgroups Association (PPA), Scottish Pre-school Play Association (SPPA), Welsh PPA, the National Childbirth Trust (NCT), local organisations such as Priority Area Playgroups (PAP) in Birmingham, or one of the churches or large national charities such as Barnardo's. PPA, for example, has experienced a large increase recently in national membership of parent and toddler playgroups (4,744 groups in December 1993).

The main aim of such informal groups is to enable parents and children to meet together and for parents to retain responsibility for their children during the sessions. Increasingly, though, and when creche arrangements can be made alongside, parents can undertake more formal discussion sessions and learning activities. The PPA is proposing a Parent and Toddler Playgroup Course focused at parents or carers who attend and, in particular, those involved in helping to run the group. The aim is to develop parents' confidence, basic knowledge and understanding so that they can meet the needs of young children and adults attending the groups, all of which will assist with individuals' own parenting skills. The Wrexham Toddler Project was set up in association with a local hospital to be run and used by parents to create parental awareness and promote self-esteem, with limited guidance and support from professionals. Snelling (1989) reports that:

the idea was to discover, through discussion, the confidence to feel good about their children, families and parenting skills, counteracting the feelings of inadequacy felt by some parents, brought on by professionals, politicians, magazines and neighbours who seem to know all the answers.

## Playbuses

The National Playbus Association (NPA) has increased and broadened the scope of its work considerably since the first bus took to the road in 1969. NPA provides support, information and training to local playbus groups who in turn work in communities with parents, providing vital support, help and information. They work with parents to enable them to enrich their own and their children's lives through informal sessions where problems and solutions can be shared. The playbus ethos is very much about working together with parents to form appropriate solutions to the stresses and strains of parenthood in the 1990s. The majority of the 270 NPA member groups work with parents and children, each group running at least eight sessions a week working with up to 20 children and 15 parents at each session. NPA suggests that:

> the informal, non-stigmatized nature of the playbus environment leads to a great deal of learning about the parenting of young children...and through gaining an understanding of the role which play takes in their children's development, and the skills to provide for changing needs and demands, parents are able to feel more confident about their child-rearing abilities (Andrea Allez, Development Officer, response to enquiry, July 1993).

The playbus approach has proved particularly valuable in taking the service to where families are, especially in their work with travellers and on housing estates in deprived and isolated areas.

## Playgroups

The PPA, established in the early 1960s, continues to emphasise the role of parents, encouraging their active involvement and offering informal support. PPA conservatively estimates that in 1993 at least one million parents were using their playgroups, although of course not all became actively involved. Similarly, in Scotland SPPA estimates that playgroup services reach 65,000 families each year. An unknown proportion of playgroups offer the opportunity for parents to meet on their own for informal discussion or more formal learning, many though are constrained from doing this by the lack of suitable space separate from the playroom. In order to take this part of its work forward, PPA has established a working group to review its role in supporting parents. 57,000 parents are currently involved in PPA courses (2.2 million student hours), ranging from short courses for parents to the Diploma in Playgroup Practice for playgroup supervisors and staff. Margaret Lochrie, PPA Chief Executive Officer, says that 'since there is a blurring between the roles of staff and parents many of the students on, for example, our Diploma course, testify to the help the course has also given them as parents' (response to enquiry, August 1993). The 10-session course focused at parents or carers of young children has the following aims:

> To recognise the needs of parents/carers and to promote their self-esteem and self-confidence. In the context of today's changing society, to assist parents/carers to come to an understanding of their role in the development of their children so that they can meet their children's needs.

The objectives of the course suggest that, in the context of equal opportunities, course members will be able to:

- explain the basics of child development and within the context of today's changing society the role of the family and a consistent adult in that development;
- recognise and respect different styles of parenting;
- explain the positive aspects of the parent's management of their children's behaviour in relation to the stages of development and the cultural background of families;
- explain the importance of play and how play develops the skills of children regardless of their abilities and disabilities;
- describe how to provide for play at home;
- identify sources of family support and the diverse forms of child care and education;
- identify their own future training needs.

PPA sees it as an important priority to increase the information they can give to parents and to increase levels of parental involvement. Experience leads them to believe that parents gain not only from education and information, but also from participation in situations where they can feel in control. 'Too often', says Margaret Lochrie, 'parents feel (wrongly) that their own knowledge or convictions are subsidiary or inferior to those of professionals' (response to enquiry, August 1993).

## Toy libraries

Toy libraries play a valuable role in support for parents in many different settings – playgroups, family centres, hospitals, schools, drop-in centres, and so on. Parents have the opportunity to make links with other parents and also sometimes with professionals, and often take an active part in the running of the toy library. Where toy libraries are set up as a school-based pre-school resource, they can be a valuable route in to developing community links. In clinics they encourage families to attend for health surveillance checks. The particular value of toy libraries is that the concept is easily used by a wide variety of organisations to help people gain access to services they might otherwise find difficulty in accepting. Parents will often join something for their children's benefit that they might otherwise reject. The Toy Libraries Association estimates that there are 1,100 toy library groups in the UK, catering for over 100,000 families and over a quarter of a million children (Glenys Carter, Director, response to enquiry, February 1994).

## Faith communities

There are a number of new initiatives in support for parents and parenting in faith communities of all kinds. In the Christian faith, for example, the Lord Bishop of Coventry (*Hansard*, 1992) commented in his maiden speech in the House of Lords:

> Church members and Christian agencies in growing numbers of places where the Church is coming alive are working to affirm parents, to help them know that they are performing a profoundly important task, to protect them from family breakdown before it threatens, to give them confidence in face of the pressures and temptations to which they and their children are increasingly exposed and to help those with poor experience of parenting in their own childhood to find new role models.

In almost every diocese of the Church of England, Family Life and Marriage Education (FLAME) has been set up. Its work is spreading beyond the confines of the Church, promoting community education in parenting, in marriage and in family life. FLAME aims to build confidence in parents, helping them to change and develop their skills. Its philosophy is to encourage 'good enough' parenting.

The Church Pastoral Aid Society published a video in 1993 called *'Help! I'm a Parent'*. Through workshops and discussions it aims to address the key attitudes and skills of family life, and answer some of the questions parents are asking.

The Methodist Church Division of Education and Youth (1994) argues that the Church has a useful role in emphasising 'parenting' rather than 'marriage and family life'. The concept of parenting makes no assumptions about the number of or relationship between parent figures; rather it looks at the relationship between child and primary carer, with a view to affirming the loving and caring that goes on in a wide variety of situations – often against great odds. The Division, in describing parenting courses, emphasises that there is no single agreed term to describe the kind of parent the courses are trying to produce. It is generally agreed that people should not expect to be or become perfect parents, nor should they be autocratic, authoritarian or permissive. Rather, they should be responsible, authoritative, assertive, positive, democratic, effective, or good enough. The Division has collaborated with the National Children's Home and Parent Network in producing a booklet *Partners in Parenting*, which suggests some of the ways in which local churches can support parents in bringing up their children. The booklet points out that the churches already have links with a large number of parents, through baptisms, toddler groups, work with children and young people, Sunday worship and learning, pastoral visits, and so on. Churches are also set within wider communities and can therefore develop useful networks. Many church members have useful skills and experience to share.

The work of the Christian-based voluntary child care agencies such as Barnardo's, National Children's Home and The Children's Society is increasingly focusing on working with whole families in neighbourhood centres and family centres such as those described in the following pages, rather than taking children out of the community and putting them into institutions.

## More specialist group support

The New Parent Infant Network (NEWPIN) is described as 'a support network for individuals who want to make positive changes in their lives and improve their relationship with children, partners and families'. Although much of their work, aimed specifically at parents, or other main carers, suffering from depression or feelings of isolation, is achieved through group workshops and therapy, recognition is also given to the value of peer group support. Each new user of NEWPIN is matched with a befriender – a carefully selected established

NEWPIN user – who introduces the user to the NEWPIN centre, where adults and children can begin to develop trusting relationships with other members. A pilot evaluation of NEWPIN in South London (Pound and Mills, 1985) found that the experience had transformed the lives of many of its members and enriched the experience of their children.

> In terms of improved mental health, raised self-esteem, quality of relationships and capacity to care for children, NEWPIN has demonstrated the value of a volunteer organisation which uses the resources of goodwill in the community to raise the quality of life within it.

A substantial reduction in levels of despair, anxiety and hostility was noted, and some 73% of those with significant mental health problems who had been involved with NEWPIN for over six months were found to have improved. A more recent study (Cox and others, 1992) concluded that NEWPIN is an important new development in services for vulnerable parents and children, providing intensive support without dependency and loss of self-respect. In an examination of changes in parent/child relationships the researchers found that there were significant improvements in the mothers' ability to anticipate their children's needs. Changes in other areas were not statistically significant and, in any case, concealed the fact that there were some mother/child pairs who changed dramatically and others not at all. The research group has now begun piloting a parent package (in London and in Scotland) based on their five 'dimensions of parenting' (anticipation, autonomy, cooperation, child distress and warmth and stimulation), using psychotherapy and a range of approaches including video to improve parent-child interactions. This is already showing increased self-confidence on the part of mothers and improved interactions between parents and children, particularly in reducing negative behaviour such as smacking and shouting (Puckering and others, in press). The majority of the children in the study have come off the child protection register.

SCOPE is an example of an organisation which offers a supportive network of care at times when families with children under five are functioning at a low ebb. The main focus of the organisation's work has been the establishment of neighbourhood groups. SCOPE started in Southampton in 1976, and has now developed to include other main towns in Hampshire, providing a valued service to over 400 families. The groups are organised into seven Units, each of which has a paid coordinator attached to five or six neighbourhood groups. Families are recommended (not referred) to the organisation by health, education, social services and voluntary organisations and coordinators then invite them to attend one of the weekly groups which meet in a variety of community centres, local halls and schools. The concept of *membership* is important in SCOPE – families are not perceived as clients, and once a family joins a group there is an expectation that it will contribute to the group's learning and strength. Each of the neighbourhood groups is convened by a member who has been trained by the Unit Coordinator. One of the tasks of group convenors is to welcome new members in such a way that they feel valued, however dire their personal circumstances may be at the time. The pioneering work of SCOPE aims to:

- provide friendship and support for parents;
- build up the confidence of parents;
- gain more knowledge about the health and well-being of children and adults;
- enable parents and children to meet others in their neighbour-hoods;
- enable families to use the services available to them effectively;
- tackle things which concern us, together.

The structure and management of the organisation by its members is used as a means of empowering people to undertake responsibilities and tasks which they may not have felt within their abilities or competencies when joining. Proof of the method's success is seen in the fact that half of SCOPE's paid workers have come from the membership and have been appointed in open competition with candidates from elsewhere, many of them professionally qualified. SCOPE's Chair (and founder), Geoff Poulton says:

> Much of our work focuses on helping individual parents to feel more valued and positive about themselves in a variety of roles, including parenthood. Our experience suggests that people who are more confident in themselves and in their ability to communicate with children and others are more likely to be effective parents. This work involves a high investment of time and energy in face to face contact, but this method seems to be more likely to succeed than other approaches which do not convey any sense of belief in the parents' potential for change. (Response to enquiry, May 1993)

For families who are undergoing especially stressful episodes in their lives, SCOPE can offer short periods of residential respite care in its Family House. Families in crisis can come to the House at very short notice, while others may make prior arrangements through their coordinators.

A parent support group for parents who are in crisis and

experiencing difficulties with their parenting is run in South Birmingham by FSU. Here, as in a number of such groups, the emphasis is on support rather than specifically on parenting skills.

## Family centres

As we have already noted, work with and support for families can be perceived as being on a continuum, with community projects at one end and intensive therapeutic work at the other. Jon Doble of Barnardo's has drawn attention to the tensions between a broader, more equitable vision of access to such services as are promoted by Part III of the Children Act on the one hand and the implications of the application of the Section 17 prioritisation criteria of 'in need' on the other (response to enquiry, May 1993). He suggests that such tensions include the way in which support services utilise approaches, methods and responses from perspectives such as:

Universal access ———— Response to vulnerable families
'Normality' of ———— Deficit approach
problems
Promotional and ———— Residual and compensatory
educational

Family centres, such as those run by Barnardo's, and also by a variety of other organisations, are situated at various points along these continua, using a range of approaches and methods of working. This has been a fast growing area of family support. Warren (1990) listed 352 such centres in England and Wales and the Family Centre Network estimated there were about 600 early in 1994. The Children Act 1989 (in the first statutory mention of family centres) describes them as centres where family members may attend for occupational, social, cultural or recreational activities and for advice, guidance and counselling. The Family Centre Network defines the term **Family Centre** as

descriptive of those approaches which bring together those who subscribe to a holistic approach to families with emphasis on the organisation of services in the locality and emphasis on maximising participation of all.

Holman (1992) suggested that family centres were of three types: the **client-focused model** which works with referred clients and has a strong 'professional/client' ethos; the **neighbourhood model** typically located in areas of high social need, offering a broad range of activities and encouraging user participation; and the **community**

**development model** (very much in the minority) characterised by collective action, local control and workers offering indirect support to community groups rather than direct provision of services. The Children Act Guidance classification is slightly different, but again suggests three types: **therapeutic, community** and **self-help**. In reality, however, any classification is likely to be too simplistic, since even within one family centre a variety of different approaches may be employed. For example, one Barnardo's centre providing structured therapeutic assessment and treatment work to families in difficulty offers this within a broader network of provision, including open access play schemes, open access women's groups, outreach work and so on, in an attempt to be as non-stigmatising as possible. Holman (1992) suggests that there may now be a period of growth for family centres, especially those of the client-focused type which are limited mainly to families showing actual or potential child abuse. However, neglect of other types of family centre – the neighbourhood model and the community development model – would be a loss, since they are both popular with users and of preventative value.

Cannan (1992), too, expresses concern about the abandonment of community work in favour of an intensive family therapy approach, with its roots in parental malfunctioning and pathology. She continues:

> [Family therapy] does not seek to understand such pathology in its own right but to see how pathological patterns of interaction in the family system have led to the victimization of a (child) member. (p 103)

Cannan suggests that the client-focused, social work family centre which social workers have tended to promote reflects, in part, their organisational needs and in part their professional interests. She goes on to propose that the most effective family centres are those which offer a range of services and resources for families, provided in the spirit of acknowledging that families – and especially lone mothers – need services (such as space, respite, day care, playgroups, welfare rights information, low-key counselling, group work and holiday schemes) and formal and informal resources if parents are to succeed as (and to enjoy being) parents.

Ferri and Saunders (1991) study of five Barnardo's centres in the north of England draws attention to the value systems by which child care and development, parental attitudes and behaviour, and the lives of families are judged. In this context, the authors suggest:

> it is important to recognise that any strategy for parental involvement which includes among its aims the improvement of parenting skills

becomes a ready vehicle for socialising parents – and children – into the norms and values of the service providers. (p130)

A study of family centres for the Children's Society (Smith, 1993) highlights the role of these centres in helping parents in their task of bringing up young children. The study concludes that the centres were 'meeting parents' needs for social contact and to share problems, and helping the most vulnerable to gain confidence and learn to cope with their children'. Smith confirmed that parents' needs were not confined only to referred users: large numbers of children were growing up in very disadvantaged circumstances. In attempting to answer the question which type of family centre is more effective, Smith concluded that 'worker style, a mix of activities, an 'adult education' approach, and the provision of scarce resources and services in neighbourhoods lacking facilities are probably more important than project 'type'. Another study, by Gibbons (1990), focused on the type of user rather than the type of family centre. Gibbons found that 'clients' (who had been referred by a social work agency) were least satisfied with the centre. 'Consumers', who had just dropped in, were fairly satisfied and 'members', who had some formal role in the organisation, spoke most positively about the centre. This finding could be interpreted to indicate that participation and satisfaction are closely related, while being a 'client' inhibits participation.

The National Children's Home (now NCH Action for Children), another large voluntary child care organisation, runs around 100 family centres which

> work with parents by building on their skills and abilities. Staff offer practical advice on matters such as healthy eating, budgeting and hygiene, importance of play – all of which help parents to develop their parenting skills. (Methodist Division of Education and Youth, 1994)

A rather different model of family centre, also run by NCH Action for Children, and working with 'high risk' families, has been evaluated by Lindsell and Pithouse (1993). The researchers conclude that the outcomes – defined as changes perceived by the families in their own behaviour, attitude or lifestyle – were positive for all families. Families felt that the centre had helped them to change by giving them a better understanding of themselves, by helping them to make positive and informed choices about which course to take and how to make the change.

The Larkfield Family Centre in Greenock is an example of a community model family centre. Run by Quarriers, in partnership with local statutory bodies, it has developed since its inception in 1987 to provide a variety of services: drop-in centre, community nursery, toddlers' group, day care unit, home link support, adult education classes, discussion groups, playschemes, good-as-new shop, and other facilities. An internal evaluation report on this group (Gill, 1992) states that the empowerment of local people is an important and integral part of this project. Through their internal management structure (a system of 'get togethers' and 'working groups'), parents are enabled to take on pieces of work as and when they wish, thus providing opportunities for women to recognise their own skills and enabling them to fulfil their own potential.

A similar empowering approach is described by Statham (1994) in her study of community-based, open access services for young children carried out for the Save the Children Fund (UK). A feature of these five family centres was the ability for users to be recipients of services at one time and providers of them at another. Many of the projects had helped parents and the local community to set up services themselves which were independent of the family centre, such as community playgroups, after-school schemes, toy libraries and playgroup workers' support groups. Statham concludes that

> the community based, open access nature of the family centres in the study allowed reciprocity to thrive, and the range of coping abilities among families using the centres allows them to support each other (and their local community) rather than merely to be recipients of services. (p 27)

Numerous other examples could be given of children's centres and family centres which provide a range of services for children and parents. One such is the Ferncliff Centre in Hackney run by Barnardo's which offers full day care for children, sharing care (home-based care with specially trained childminders), playgroup sessions, parent and toddler group sessions, toy library sessions, holiday play schemes for children with severe disabilities, parents' groups, welfare rights advice, child assessment and speech therapy sessions. Another is the Pen Green Centre in Corby, Northamptonshire, which has a long tradition of support for families. The methods used in this centre to promote children's learning and development are referred to in chapter 4 and are graphically described in Whalley (1994). The Centre's development to become a focus for adult learning too is described later in this chapter.

The variety of approaches adopted by family centres reviewed here, together with the family centre or children's centre approach now being adopted by an increasing number of local authority day nurseries suggests that there is scope here for further studies on the effectiveness of the particular type of intervention. As the Audit Commission report (1994) notes:

> Intensive intervention work such as specialist training in parenting skills and counselling should be evaluated for effectiveness. A mix of open access with a quota of referred families is preferable to a closed system. (p 40)

# Parenting education groups and courses

## Open access parenting education groups and courses

Writing in 1984, we noted that:

> Structured schemes and 'schools for parents' have never really caught on in Britain to the extent they have elsewhere. Schools for parents have been criticised for their restrictive appeal, tending to draw an 'educated and middle class elite' (Stern 1960), and even parent-teacher associations in schools have played a minimum role in this respect in comparison with similar bodies elsewhere in Europe and in countries such as New Zealand and Japan. (p 145)

We quoted a DHSS (1974b) report which concluded that:

> the majority of parents would not participate in the parent education movement or attend formal further or adult education classes even if, as was suggested, they were given a financial incentive to attend. Some less formal approach was needed.

Some of the informal approaches identified ten years ago are still in evidence – for example the Calderdale Association for Parents, set up in 1968 for the

> advancement of education in the practice and methods of child upbringing in order to foster healthy growth and development amongst children; and to provide guidance for parents and to encourage the pooling of experience in child upbringing, particularly in the preschool years and in the light of the changing social scene.

Based on the French *écoles des parents*, the Association has a parents centre in a small council house in Mixenden, run by parents, and is still the only group in the UK affiliated to the International Federation for Parent Education.

The parent education courses published by the Open University over a ten-year period – *The First Years of Life* (1977), *The Preschool Child* (1977), *Childhood 5-10* (1981), *Parents and Teenagers* (1982) and *Pregnancy and Birth* (1985) – provided a wealth of material on parenting from pregnancy and birth to parenting adolescents. The underlying philosophy of the parenting packs can be summarised as follows:

- parents have the best knowledge of their own situation, what they want to happen and what they feel most happy doing;
- parents have a wealth of experience and ability to put into their families, but many need encouragement to recognise this;
- most parents feel inadequate at times and need help to build confidence in their own abilities;
- with support, parents can critically examine and learn from expert opinion and theory;
- through a process of reflection and action, parents can be helped to build up their skills;
- building skills and confidence in parents leads to them taking a more active role in the wider community. (Open University, 1992)

The study packs were published as magazine-style booklets containing short topics – later bound into a single volume. Study packs also included audio-cassettes and posters and were linked to BBC radio and TV programmes. The materials have been used extensively not just as structured learning materials for parents to use on their own at home, but also as the basis for group discussion by health visitors, social workers, teachers, playgroup leaders, and adult education tutors. Over 250,000 students used *The First Years of Life* and *The Preschool Child* and about 30,000 *Childhood 5 – 10*. The *Parents and Teenagers* course has been less successful, partly because the informal networks do not exist at this stage, partly because parents of teenagers do not seem drawn to such courses, and partly through lack of a professional network to use the materials (Open University, 1994).

In addition to the main materials, a project funded by the van Leer Foundation worked with community groups in Birmingham, Coventry, Liverpool and the Western Isles of Scotland to produce materials which were more accessible to those who had difficulty with the written word. *Women and Young Children, The Developing Child, Family Relationships*, and the *PPA Pack* (1983) have sold over 25,000 copies. Other 'spin-offs' include a Welsh language version of *The Preschool Child (T Plentyn Bach)*, a pack for childminders *Childminding: Materials for Learning and Discussion* (1986) and extracts used for the Scottish *Book of the Child*, which went to 350,000 pregnant women.

Follow-up surveys of individual learners and group leaders show benefits in a number of areas: knowledge gains; a better understanding of children; enhanced skills; changed attitudes (more tolerant and sympathetic); changes in practice; increased confidence in themselves as parents; social and community benefits, through bringing together parents who were isolated or lacking in confidence; and usefulness of the training resource to the many professionals using the materials (Open University, 1986). The Open University has undertaken extensive evaluation of all courses and materials (Open University 1986, 1992), and concludes that:

- an impressive number of parents have been reached and helped to develop their parenting skills;
- a model of 'learning for everyday life' and developing important lifeskills has been developed and refined;
- an approach to facilitating learning groups in the community has been developed and disseminated.

The model devised over the last 15 years is now to be developed in an ambitious new *Parenting and Under 8s* programme to start in 1994.

The last ten years has seen a considerable expansion in other published materials and in parent education groups, some widely available and others restricted to parents expressing particular difficulties.

The Family Caring Trust, for example, founded in Northern Ireland in 1986, has published a range of materials in its Veritas Basic Parenting Programme and estimates that in the past seven years its courses have been attended by over 135,000 parents in Britain and Ireland. The main emphasis in the programmes is on

improving respectful communication and effective discipline in the home. Parents are encouraged to appreciate their own strengths and discover what methods work best for them – rather than be over-dependent on experts.

The project sees three essential planks in their approach – parent education, community development and leadership enablement – and stresses the importance of parents taking an active part in leading their own self-help groups, not just being put into a 'helped' role. 'No one in the group is in a position to tell someone else how they ought to parent their children' (Gamble, 1994). There is thus emphasis on empowering people from all backgrounds to lead groups, and the Trust prefers to work through existing structures in the community – churches, voluntary organisations, social services, schools – rather than create its own structure.

Drawing on the work of parent educators such as Gordon, Adler, Dinkmeyer and Dreikurs (see chapter 3), the materials support discussion groups usually held for about eight sessions on a weekly basis and lasting for about two hours. They focus on issues such as taking responsibility, encouragement, listening, good communication, discipline, talking things over, self-respect and assertiveness. Published materials include *What Can a Parent Do?* (Quinn, 1988) *Being Assertive* (Quinn, 1992) and *Teen Parenting* and *Parenting and Sex*. Voluntary groups and churches using the parenting programme include the Children's Society and the Anglican Church in Wales, where the materials have been translated into Welsh, and Barnardo's and the Anglican, Methodist and Roman Catholic churches in England. There has been no external evaluation of these materials, although the organisation's publicity material cites enthusiastic parents, and church workers and health education workers in many parts of the country describe the groups as 'snowballing'.

Parent Network was also set up in 1986, drawing eclectically on similar writers to:

> provide parents with opportunities to enable them to understand their own social, emotional, psychological and physical needs and those of their children and enhance the relationship between them.

Parent Network operates through the Parent Link programme, which aims to develop self aware and self confident parents. Courses follow a pattern of twelve weekly group discussions facilitated by a trained parent who has received over 100 hours in training from Parent Network. Topics covered include meeting parents own needs, appreciating our children, acknowledging feelings, listening to children, and helping children solve their own problems (Sokolov and Hutton, 1988). About 5,000 parents have been through the Parent Link programme, and there are 190 coordinators operating in 30 local areas. A project for expectant and new parents – PIPPIN – which has developed from Parent Network, is described in chapter 5.

Waltham Forest aims to run 15 – 20 Parent Link courses each year, supported by the education and social services departments, as part of a broader strategy of supporting parents' role in education. The course is being translated into Urdu, Bengali and Turkish and courses are currently running in a number of primary and nursery schools. An East London African-Caribbean Action Research Project was also set up, with one all black group, in addition to the support offered to groups which included black and white parents. The report of this project comments that there was not felt to be a clash of values between Parent Link and the African-Caribbean community because 'the notion of empowerment is familiar to young black people' and found that:

> the fundamental Parent Link attitude that each family needs to find its own solutions to its own dynamic problems postulates an acceptance

and respect for 'differences' that embraces acceptance and respect for different cultural experience. (East London African/Caribbean Action Research Project Report, 1992)

An independent evaluation (Baginsky, 1993) reports that the courses have led to:

significant benefits to the parents in terms of confidence, better communication with their children, improved understanding of children's feelings and emotional needs and improved handling of children's behaviour.

The LEA community education officer who supports the project describes the most important aspects of Parent Link as being the fact that it is run by parents for parents; and that it builds on parents' own experience to develop confidence and skills, particularly in the area of communications and emotional problem solving.

In Exeter the first Parent Link family centre opened in 1992, with facilities including a family workshop, a parent and toddler group, a drop-in centre, a playgroup, and parenting groups. It is ironic that in 1994 it is under threat of closure, as the local authority reviews its funding priorities (*Guardian*, 1994). Their first newsletter described a new fathers group (part of the Parent Network fathers' project), a support group for parents of teenagers, and workshops on sibling rivalry.

Speaking at the Network's fifth anniversary reception in 1991, Richard Evans of the Artemis Trust, which initially funded Parent Network, described the Network as filling

that vital gap in parental education and support which Gillian Pugh and Erica De'Ath identified in the 1984 study for the National Children's Bureau of parent education and support in this country. I'm heartened to know that Parent Network meets their suggested requirements almost exactly.

Exploring Parenthood, established in 1982, derives its focus from a psychodynamic approach to parenting (Schmidt Neven, 1990). Driven by a wish to 'mobilise parents' own capacities for change', Exploring Parenthood uses the therapeutic skills more usually found in child guidance clinics to provide a more widely accessible service to parents. Much of its work takes place in workshops for parents, but it has more recently taken on a broader role, setting up an advice line for parents, training other professionals in group work techniques, and establishing a number of specific projects. These include working with parents through schools, working with men in prison, the Moyenda project which supports parents from minority ethnic groups, working with parents whose children are in trouble, work with parents with disabled children, and a counselling and advice service for employees, established with IKEA.

A tenth anniversary multi-agency symposium *Responsible Parenting Requires a Responsible Society* (Exploring Parenthood, 1992) led to a ten point vision and, during 1993, to the establishment of an All Party Parliamentary Group on Parenting.

In addition to these three organisations with their national networks, a number of smaller local schemes have been established, for example those set up by voluntary groups, such as Portsmouth Area Family Concern which has published two *Positive Parenting Packs* (PAFC, 1992); and Parents & Co run by the Elfrida Rathbone Association in Camden for parents with learning difficulties (Binning, 1994). The Effective Parenting Programme has been developed by a parent and a teacher and is currently being piloted in 18 primary schools in Barnet and Hertfordshire, where teachers are being trained and supported to run 'coffee and chat' groups for parents. (Hartley-Brewer, 1994; Hartley-Brewer and Hills, 1994; Kahn, 1994b). Another interesting new initiative in Plymouth is Parentwise, a multi-agency community based project coordinated by a community educational psychologist. Working with health visitors, parent education workers and others the project is developing parentcraft workshops which bridge the gap between ante-natal classes and school entry, as part of a community based parent and child support programme.

## Specialist parenting courses

The projects noted above are open access, for any parent wishing to think about and discuss their own approach to bringing up children. But as noted in chapter 3, there has also been a considerable interest in recent years in the use of behavioural approaches for training parents. Topping (1986) for example reviewed over 600 research reports on the effectiveness of parent training programmes in a wide range of areas, including work with children with learning difficulties, developmental delay, and difficulties over reading. It is in the area of handling behaviour difficulties, however, that a growing number of schemes are currently in operation, many of them run by educational psychologists and social workers, and often taking families referred by health visitors and social workers. There is an extensive literature on psychological approaches to training parents in behavioural methods of managing their children in order to reduce the frequency of behaviour problems (for example, Forehand and

McMahon, 1981; O'Dell and others, 1977; Patterson, 1982; Herbert, 1981). Much of this draws on a social learning/behavioural framework to train parents, building on parents' ability to reinforce good behaviour by expressing warmth and approval, with time out for non-compliant behaviour (see chapter 3).

Hinton's behavioural management workshops for parents of young children, for example, have been run over many years in nursery and infant schools in Surrey, based on an ABC of change (looking at antecedents, behaviour and consequences) (Hinton, 1994). An evaluation (Hinton, 1987) showed significant reduction in problems at home and at school, and the development of a problem solving approach. Another scheme, EPIC – Everyday Problems in Childhood – has published materials and tapes which have been used by groups, mainly in the Brighton area. Most recent work has been with parents of children with special needs (Clench, 1993) who have reported very positively on the sense of empowerment the group has given them.

Other approaches use the *Assertive Discipline Course for Parents* (Canter, 1988), developed from American materials but now adapted to 'meet the needs of parents living in deprived city areas in the UK'. The Coping with Kids project in Bristol is run by the psychology service, offering five workshops for parents, and linking into assertive discipline courses in schools. The materials are only available to course leaders who have been trained by Behaviour Management Ltd, and the main advantages of the package are described as:

> clear communication; planned, structured and agreed sanctions or consequences for misbehaviour; and praise, approval and love, without an over-emphasis on tangible rewards. (Robinson, 1994)

Other projects drawing on this approach include two schemes in Leicester involving psychologists, social workers and health visitors, one at de Montfort University (Sutton, 1992; 1994) in which materials have been developed and health visitors are being trained to work with parents; and the other at the Centre for Fun and Families (Gill, 1989). An independent evaluation of Sutton's pilot study showed success through phone counselling, individual and group work, and identified key factors in the success as the availability of family support, competence in using time out, and the use of training materials (Sutton, 1992).

Other approaches are by clinical psychologists and health visitors, such as the Parent Education Package developed in Bristol (Hewitt and others, 1991). This package, prepared by clinical psychologists, was used by health visitors with parents of children between one month and two years, in their own homes, and aimed to prevent behaviour problems. The evaluation showed that the parents enjoyed the programme but the intervention did not produce a reduction in problematic behaviour; on the contrary some parents reported more problems. The report concludes that it may be better not to try to prevent specific problems which may never arise, but to foster more positive attitudes towards children.

Working with Parents for Change in Strathclyde (Edwards and Townsend, 1993) has trained nursery workers to apply appropriate management techniques designed to modify behaviour. These workers have gone on to run courses, some of which have led to parents setting up support groups, doing Open University Courses etc. The project reports encouraging results over two years, including successful piloting in a primary school. A training pack *Working with Parents for Change* has recently been published.

Other projects include work with parents on their children's school attendance in the Marlborough Family Service Education Unit (Dawson and McHugh, 1986); and a project in Kent on managing sleep disturbance (Quine, 1991).

Work with children with severe behavioural problems at the Maudsley Hospital's department of child and adult psychiatry adopts a similar approach (Jenner, 1992; Jenner and Gent, 1993) using the parent/child game developed by Forehand and McMahon (1981). Once or twice weekly sessions take place in a video suite, with the therapists observing the parents and child through a one way mirror and talking to them through a small microphone. The parent is encouraged to express warmth and approval when their child's behaviour is acceptable, ignore unacceptable behaviour, is shown how to give clear commands, and how to enforce time-out for non-compliance. A preliminary evaluation has found lasting improvements in behaviour, and developing mutual trust between child and parent. Two BBC television QED programmes showing Jenner's work (BBC, 1993) have aroused considerable interest.

Drawing on a theoretical framework developed by Bavolek and Comstock (1983) in their 'nurturing programme for parents and children aged 4-12' the Family Nurturing Network (formerly the Oxford Family Skills Development Project) is working to prevent and reduce physical and emotional abuse in families, by focusing on four key elements common in abusive families: inappropriate expectations of children, lack of empathy, a strong belief in corporal punishment, and role reversal. Run by a clinical psychiatric nurse, a health visitor and a clinical psychiatrist, the project works with groups of families in up to 12 weekly sessions, with children and parents working separately, but with a joint 'nurturing time' in the middle of the session. An evaluation of the pilot phase is currently underway, with funding from the Joseph Rowntree Foundation. The work evolving from NEWPIN (p168) combines a number of different skills and techniques, some focusing on parents and some on parents and children together, and early results are very promising (Puckering and others, in press).

Schemes for parents and children with learning disabilities are discussed on p193-196.

Although some of these projects, schemes and programmes outlined above have been independently evaluated, many seem to be developing without drawing on the experience of others. Given the extent to which such projects are increasing, an external evaluation of the effectiveness of different approaches is urgently required and, would provide the basis for decisions as to which approaches are likely to be most appropriate for which parents.

## Home-school liaison

This section describes some of the ways in which parents, through their children's schools, can be helped to support children, to understand their learning and to take opportunities to extend their own learning. Space permits us to touch on just a small selection of the widespread schemes available to parents.

Over the years a number of local authorities (Liverpool, Waltham Forest, Humberside, Coventry, Birmingham, Cambridgeshire, Cleveland and Devon are some of those noted in Bastiani, 1993) have adopted an overall policy approach to parent support and home-school links, including support for community education. However, legislation, policy and funding changes make the continuation of such policies far from certain. In an attempt to secure a sounder basis for support for the recognition of parents as their children's first educators, a group convened by Waltham Forest Teachers' Centre campaigned for a parents' amendment to be included in the 1993 Education Act. The amendment failed, but the same group is working to introduce a similar amendment into the 1994 Education Bill setting up the Teacher Training Agency.

A growing number of individual schools, and teachers, have been putting considerable commitment and energy into working with parents, families and their local communities. This activity in the field is now paralleled by an unprecedented level of political interest in the relationships between parents and their children's schools, culminating in a new body of ever changing legislation and guidelines for schools to implement. Parents now have a right to express a preference about which school their child should attend, receive information about the school, receive information about their children's work and progress, participate in the management of their children's schools and be involved in the assessment and review of special needs provision for their children. There is much of mutual benefit to be gained by this home-school partnership and, as the Community Education Development Centre comments:

> the bottom line is that the education, welfare and development of children growing up in the nineties is too great a task for either families or schools to undertake on their own. Each needs the other. (1993)

Wolfendale (1992) cites evidence to show that there has been in recent years a significant shift towards increasing parental involvement in schools and 'in some quarters a realignment in the power balance, towards an approximation of power-sharing.' Parental involvement is seen by some as a reflector of the ethos of a school, and by others as an indication of the effectiveness of a school. Wolfendale tentatively predicts that, although schools will be forced to adopt strategies to promote parental participation, these are unlikely to be of the kind which promotes equality in decision making.

A directory of home-school initiatives in the UK (Bastiani, 1993) is a valuable source of knowledge about the current state of policy and practice in this area. Some 30 descriptions of local education authority policies and activities in England and Scotland are provided, together with descriptions of 20 home-school liaison projects and initiatives and 19 special programmes (mainly with Section 11 funding – Home Office funding to assist local government services to minority ethnic groups under Section 11 of the 1966 Local Government Act) across the UK. Seven national organisations are listed as being concerned with the initiation, coordination, support and development of home-school activity. Finally, the work of 30 agencies which are responsive to the interests and concerns of parents, parent/teacher initiatives, parent groups and organisations is reported.

The examples we give in this section can be broadly separated into those which **encourage parental participation in school life**, those which aim to facilitate and extend **parents' role in their own children's education**, and those which aim primarily to **extend and develop parents' own learning**. There is, of course, often some overlap between these areas, as demonstrated by the 70 Family Education Projects in Devon which include family workshops, family groups, parent education projects, parent support groups and other learning projects.

## Increasing parental participation in school life

For many years parents have had opportunities to partake in the school life of their children, whether it be in fundraising activities, outings, helping in the classroom, or more formally through parent-teacher associations. The Education Acts of 1988, 1992 and 1993 have given parents rights over choice of school and access to information on their children's progress, and also responsibilities, as set out in the Parents' Charter, and required schools to work more in partnership with parents. As part of the debate on the overall effects of these changes in the education scene, Bastiani (*in* Munn, P (ed), 1993) notes the 'complex and elusive' nature of partnership, suggesting that it may be better seen as something to work towards rather than something that is readily achievable. In the same publication Jonathan (1993) questions whether the granting of parental rights, of choice and control, are to be universally welcomed, given that, as she shows, rights for individuals may result in the curtailment of the wider social rights of the adult community.

## Parents as their children's educators

Whilst parents are often described as their children's first educators, it is only comparatively recently that attention has been paid to supporting and exploring this role. Easen and others, (1992) describe an approach to working with parents which emphasises the parents' own learning process and which might be termed 'developmental partnership', through which parents are explicitly acknowledged as the primary educators of their own children, and parents, educator and children learn and work together. This study, undertaken by two community teachers in the north east of England, focused on the creation of a dialogue around parents' interpretations of their children's play and development. In this way, the authors claim, these experiences then become directly relevant to parenting and central to the parents' learning process. Parents' self-esteem and confidence in their role as a parent is enhanced, and a partnership of mutual trust and respect is built.

Such an approach can start at the pre-school stage, and in East Sussex the County Council runs nine Playlink schemes in areas which demonstrate greatest need and are poorest in provision of relevant services. These schemes follow on from an earlier pilot scheme, the East Moulsecoomb Pre-School project, the evaluation of which (cited in Daines and Gill, 1993) concluded that the project clearly demonstrated that the Pre-School Project successfully combats the dependence and passivity that were the original cause for concern. The Project children were found to be more competent at, and more orientated towards, interaction with both adults and the material environment. The children were found to be more socially skilled, showed greater confidence and concentration, and made more use of language when compared with a matched control group of children from the same estate who had not been offered the project.

The Playlink schemes have two main, interlinked, practices. First, the provision of a home visiting service by Pre-school Visitors. The Visitors go to the homes of all children between the ages of 18 and 30 months for one hour per week. The aim is to support parents, and enhance their relationship with their children, primarily through the activity of shared play. Second, the schemes link families with their communities by connecting individual families with each other, and to outside activities; creating activities and new services in response to need; and introducing families to the range of services at their disposal.

Evaluation of these schemes (Daines and Gill, 1993) has indicated that all had high take-up and low 'leaving' rates, suggesting 'a match between scheme design and the needs of parents, as parents.' The schemes were popular with parents, and the enhancement in children's behaviour (specifically concentration and language development) appeared to match that shown in the earlier Moulescoomb evaluation. The philosophy and practice of the schemes appeared to be widely understood and welcomed both by professionals and by the target communities. The evaluation concluded that the Playlink schemes offered a highly portable model which had relevance to the needs of parents and children, and benefited from a shared inter-agency co-working and ownership approach.

The Home Based Early Learning Project (HELP), designed to involve parents in an educational dialogue on all aspects of child development by making available creative materials to parents of young children, was evaluated in Coventry and Hounslow (Macleod, 1984). The HELP project demonstrated the effective use of 'everyday professionals' – volunteers, themselves parents, who were able to relate easily to other parents. In both areas the project helped to establish new kinds of links between parents and professionals such as health visitors, nursery and school staff members.

Parents as Teachers (PAT) is a programme first developed in Missouri, USA in the early 1980s. A 1989 evaluation indicated that children who participated in PAT were significantly ahead of other children in academic performance at the end of their first year at school, and that parents of PAT children were more involved in their children's schooling. A further evaluation (Pfannenstiel and others, 1989; 1991) found that at age three PAT children on average scored significantly above the national norms on measures of school-related achievement. In the UK the PAT programme now operates in a County First School in High Wycombe in Buckinghamshire. The programme is designed for parents of children from birth to age three, and incorporates home visits from Parent Counsellors (certified by PAT), child development information, monitoring of children's development and group meetings. The PAT programme has extended to other American states and to some other countries, including New Zealand, where it has been the subject of some criticism on grounds which include the over-emphasis given to parents' (that is, mainly mothers') natural role as children's first educators, the focus on the home and the focus on 'trained' parent educators who give advice as 'experts' (Dalli, 1992).

A somewhat similar scheme, Home Early Learning Project (HELP), based in four Leeds schools, operating under the umbrella of Leeds Education 2000 and funded by local businesses, aims to:

- provide opportunities for parent/carers to understand and be fully active in their vital role as the first and most important educator of their children;
- provide opportunities for parents/carers to value their own skills and knowledge and gain confidence in their own learning potential;
- make provision in the community for parents/carers to meet and discuss aspects of parenting, education and other issues affecting them in a mutually supportive and non-threatening environment;
- provide children aged birth-three with increased and wide ranging opportunities for learning in the home and in groups.

Different approaches are used in different schools. In one where 90% of the pupils are Muslims, for example, there is a focus on sharing children's own experiences of childhood and building on the importance of the pupils' own first language. A report (April, 1993) on the progress of this scheme throws up two important lessons. First, that regular project reviews are vital to promote an open culture and establish trust, and should be built in from the start. Second, a realisation that projects such as HELP are considerable undertakings for schools already overburdened by statutory obligations and require extra time, energy and intellectual commitment from the staff involved.

In Liverpool the Parent School Partnership (PSP) is a well

established advisory and supportive resource for developing parental involvement in all Liverpool schools. In 1991 the LEA adopted a policy for all schools to encourage parental involvement in education. An essential aim of PSP is to work with parents as partners in the education of their children, working alongside their children in the classroom, contributing their many skills to curriculum development and sharing with teachers their knowledge of their child's learning at home and in the community. Parents have the option of gaining formal credit for this experience through the Parents as Educators course validated and accredited at Merseyside Open College Federation. Other activities have been initiated to recognise and support children's learning in the home. For example, shared reading and maths work, paired reading, computer clubs and home science kits. All these reinforce and develop learning that takes place in school and help to bring home and school together, easing the child's transition from one to another. A review of PSP included the views of 500 parents (PSP, 1992), 80% of whom spoke of increased confidence and 53% recorded access to further education opportunities through PSP. One woman wrote: 'Given purpose to life, friends, confidence, self-esteem, skills, certificates and how I share skills with the school. Feel more confident with my children.'

In 1991 Knowsley Local Education Authority secured Urban Renewal Funding to support and develop parental involvement in schools. Parental involvement coordinators were identified in schools, whose role was to:

- develop the partnership between parents and teachers;
- give parents opportunities to further their own education;
- increase parents' understanding of the educational process to enable them to better support their children;
- find out about and link more effectively with other agencies.

A newsletter describes some of the ideas and strategies tried by some of the schools during the first phase of this three-year project (Parental Involvement Project Newsletter, summer 1993).

Another local education authority active in the field of home-school liaison is Humberside, which in 1992 reported a number of initiatives, including the involvement of parents in the school curriculum. Schemes have included: pre-school literacy development, pre-school learning packs, home-school reading, home-school speak and listen, home-school spelling, home-school maths, home-school science and home-school European awareness.

An interesting initiative in Sweden which has reached 100,000 parents since it started some ten years ago, Growing Up Together, has developed new ways of encouraging parents to become involved in their children's education. The approach is based on 'study circles' involving both parents and teachers discussing topics described in an accompanying book. The parents of some 70-80% of children in participating schools are said to have taken part in these study circles (Lund, 1987).

In Leicester the Adult Basic Education Unit provides support for teaching staff who are trying to encourage parents to be more involved in their children's education. The Unit can offer consultancy, staff INSET training, advice on school-to-home communication and short courses for parents to support them in helping their children with school work.

The involvement of parents more directly in the curriculum, particularly at the primary stage, is demonstrated by the successful IMPACT maths scheme in which parents become involved in home-based activities closely related to the teaching which goes on in school. Similarly PACT (Parents and Children and Teachers Working Together) and its sister project PICC (Parental Involvement in the Core Curriculum), both of which operate in London Borough of Hackney schools, have been successful in demonstrating measurable reading gains in children. In Hackney, with its multi-ethnic population, it has been necessary to produce a wide range of materials in languages other than English in order to help parents understand educational methods. Such cooperative ventures between schools and parents have now extended to the science area, with SHIPS (School Home Investigations in Primary Science) from which both parents and children can learn in an enjoyable way. The success of these ventures, as the publication *Parents as Co-educators* (CEDC, 1993) states, depends on common purposes and shared goals which need to be established within schools.

## Parents extending their own learning

Adult education starts from a basis of mutual respect and learning among equals, and it is thus ideally placed to respond to people who through lack of confidence may feel there is no way in which they can alter the circumstances of their own lives. The 'traditional' adult education model may not always be the most accessible for some parents and, in fact, the more informal course, with negotiated content, has tended to be more successful in meeting many parents' needs, particularly for people whose own school days are not remembered as the 'happiest days of their life'. Adult education agencies have been providing family education programmes for some years, predominantly in the field of parents and their care of young children, home visiting schemes and family workshops. As we noted in chapter 4, recent legislation (Further and Higher Education Act 1992) now allows schools to provide further education, which may further increase the opportunities for intergenerational learning. As Clyne writes (discussion paper, January 1994):

> By starting from where people are in their family settings and relationships, family education can be seen to be a vivid example of the best adult education traditions... In the years to come...the processes of developing family education programmes will themselves be enriching and learning experiences for the participants.

A particularly interesting initiative, the Minus 1-5 Project, set up on a multidisciplinary basis through Community Education, was launched in early 1994 in Huntingdon, Cambridgeshire. Three primary schools are used at weekends for family education workshops from which it is hoped that other community education initiatives will develop.

The Adult Literacy and Basic Skills Unit (ALBSU), in recognition of findings which indicate that low achievement in basic skills is often passed from one generation to another (ALBSU, 1993), recently proposed an extensive programme of family literacy schemes. In fact, the DFE is currently funding five pilot projects (Developing Family Literacy) – in North Tyneside, Liverpool, Newham, Norfolk and Cardiff – which aim to encourage parents to play a more active role in their children's learning as well as improving their own standards of literacy and numeracy. In Shiremoor First School, North Tyneside, for example, each 12-week course provides parents with 12 hours of tuition linked to City and Guilds Communication Skills, their children with 72 hours of early language and literacy development, and parents and children with 24 hours of joint activities. This initiative also includes over half a million pounds in 1994/95 designated for funding for local work through a Small Grants Programme.

The City Lit Parent and Family Education Unit works with parents in Tower Hamlets schools under the Parents into Primary Schools (PIPS) initiative, supported by Bethnal Green City Challenge and GEST funding. This team works in five Bethnal Green schools supporting groups of parents mainly from the Bangladeshi community. The focus of the work varies and depends on the priorities of schools and needs and wishes of the parents, covering topics such as science workshops, story writing and illustrating, bi-lingual alphabet sound books, reading games and maths games.

Another, long-established service, which also places much emphasis on the involvement of parents in managing its activities is the Newham Parents Centre in the London Borough of Newham (Phillips, 1992). Under its basic principles, that parents are the first and main educators of their children and need to be given support and resources to improve their skills as educators, and that parents them-selves need better educational opportunities to enhance their self-esteem and general well-being, the centre acts as a resource and advice centre for parents, and runs a number of education and training activities.

The Pen Green Centre in Corby already referred to is an example of the way in which such work can empower parents. The Centre has a clear philosophy that 'parents bringing up young children [have] the right to personal space and self-development' (Whalley, 1994). Parent areas were set up in the nursery and parents' rooms, drop-ins and parent group rooms provided to offer parents (initially women) spaces for their own learning and development. These spaces appeared to be far more accessible to them than the traditional classroom environment, and the community education programme has continued to evolve over the last ten years with the support of the Workers' Educational Association and a local college. The Centre now offers a programme of GCSE and 'A' level courses, in addition to a range of educational, support, health and self-help groups designed to meet the needs of parents and negotiated with them.

Overall, it would appear that there have been significant cutbacks in support for family life and parent education in the traditional adult education sector (MORI report due mid-1994). These cuts have, however, been to some extent counterbalanced by increased activity in the voluntary sector (especially PPA courses) and by the churches (see the Veritas programme already referred to) who, ironically, are finding it increasingly difficult to fund courses because of reductions in grants.

## Support to meet particular needs

Many of the services and support projects described in the foregoing pages of this chapter are intended to meet the various needs of a broad spectrum of parents. Despite this, there are some parents, and other people who have parental responsibility for children, for whom such services may not be accessible or may not be relevant. To meet these specific needs, a whole range of specialised schemes, organisations and projects has grown up. It is these which are described in this next section.

## Parents of teenagers and adolescents

> When I was 14 my father was so stupid I could hardly stand to have him around. At 21 I was astonished at how much he had learned in the past seven years. (Mark Twain)

Puberty and adolescence can start as early as ten or as late as 16, and can be a turbulent and stressful time both for the young people and their carers. Brannen and others, (1994) refer to the struggle to independent adulthood of young people, and parents' concerns to control and shape this process, needing to get the balance right between care and control. There are few natural meeting places for parents of older children – such as outside the primary school gate, at the health clinic or playgroup which exist for parents of younger children. There is a need for more opportunities to meet with other parents to share experiences, discuss common concerns and develop a better understanding of young people's transition to adulthood. It is important to note, however (Burnell, 1993; Coleman, 1993), that although adolescence is popularly seen as a difficult time for parents, the psychological literature tends to see this period as a 'transition' rather than a 'crisis'. A review of research (Hill, 1993) suggests that less than 20% of families suffer severe inter-generational conflict. Nevertheless, the teenage stage can be stressful for many parents and many of the courses already mentioned contain elements on bringing up teenagers. Although there is still comparatively little available for parents and teenagers, there are also some specific opportunities for advice and information at this stage, for example:

---

- *RELATE course offered through RELATE centres, for example, 'Living with Teenagers', 'Parents of Teenagers'.*

- *Trust for the Study of Adolescence: Teenagers in the Family; Teenagers under Stress, Teenagers and Sexuality.*

- *Course run by St Neots Youth and Community Centre, Cambridgeshire: 10 session course for parents of teenagers, covering:*

  - *participants' own experiences;*
  - *physical, psychological and emotional development of teenagers;*
  - *home-school links;*
  - *career planning;*
  - *stress;*
  - *drug awareness;*
  - *sex education and relationships;*
  - *bullying and anti-social behaviour;*
  - *young people and the law.*

- *Veritas course on **Teen Parenting.***

---

## Fathers

Despite employment changes which have moved towards the abandonment of the traditional role of man as breadwinner and woman as home-based wife and mother, the majority of support projects and centres still focus mainly on mothers and their children. Men have, overall, lost their position of power in the family and still have to face feeling embarrassed or awkward at entering the female territory of child care. Furthermore, concerns over males as perpetrators of child sexual abuse have made their entry into the world of child care even more difficult.

In recognition of some of these difficulties, and of the importance of effective fathering, some family centres and other support projects have begun to introduce fathers' groups. One such is the fathering group at the Lawrence Weston Family Centre in Bristol run by Barnardo's. Unemployment in the area is high and the centre runs groups for women, parents and children, and also men. The men attending the family centre also have access to counselling around issues like violence and feelings of anger. Men have been encouraged too at the Pen Green Centre already referred to, with fathers attending a men's group (Chandler, 1993; Whalley, 1994) or one of the mixed gender groups set up at the centre. Interestingly, the men's group has proved difficult for nursery children's fathers to attend – the members have been mainly from outside the centre, foster carers or fathers whose children have left the centre. Representatives from Pen Green have joined a number of colleagues from all the member countries of the European Union to discuss men as carers for children – both as fathers and as workers – as part of the European Commission Childcare Network (1990). As noted in chapter 1, increased participation by men in the care and upbringing of children is one of the four Childcare Recommendations from the Council of Ministers.

The project already described at the retail firm IKEA, encourages fathers to participate in the day-to-day responsibilities of child care and helps them adjust to parenthood.

Families Need Fathers is a voluntary self-help group set up in 1974 which has a network of local groups providing advice and support especially on aspects of post-separation and post-divorce parenting, and in particular to parents who have problems maintaining a relationship with their children. Some local groups arrange Sunday groups which provide a venue for contact visits with children. Many fathers appreciate the chance to get together with their children in a place where toys and games and facilities for preparing drinks and meals are available. Parenting courses are run in the Norfolk Family Life Group.

## Families with children with special needs

> Motherhood has a single long-term goal, which can be described as the mother's own eventual unemployment. A successful mother (and father) bring up their children to do without them. But if a child has a disability or special need, there may be no longer term unemployment. In effect the 'life-plan' which all parents make for their children will be **different** for the child with special needs. Some parents... may find the adjustment to disability too difficult to cope with. They are not bad parents. They do care. But somebody has to care for **them** as people before they can enter the wonderful new world of partnership between parents and professionals that we all hear so much about.

This parent of a disabled child speaking at a Parent Workshop (Russell and Flynn, National Development Team, 1991) expresses exactly why such parents have a special and particular need for support services.

It is estimated that in the UK there are about 360,000 children of 16 and under with disabilities (OPCS, 1989), representing about 3% of the child population. All but 5,000 of these children are living at home with their families who are in need of a range of support services in order to help them carry this extra burden of care. The OPCS study suggested that not only do parents find the care of their disabled children difficult to cope with, but a high proportion felt that the care of their **other** children was adversely affected by competing interests. The same study, cited in Philpot and Ward (forthcoming), found that only 38% of parents with a disabled child belonged to or knew of a disability organisation which might help them. Respite care was only available to about 4% of families, although there were strong messages about families' needs for additional practical support.

Support for families with children with disabilities has to be seen in the context of the Children Act 1989 which emphasises the need for such families to lead lives which are 'as ordinary as possible', and the resulting expectation of parents that community-based services will be sufficiently adequate for this to occur (Russell, 1994). Russell also points out that the successful parenting of a child with special needs will not only depend upon the quality of the early education or child health programmes which are available: a number of studies have shown the increased pressures placed upon families by the care needs of their children. The resulting concerns have led to a number of initiatives to provide counselling, practical support and an educative role for parents. Cunningham (1989), for example, has found that trained home visitors offering regular support can make a major impact on parent involvement in education and community activities. Cameron (1982) has noted that parents need, firstly, to understand how to teach children everyday life skills and, secondly, help in managing difficult or disruptive behaviour which the child may acquire. A further consequence of Children Act and 1993 Education Act legislation is the opportunity provided for assessment and care management systems which acknowledge the importance of holistic support for all children with special needs, and therefore also for their parents.

Portage home visiting services were first set up in the UK in the 1970s, and have become increasingly popular. A recent survey (Kiernan, 1993) described 190 services across the UK, most operating on the familiar model of trained home visitors working in partnership with parents to meet the all round developmental needs of their young children with special educational needs. In that sense, comments the National Portage Association, these services play a role in educating as well as supporting parents. Kiernan's survey identified one service in Cornwall, the 'Special Parenting Service', which was specifically targeted at parents who themselves had a learning disability and whose pre-school children also showed developmental delay. This small service served eight children, with four on the waiting list. Three services were school-based, using both work in the school and home visiting, with a team of staff and parents as Portage workers.

The features of the Portage method include the fact that it involves the strengths and knowledge that parents already hold, and enable parents to select their own priorities. Portage, then, has a major role in supporting families and is increasingly being diversified into school as well as pre-school settings.

A scheme which started as a Portage service in the early 1980s, Haringey Home Intervention Scheme (HINTS), has developed so that the needs of parents are very much more to the fore. HINTS is part of the local authority social services department and has a team of trained visitors who work with families in their own homes to help in the child's development, by placing a great emphasis on the relationship between the visitor and the family. The approach is essentially flexible to the individual needs of the family, and negotiated openly with the family. Some 40-50 families receive this service at any one time and HINTS also operates an integrated toy library and playgroup once a week. It also runs a behaviour management group in collaboration with the educational psychology service, and in 1993 set up a group for Turkish and Kurdish families.

The authors of a paper describing this scheme (Silverman and Stacey, 1989) make a plea for professionals to:

> listen more attentively to parents and, indeed, to whole families. We must listen to their emotional and psychological needs as well as their practical needs.

The Rathbone Society, working in Leicester and North West Leicestershire promotes the welfare of children, young people and adults who have moderate learning difficulties. The family support is mainly provided by Family Support Workers who spend time with parents in their own homes, helping parents work out ways of tackling their troubles, which might include concerns about a child's behaviour or development, anxieties about being a new parent or finding out where to go for help. Rathbone Family Support Workers aim to develop the skills and confidence of people with learning difficulties so that they are better able to cope with the responsibilities of parenthood. As parents grow in confidence they can be encouraged to fulfil their crucial role as partners in the education of their children. Families also have the opportunity to attend Rathbone groups at which members can share interests and experiences and give each other support. Parents & Co (see p159)runs an advocacy service which was set up in 1987 to provide independent information, support and advice to parents of children being assessed for special educational needs under the 1981 Education Act.

Contact A Family, founded in 1979, is one of a number of self-help organisations which help to bring together families who have children with special needs.

> Discovering that your child has a special need or disability is probably one of the most devastating experiences that a parent will live through. The feeling of isolation – both physically and emotionally – can often be acute. However, experience tells us that some of this pain can be relieved by sharing thoughts and fears with other families in a similar situation

writes Contact A Family (Contact A Family leaflet). This organisation works, directly and indirectly, with about 50,000 families a year, mainly through over 800 local groups and networks involving families whose children may have any type of special need, disability or serious illness. Over 300 of these groups concentrate on families whose children have specific conditions, rare syndromes or genetically inherited disorders. These groups are organised by parents' committees and membership numbers vary depending on the condition. In addition to providing contact with other families in similar circumstances, this organisation has a team of development officers who can offer advice on setting up and maintaining parent support groups; a range of factsheets; and several local community projects in London offering support to families and a range of activities such as integrated playschemes and parent workshops. Other examples of such support organisations are SNAP, Network '81 (a national network of parents of children with special needs seeking to implement the 1981 Education Act in full) and Parents in Partnership.

A number of UK-wide organisations offer advice and support to families whose children have special needs or disabilities. For example, each year approximately one thousand babies are born with Down's Syndrome and the Down's Syndrome Association has a key role in giving information, support and advice to parents of people with this particular disability. The Association has a network of branches and groups throughout England, Wales and Northern Ireland and has a sister organisation, the Scottish Down's Syndrome Association. The Royal Society for Mentally Handicapped Children and Adults (MENCAP) has an early years project which aims to provide an up-to-date information and advice service for parents, carers and professionals. This project also provides accessible, low cost joint training for these groups of people and is developing training packs and designing training specifically for parents. A short course is being piloted in Camden for parents and carers of children with disabilities. The objectives of the course include encouragement to participants to deal more assertively with the various problems that they face, and to help participants develop interpersonal skills to offer support to other parents/carers.

## Parents with disabilities

The disability organisations have become increasingly interested in issues relating to disabled parents. The Maternity Alliance, for example, has a subcommittee on disabled parents, the National Childbirth Trust has a Parentability group supporting pregnancy and parenthood in parents with disabilities, and many organisations such as Parkinson's Disease Society and the Multiple Sclerosis Society also work in this field.

The Special Parenting Service (SPS) already referred to above was started in 1988 in order to address some of the perceived deficits in lifeskills of parents with learning disabilities. As a result of careful assessment (McGaw and Sturmey, 1993, 1994 and McGaw, 1993) and the use of a specific teaching programme parenting skills have been shown to improve markedly. The main work of the SPS is its specialist teaching which is provided to families in their own homes once or twice a week, often starting when the mother is pregnant and continuing until the child enters mainstream school. Parenting is also taught to school-leavers in special schools, covering topics such as decision-making, relationships, contraception, life-skills and children's needs.

There are some complex issues around parents with learning difficulties. Of course, noone can tell anyone they cannot become a parent, but there are ethical issues about the way in which the quality of parenting is assessed. The evidence suggests that most parents with a disability will, with appropriate support, be excellent parents. However, there is still little evidence about how parents with learning disabilities cope with older children, when they need wider stimulation and language and socialisation.

## Lone parents

As we noted in chapter 1, there has been a dramatic increase in lone parenthood during the ten years since *The Needs of Parents* was published,and lone parent families now make up 19% of all families with dependent children in Britain, with lone **mothers** comprising over 90% of all lone parent families. Many of the families involved in all the services described in this chapter will therefore be headed by a lone parent, but some schemes are designed specifically for lone parents. Cannan (1992) and Warren (1990), for example, have both noted that the majority of family centre users are lone parents, probably indicating the need of such parents, many of whom are living in deprived circumstances, for particular support, both for themselves and for their children. In FSU family support projects, 53% of users are headed by a lone parent (FSU Profile Report, 1992).

Gingerbread, founded in 1970, is the leading voluntary organisation providing information and advice to lone parents in England and Wales. The central Gingerbread organisation supports a network of 250 local self-help groups, which provide a variety of advice, friendship and opportunities to develop new personal and professional skills. Recent developments within Gingerbread include the launch of an out-of-school initiative and also 14 family service projects, such as the one at the Bradford Gingerbread Centre. The services offered by this project include an adult learning facility, known as Gingerale, which runs a variety of courses, and a purpose-built housing development offering short-term accommodation for lone parents. Other family support projects offer drop-in facilities, a clothing and furniture store, holidays and child care.

---

*Examples of services particularly focused on the needs of lone parents are the following:*

- *A lone parent volunteer befriending scheme in West Leeds, in which a coordinator is employed to recruit and train volunteers who befriend lone parents. The support is low-key and practical and the scheme hopes to be self-generating, that is, those who are being supported will go on to support others.*
- *The Scottish Council for Single Parents provides counselling from its head office in Dundee, produces publications and runs family centres, such as the one in Tayside which has lone parent groups, one of which is aimed particularly at young mothers and concentrates on parenting skills. This centre also runs a lone fathers' group.*
- *Family Link is a scheme run by Family Care, a social work agency based in Edinburgh. The scheme links lone parent families with volunteers, who work flexibly to provide appropriate support – the important part of this scheme is that family and volunteer commit time regularly to getting to know each other and that the parent knows that the volunteer is someone on whom they can rely (Family Link leaflet).*
- *A health visitor and a social worker established a group of lone mothers, all of whom had been in contact with social services, in Pontefract, Yorkshire, in order to look at issues such as trust, self-esteem, parenting experience, expectations and sexuality. The group achieved its modest aim of exploring issues and did result in a dropping off in clinic attendances and less contact with social workers (Brown, 1989).*

---

## Teenage parents

We have noted in chapter 1 the fact that Britain still has the highest teenage pregnancy rate in western Europe. The use of the blanket term 'teenage mother' might be assumed to imply that early motherhood is uniformly distributed throughout the teenage years. This is in fact not the case as Phoenix (1991) explains. Teenage mothers are predominantly 18 and 19-years-old and are, therefore, legally adults. Similarly, the term 'teenage parents' can include distinct groups with differing needs, for example, schoolgirl mothers, single mothers and teenage couples who are parents. However, because of their particular vulnerability, these young parents often need many of the schemes and services described in this book all at the same time: because of their **age** they need the type of education and preparation for parenthood provided (to a limited extent) in schools and the youth services; because of their **status**, they also need the various opportunities and supportive services described in this and the preceding chapter. Phoenix suggests that because they tend to straddle the different services and stages teenage parents are in danger of being forgotten or ignored. Their needs as young people may be different from their needs as parents and it may be difficult to strike a balance between the two.

The Teenage Parenthood Network, an umbrella group for projects involved in teenage parent support, was established in 1990 and publishes a newsletter three times a year covering issues relevant to teenage pregnancy and parenthood.

---

*The Trust for the Study of Adolescence and the Maternity Alliance joined forces in 1993 to publish* **The Really Helpful Directory: Services for Pregnant Teenagers and Young Parents.** *This directory lists approximately 350 separate projects for young mothers, 130 of them being residential, 50 educational, 30 antenatal/parentcraft provision and 140 support and information projects:*

- *residential accommodation includes all those which encourage admissions from young mothers or pregnant young women;*
- *educational facilities are almost exclusively educational units specifically designed for schoolgirl mothers, usually as part of a wider Home and Hospital Teaching Service;*
- *antenatal and parentcraft provision is usually located in hospitals and health centres;*
- *support,information and advice is usually located in support groups, most often supported by the Youth Service.*

---

A number of local authorities have developed specific projects for young parents. Sheffield Youth Service, for example, runs a project on teenage parenting and sexual health in four areas of disadvantage in the city. The service includes project-based work with young people to promote parenting skills and understanding of parenting, alongside the core youth work which addresses personal and social awareness and confidence. Health, assertiveness, advice and benefits, and also child care, feature regularly in these programmes. A further example, also from Sheffield, is The Gap project which undertook a major initiative on motherhood using arts and drama as the main vehicle.

The work was presented in an exhibition and included a video made by the young mothers on their life experiences. Other examples are the Teenage Parenthood Network based at the Larkfield Centre in Glasgow, and in Bristol the Young Mothers Information Project.

---

*The YWCA have published an education pack, **Teenage Parenthood**, focusing on 'unplanned, premature parenthood', to be used as part of a wider social and sex education curriculum. Areas included in the pack are:*

- *a realistic consideration of teenage parenthood, focusing on the experiences of actual teenage parents;*
- *information and exercises relating to health, education, housing, finance, young fathers, the roles and responsibilities of parenthood and sexuality, including the right to say no;*
- *ideas for creative writing, role play and poster design;*
- *resource list and suggestions for further reading;*
- *letters to teenagers, written by teenage parents.*

---

## Families from black and minority ethnic groups

There is comparatively little research on parenting issues and stress factors for black and minority ethnic groups but many black parents find that the mainstream services available for parents are not so accessible to them because of their particular religion, language, culture or ethnic background. The Moyenda Project has been set up by Exploring Parenthood as a means of researching and identifying the needs of black parents (Asian and African-Caribbean) with regard to support, information and counselling in parenting. It intends to develop materials and resources to meet those specific needs. The following issues have emerged so far from the research element of this project (Grant, 1993, in preparation):

- cultural conflicts in bringing up a child in a different culture;
- particular problems for Asian teenage girls;
- language barriers and lack of awareness of the services available;
- racism;
- parenting in a racist society;
- helping children deal with racism.

Some examples of support services developed with the needs of black and minority ethnic parents particularly in mind are:

- *Multicultural Resource Centre, Cardiff. Run by Barnardo's and doing work with Chinese, Vietnamese and Somali communities.*
- *Asian Women's Parents Group in Waltham Forest, London. Run by FSU. Emphasis on support rather than on skills development.*
- *Bradford Skill Share, run by FSU. Asian parents are taught skills which will help them gain employment as a way of providing family support.*
- *Hopscotch Asian Women's Centre founded in 1979 and jointly funded by London Borough of Camden and the Save the Children Fund as a drop-in centre for Asian women. The aim is to work with the women and their young children by promoting their independence and confidence and acting as advocates on their behalf. Includes parents' workshops – discussion sessions with mothers on their children's development and progress in health, education and other areas.*
- *Deptford Family Resource Centre (Lewisham, London) runs Vietnamese and West African Women's Groups.*
- *Parents & Co are working with Bengali families in the London Borough of Camden, especially with families with children with special educational needs.*

As already noted on p177, in 1992 Parent Network set up the East London African-Caribbean Action Research Project in an attempt to redress the imbalance between black and white participants in Parent Network programmes. A second aim of the project was to support the few black parents already in the network, but who were under-represented and under-supported. In the event, two black trainee coordinators emerged as a response to being invited to assist in the project. The research project attempted to:

- assess the value of Parent-Link courses for African-Caribbean parents;
- assess the conflict, if any, between the values of Parent Link and those of the African-Caribbean culture;
- explore the image of the Parent Network as seen from an African-Caribbean perception;
- assess the effectiveness of all-black as opposed to ethnically mixed Parent Link groups.

Work with young women with children in Sheffield revealed the need to develop specific work with white young women with children of mixed parentage. Workers found that there was little support for white young mothers of mixed parentage children when addressing issues of ethnicity and culture. For some there was very little contact with the communities of which their children's fathers were part, which might mean that the young women could not ensure that their children were given the opportunity to develop an identity that integrated and reflected their multiracial/multicultural heritage. Work with these young women has meant that they are now able to address issues of ethnicity, gender and class, and in so doing are able to address their own perceptions and stereotypes of black people and be better equipped to challenge the way in which society and institutions respond to them as parents of black children, as well as sexism and racism within the context of their lives and the lives of their children. The Youth Service has responded to this need by developing a number of group work initiatives in the Park Hill/Wybourn, Kelvin and Parson Cross areas of the city (response to enquiry, September 1993).

## Parents in temporary accommodation

Parents in temporary accommodation, often with young children, are frequently living in overcrowded and limited space with few facilities. Some agencies have set up parent and toddler groups, drop-ins and toy libraries to help parents who, although in a 'temporary' situation, may be in such accommodation for a considerable period of time. The Child Accident Prevention Trust and Save the Children Fund, conscious of the unsuitability of such accommodation, have produced a booklet advising parents on how to improve safety for themselves and their children.

## Parents of children in trouble at school or with the police

Exploring Parenthood launched Parents Against Crime in 1993 in West London to help parents of 10 to 14-year-olds who have already had a 'brush with the law'. This organisation runs a series of workshops (partly funded by the Home Office) aiming to enable parents to listen better to their children, set boundaries for unacceptable behaviour, deal with stress, cope with adolescence and develop consistency in their relationships with their children.

## Offenders

There are some 7,000 young offenders in custody in Britain, of whom perhaps two-thirds are already, or are to become, young fathers. Some

20 Young Offender Institutes (YOI) run parenthood courses for young fathers and fathers-to-be. One example is the ten-week course at Deerbolt in Co Durham, which begins with practical skills such as bathing and feeding, and moves on to questions of responsibility and relationships, attitudes to parenting, to partners and to participants' own delinquency. At the recently opened Lancaster Farms Young Offenders Institution young men can volunteer to attend a nine-week (one full day per week) Education for Parenting course. The course developed from the realisation that many of the young men had not had good experiences of parenting themselves. Many had suffered emotional deprivation, neglect, physical abuse; fathers had been around very little or not at all, so that good role models were absent from many of their lives. The course aims to empower these young fathers so that they can feel more committed to their children and have a sense of self-esteem in their abilities as fathers. Interviews carried out with male YOI trainees before and after attendance at parenthood training courses (Caddle, 1991) indicated that the courses had increased their knowledge of child development and brought about positive changes in their attitudes to family relationships. In particular, attitudes to the role of the father in maintaining parental discipline showed most susceptibility to change following the courses – the courses were successful in suggesting a wide range of ways of maintaining discipline.

Work with male inmates in two prisons in Scotland began in 1983, using the two Open University Community Education courses *The Pre-school Child* and *Family Relationships*. The short courses proved extremely popular with the prisoners who undertook them, despite certain difficulties caused by the obvious differences in the type and situation of families portrayed in the materials from the prisoners' own family situations. The students made efforts to surmount the restrictions of their imprisonment by finding ways to use new ideas from the course material to brighten up visiting time for their children and to make more use of letters and drawings between visits. Preparation for liberation and reunion with the rest of the family also required thought in the context of the parent education course. One interesting conclusion of the internal evaluators of this pilot scheme (The Open University in Scotland, 1984) was that considerable insight had been gained by prison staff into the effect of prison regulations on prisoners and their families.

A Probation Centre for serious offenders in Bristol is an example of probation officers working with a group of adult male offenders (almost all fathers) where much of the work is focused on links between masculinity and offending.

One of the few Mother and Baby units in prisons is in Styal prison, and aims to prepare the 22 inmates for independent motherhood when released from prison. Women follow a basic child care course, supplemented by sewing and cookery, and look after their babies up to the age of 18 months, after which they have to leave the Unit and their children are cared for outside the prison.

# Support for people in particular parenting relationships

There are a number of 'parenting' situations in which the person fulfilling a parenting role may not be the natural parent of the child; grandparents, adoptive or fostering parents and step-parents, for example. Support for these groups is considered in this section.

## Grandparents

Family breakdown and divorce are very distressing for grandparents. There may be real fear of losing touch with grandchildren, through no fault of either child or grandparents. The loss of contact can be like bereavement (the child is lost and grieved for, but grandparents also long to get in touch). Children may feel hurt and bewildered at being separated from grandparents. The Grandparents Federation was originally set up for grandparents of children in care, but has more recently started providing support for people who have lost touch with their grandchildren through family separation.

## Foster parents

The National Foster Care Association (NFCA) is the main support organisation for foster carers, offering everyone involved in fostering the opportunity to share experiences, through information, training and a variety of support services. Of particular interest to foster carers are two of NFCA's training courses *Choosing to Foster* and *A Problem Shared*. In addition to a number of core sessions, *Choosing to Foster* includes additional sessions focusing, for example, on partnership and teamwork and managing difficult behaviour. *A Problem Shared* is a study pack dealing with the practical management of difficult behaviour in foster placements.

## Support for parents following separation and divorce

Reference has already been made to Gingerbread, the National Council for One Parent Families and Families Need Fathers, all of whom provide support for parents whose marriages or partnerships have broken up. A new form of support for separated parents is the Network of Contact and Access Centres, currently around 55. Many are based in church halls and run by churches, local voluntary organisations and linked to some of the mediation services.

## Step-parents

Support for non-residential parents and step-parents may become increasingly important in helping children to adjust to so many transitions through their childhood.

In some parts of the country RELATE have started offering courses for step-parents. Other agencies and professionals are aware of the impact of shifts in family patterns and assessing what additional services they could provide. The Health Promotion Service in Milton Keynes, for example, runs a rolling programme of two workshops a year on stepfamily issues, such as *A New Baby in a Stepfamily*. They also offer a one-day workshop for step-parents looking at general issues for stepfamily life, role definition, conflict resolution, communication and negotiation skills. In other places two groups are held every year for step-parents who are thinking of adopting their stepchild.

The major source of support for step-parents is STEPFAMILY, the National Stepfamily Association, set up in 1983 by a group of step-parents and stepchildren. This membership organisation has built up a range of services including a counselling Helpline available six hours every weekday, specialist publications, two newsletters – one for adults and one for children – a network of local contacts and groups. They also run conferences, training events and hold an annual research seminar to encourage more understanding of the needs of children and adults in stepfamilies. Many head teachers are conscious of the impact of family transitions on the performance of children in class and some schools have invited STEPFAMILY to provide speakers for parent meetings and workshops for teaching and administrative staff. STEPFAMILY is producing an informal training pack, similar to the Veritas materials (see p176), to enable parents, step-parents and group leaders to run a series of six weekly meetings on step-parenting and being in a stepfamily.

Support is also available in a more general way from other parent organisations such as Parentline and Parent Network who estimate that as many as a quarter of their groups and volunteers may be in stepfamilies. Exploring Parenthood offers occasional workshops as part of their programmes of events for all families and some family centres have local self-help groups.

## Summary

This chapter has examined a range of schemes and services which aim to respond to parents' needs for companionship, for information, for increased self-confidence and for greater knowledge and understanding of themselves and their children. Some forms of support are very informal, offering opportunities for mutual learning and peer support. Others, such as playgroups and some family centres and home visiting schemes, have enabled parents to move beyond the provision of facilities for their children, to opportunities for their own involvement (often with some form of training), and then to widening their learning horizons further.

Some schemes, working further along the support continuum, have worked with more vulnerable families or those going through particular crises in their lives. Many of these have been successful in keeping families together and raising parents' self-confidence. Although some are apparently less successful in changing relationships within families, some recent reports have described improvements in parent-child relationships. Family centres operating an 'open door' policy rather than taking referrals only have been particularly welcomed by parents.

There has been a growth in the number of parent education and more formal 'parent effectiveness training' schemes, using a number of different approaches, but many of these are not widely available, and their effectiveness, although often encouraging in the short-term, has not yet been assessed over a long term period.

Opportunities for parents' involvement in their children's schooling, whether in a general way, or as their children's educators, or in extending their own development and learning, appear to have increased in some localities and to have had positive outcomes for both parents and children. Some good practice examples have been described. However, we have found it less easy to find examples of adult education involvement in the parent education area.

Although all parents have a need for a 'base level' of support, there are some for whom this needs to be adapted to their particular needs, and we have been able to cite good examples of work with families with disabled children, with disabled parents, with lone parents, teenage parents, parents in custody, black and minority ethnic families and with fathers. These types of support are, however, by no means universally available and it is with the last group, fathers, where perhaps there is least provision. Most support services tend to be gender-biased and focused especially at **mothers** and their children.

Overall, we have found a wide range of support services for parents. However, there is little evidence of a coordinated approach to such provision in a locality; concern about cuts in funding for statutory services; emphasis on targeted rather than universal services; and extensive reliance on a sometimes insecurely funded voluntary sector.

In order for parent support to be available to all who want it, at the time they want it, and in the way they want it, it will be necessary to move beyond this somewhat 'ad hoc' approach.

# Part III: A policy for parent education

# 7. Summary and agenda for action

In returning to the broad canvas of preparation, education and support for parents that we first painted in 1984, we have again taken a bird's eye view and have attempted to detect some of the main trends and pick out some of the key issues, noting in particular changes over the last ten years that have impacted on parents' abilities to bring up their children.

As a society we depend on the children of today to be the citizens, workers and carers of the future, and we began by examining the context in which parents are bringing up children. Families are of course the main educators and care-givers of their children and create the social and moral climate in which children grow slowly towards independence and think about taking on parenting responsibilities of their own. But family patterns are changing, and the circumstances in which families live are also changing. Whilst research confirms that children are more likely to thrive in a stable environment where two parents can provide sufficient income, appropriate housing, wholesome food, unconditional love, and adequate stimulation and protection, for many parents this is proving increasingly difficult.

The shape of families is changing. The birth rate is falling and increasing numbers of children are being born outside marriage. Although 70% of children are growing up with both their natural parents, there is an increasing rate of divorce and remarriage. One in five families are headed by lone parents, and 8% of families now include a stepchild. Family disruption is thus experienced by growing numbers of children, who may or may not cope well with such changes, according to their own resilience and the maturity and capability of their parents.

Whilst parents retain the prime responsibility for bringing up their children, they can only fulfil these responsibilities if the state provides adequate support, through universal health and education services, and through more specialist services to meet particular needs. Major legislative changes over the last decade are requiring health, education and social work agencies to rethink the way in which they relate to and provide services to families.

There are now nearly as many women working as men, and this period has seen dramatic changes in the lives of many women. However, shortage of day care and lack of parental leave and flexible 'family friendly' policies and employment policies, mean that many parents – both mothers and fathers – are struggling in their attempt to balance work and family responsibilities.

Economic and social policies have not on the whole made life easier for families, tending to favour single people and wealthier couples, rather than couples with children. High levels of unemployment, increasing numbers of lone parents and a growth in the incidence of low pay have contributed to the alarming increase in the number of children living on or below the poverty line during this period – now estimated to be nearly one in three of all children. Whilst most parents share similar goals for their children, material constraints prevent some parents from being able to achieve them.

Despite these many changes, research has shown that relationships within families (between parents, and between parents and children) and the quality of parenting are more important to children's development than particular family structures, and it is these that must be supported.

Parenting is a challenging job, surrounded by high expectations and requiring considerable knowledge and a wide range of skills. Recent legislation has confirmed parental responsibilities rather than rights, but social and welfare policies have not been supportive in providing the permitting circumstances needed by children and parents. The transition from partner to parent can be stressful and parents need information and advice on how best to meet the needs of children. Parents' levels of self-confidence and understanding of themselves will also have an impact on how they bring up their children, as will different styles of parenting, and cultural and gender differences.

In looking at the historical development of parent education, it is evident that countries across the world are concerned at the need to support families as they bring up the next generation, and are increasingly aware that any such support must be multi-agency and multi-dimensional and must build on the strengths, values and customs of the families for whom it is intended. International Year of the Family in 1994 has refocused interest on parenting, as have renewed attempts to reinforce parental involvement in their children's schooling, and to reduce levels of juvenile crime, delinquency and truancy, by exploring the links between the way in which parents bring up their children and their children's behaviour.

Although some still believe that parenting should be 'caught rather than taught', and there is a general reluctance nationwide to seek help, there does now appear to be a growing acceptance that parent education and support can offer families a range of knowledge, skills and opportunities for developing self-confidence and discussing attitudes and approaches towards parenting. It must however be based on principles which value and respect different approaches to bringing up children, and which are relevant and appropriate to fathers as well as mothers.

Parent education is seen as encompassing a range of educational and supportive measures, with a different emphasis at each stage of the life cycle. Work with young people should focus on enabling them to develop trusting and responsible relationships and make choices about their lives, including the choice not to become pregnant. The transition to parenthood is seen as being a particularly vulnerable period for many new parents, where there is a greater need for emotional support and health education that is more closely geared to the needs of both parents. For parents with children – of all ages – a range of support is needed, from informal groups which can help reduce isolation and provide opportunities for sharing experiences and information on bringing up children, through parenting discussion groups to more highly structured parent education, designed to teach new skills and to change unhelpful patterns of behaviour.

There are many approaches – including use of the media, individual one-to-one work, and group work – and all offer something different. There are also many different professionals and parents involved in such schemes, and a growth in the number of parents who are being trained to run parent support schemes and groups. But whilst parent education may be many people's concern it is nobody's responsibility, and there are still few people for whom parent education is their main job – for most it is still something to fit in when there is time. The key skills required of those working with parents are identified as including handling groups, communication skills and counselling skills.

Although a number of evaluation studies have pointed to the effectiveness of parent education schemes in increasing self-confidence and enjoyment of bringing up children, such studies are limited in number. Research from the United States showing some success in changing 'poor' patterns of parenting, is now being used as the basis for a number of courses and projects in this country. Further work is required to assess which approaches are effective with which parents.

It is difficult to prove the cost effectiveness of parent education and support work, although when prevention work is put against the cost of crime, or of taking children into the care of the local authority, or of the personal hardship caused by depression and family breakdown, the costs of the schemes described in this book are relatively small. In using research to prove that good quality early childhood education makes long term savings (for example, Schweinhart and others, 1993) it is relatively easy to describe good quality early childhood education. Parent education however, if based on principles of responsiveness to parental need and the broad range of support we describe in this book, is much less easy to describe and to cost. However, a number of approaches to costing are used, and it is suggested that a sum equivalent to 0.5% of the total education budget could create an excellent network of support at each stage of the lifecycle in every community.

Alas, no such lifecycle project has been established since the 'Job for Life' project undertaken by the Bureau following the publication of *The Needs of Parents* and funded by Hampshire County Council and Winchester Health Authority. There is an urgent need to develop a coordinated approach to parent education and support at national as well as local level.

Chapters 4, 5, and 6 provide up-to-date information on services for parents and prospective parents over the last ten years. In some areas there have been developments – for example there now appears to be more accessible information for parents on the availability of services, and a mushrooming of informal groups such as parent and toddler groups, as well as an increase in the number of groups and courses focusing specifically on the challenges and skills of parenting. However, as we noted ten years ago, where interesting and relevant work is in progress, it is all too often due to the energy and enthusiasm of an individual worker, rather than as the result of a policy decision to commit resources to preventive and educational work. In many such instances, the scheme stops or the funding ceases if the worker moves on.

Although the cross-curricular themes of the original National Curriculum documentation provided a good framework for family life education in schools, there is still little evidence of a coordinated approach to such education either in schools or other youth settings. To a large extent, the provision of personal and social education, health education and lifeskills work has been the victim of a series of legislative changes, leading to expansion of a core curriculum and allowing less time for broader subjects related to education of the whole person. It would also seem that the child development option, now part of Technology, has dwindled to the point where there is some doubt as to its future viability. Although sex education has survived the reorganisation and does provide one important element of family life education in schools, parents are now entitled to withdraw their children from sex education lessons.

It has proved difficult to obtain a comprehensive picture of what is actually happening in schools, following the introduction of local management of schools and the diminished role of local education authorities. It would appear, however, that what is ongoing is very dependent on the interests of individual teachers with the support of heads and governors. It also seems likely that training and support for teachers in this area is still inadequate, as it was ten years ago, and this has been exacerbated by cuts in in-service training.

Despite this somewhat disappointing scenario, there was widespread support from most of the organisations that we contacted for the view that schools should continue to provide preparation for family life; and there are clear indicators in the Department of Health's *Health of the Nation* targets and in the overall requirements of the National Curriculum that this is a priority for government. We return to this issue in our **Agenda for Action**.

The Youth Service, whilst providing educational opportunities which are participative and empowering, is not a major provider of family life education, and its role is unclear, despite recent moves towards a more common purpose. Opportunities for family life education in other 'out-of-school' settings appear to be limited.

Moving on through the life cycle, we note that the transition to parenthood is far more complex than just the arrival of a baby. There may be fundamental changes in relationships between parents, both practically and emotionally; and there may be economic changes caused by the mother or father giving up work, returning to work and paying for day care, and of course the cost of supporting the child. Although ten years ago we noted the need for pre-conceptual care and commented on the importance of embarking on pregnancy while fit and healthy, there is still little advice and information for parents during this phase.

Although the majority of women do now attend antenatal clinics, recent studies confirm all the key issues we identified in *The Needs of Parents*. Classes and clinics are still aimed mainly at mothers, so that fathers may have particular difficulties in preparing for the change in lifestyle; parents' needs for education during this antenatal period are still not being efficiently met; needs and provision are often mismatched; certain parents (in addition to fathers) are still missing out – for example, young women, lone women and women from minority ethnic groups; and the focus tends to be narrow giving too little time to social and emotional aspects of parenting. Opportunities for education during antenatal health checks in clinics are often missed. Parents are not given sufficient information, either about antenatal care or birth, and continuity of care before and after the birth though valued by parents is not always evident. One study found an average of 20 health professionals were in touch with each pregnant woman.

In view of the levels of parental dissatisfaction with antenatal care and education, and the extent of postnatal depression, postnatal care takes on a particular importance. Whereas the health service has been the main provider of care during the antenatal period (supplemented by some voluntary organisations), other providers play a much more important role after the birth: indeed the availability of continuity of care from the antenatal to the postnatal period, a network of supportive friends and health personnel, and a good relationship with husband or partner have been found to be key factors in a happy and successful transition to parenthood. The value of informal groups offering support and companionship, together with some specific groups enabling parents to discuss the emotional aspects of transition to parenthood have both been identified as of particular value.

Particular support services also exist – mainly through the voluntary sector – for especially vulnerable parents, such as those who have suffered loss, whose babies die, or those born prematurely. Teenage parents and parents from some minority ethnic groups, for whom mainstream support may not be appropriate, have particular needs during the perinatal period, but care must be taken to ensure that all cultural groups are not treated homogeneously.

The extent of support services for parents is now considerable, although many focus on the early years of a child's life, and few are specifically concerned with the skills of parenting. A wide range of schemes were described in chapter 6 which aimed to respond to parents' needs for companionship, for information, for increased self-confidence and for greater knowledge and understanding of themselves and their children. Some forms of support are very informal, offering opportunities for mutual learning and peer support. Others, such as playgroups, some family centres and home visiting schemes, have enabled parents to move beyond the provision of facilities for their own children, to opportunities for their own involvement (often with some form of training), and then to widening their learning horizons further. The churches have taken a much more active role in education and support for parents over the last ten years.

We noted a growth in advice and information services, and in telephone helplines which can provide confidential advice as and when it is needed. There has also been a growth in parent education schemes, some open access and some more structured schemes using behaviourial approaches, all focusing on developing self-confidence, skills and understanding. Many of these are not widely available however, and their effectiveness in this country, although often encouraging in the short term, has not yet been assessed over a longer period. There has been an extensive increase in family centres, following the requirements of the Children Act to provide for children 'in need', and these represent a whole continuum of approaches from community based centres empowering parents to take a greater control over their lives, to a more therapeutic approach to the teaching of parenting skills. Some concern has been expressed that family centres which aim to improve parenting skills may become a vehicle for socialising parents into the norms and values of service providers and that what many parents really need are decent housing, jobs and child care. 'Open access' community-based centres have been well received by parents.

Many schemes such as these have been successful in keeping vulnerable families together, increasing self-confidence, enabling families to gain some control, and to use existing services and networks. Although some research suggests that they may be less successful in changing relationships between parents and their children, recent studies have shown more promise in this respect, particularly where they are able to work both with parents on their own and with parents and children together. US research suggests that for long term effectiveness, programmes for families with young children must also provide high quality pre-school education.

We have also noted an increasing interest in parenting programmes by those concerned with crime prevention. We would agree with a forthcoming report from Crime Concern (in preparation) that concentrating family support services on geographical areas (normally those characterised by high crime and social deprivation) offers a less stigmatising approach than attempting to single out families at risk.

Despite these developments, however, broader approaches to family support, with an emphasis on promoting positive parenting, still receive a much lower level of priority – and therefore funding – than 'heavy end' protective services. This concern has been a central theme of the recent Audit Commision report (1994) on services for children in need.

Opportunities for parents to become involved in their children's schooling, whether in a general way, or as their children's educators, or in extending their own development and learning, appear to have increased in many parts of the country and have had positive outcomes for both parents and children. It has been less easy to find many examples of adult education supporting parent education initiatives, an area in which a number of promising initiatives appear to have been cut back.

Although all parents have a need for a basic level of support, there are some for whom this must be adapted to their particular needs, and we have found examples of good work with fathers, with families with disabled children, with disabled parents, with lone parents, with parents from black and minority ethnic communities. Such support is, however, by no means universally available and it is fathers for whom there is least provision. Most support services tend to be gender-biased and focused especially on mothers and their children.

Although, as noted above, approaches to parent education and support are not coordinated, the range of providers is striking: education authorities and establishments – nurseries, schools, further education colleges, adult and community education; social service departments usually through family centres and other services for children 'in need'; health agencies – through health visitors, general practitioners, educational and clinical psychologists, child psychiatrists and psychotherapists, paediatricians, school nurses and midwives; the youth service; voluntary organisations (large, small and self-help); the churches and other faith communities and employers. The key issue now is to develop strategies for welding these many approaches into a coherent whole. Bearing in mind our concern that schemes should be sensitive to cultural differences in the bringing up of children, it is gratifying to find that a number of projects have successfully recruited workers from the communities that they serve, and that a number of specific projects have been established. This is an encouraging start, but more needs to be done.

## Some common themes

A number of themes have recurred throughout these chapters, and these are now summarised.

## Policies for families

Central to all that we have discussed in this book is the need for a government policy which looks at legislation and at the way that society is ordered and organised with an eye to how it supports or undermines family life. We have referred to the need for what in chapter 2 we call 'permitting circumstances', and a considerable body of evidence now points to the adverse effect on family relationships of such factors as bad housing, unemployment, poverty, isolation and depression. Family insecurity and poor employment prospects are combining to create for many young people an uncertain future, and it is surely unrealistic to expect that parent education and support can, on its own, relieve complex social problems and alleviate stress. Policies are needed that will enable **all** families to enjoy a basic level of income, commensurate with what is acceptable within a developed society, that will give them some genuine choice in how they live their lives and bring up their children. This will need to include a redistribution of resources through improved benefits and a reorganised system of taxation, and a swift rethinking of current policies which assume, as public services are cut back, that all families are able to be self-sufficient and that all citizens are equally well able to stand on their own two feet. It will also need to ensure that both men and women are able to combine parenting and employment, through the adoption of policies on parental leave, adequate child care and 'family friendly' employment practices.

## A policy for parent education

The lack of a coherent policy on parent education, whether in schools, antenatal services or the community, is due in part to a lack of clarity about what constitutes 'good enough' parenting, together with the need to see bringing up children within the broader context of community support and 'permitting circumstances'. It is evident from our account so far why so little progress has been made in establishing such a policy: if parent education and support has to be sensitive to the needs of parents and prospective parents and build on their strengths and interests, then it is difficult to be specific about what exactly it is that is required, and who should provide it. A range of measures are required, supporting parents and prospective parents in developing skills and understanding and building on relationships within families; and many agencies – statutory and voluntary – will be involved. We spell these out in our **Agenda for Action**. Evidence of research from this country and overseas shows that such measures reap rich rewards in terms of children's social, emotional and cognitive development, family functioning, parents' emotional health, skills and satisfaction, and prevention of family breakdown and criminal behaviour. The key is a very much stronger commitment to preventive rather than remedial work, recognising that a fence at the top of the cliff is far more effective in human and financial terms than an ambulance at the bottom.

## The value base of parent education

A return to the 'back to basics' doctrines of the moral right have given new immediacy to the conflict between the family's right to privacy and self-determination as against the State's need for healthy and productive citizens. Is parent education a means of social control, whereby gender stereotypes are reinforced, the family is two married parents with two children, adolescents are urged to conform to socially-accepted norms of behaviour, and white middle class approaches to childrearing are promulgated? Or can it be a means to social change and personal growth, whereby individuals are given increased encouragement and self-confidence to take greater control over their lives, to break out of traditional roles and to question the status quo?

We have argued that parent education must start from the concerns and interests of parents and respond to their needs, respecting the social and cultural context within which parents are living. But if women are to explore and question the nature of their dependency and their roles as mothers, what are the implications for relationships within their families, and society as a whole? And what of fathers, as they seek to redefine their own roles when many no longer have the traditional opportunity to be the breadwinner?

## Role of professionals

Related to the questions of policy and commitment is the issue of professional involvement in parent education and support, for we have noted on the one hand the very wide range of workers involved in these schemes, and yet on the other, the fact that few see it as an integral part of their work-load. Individual energy and enthusiasm are important ingredients, but if a commitment to parent education is not built into policies at local authority or health authority level, projects tend to be ephemeral and short-lived. The lifecycle approach we have traced in the book has implications for agencies, and for professional workers. For agencies – education, health, social work, voluntary and private, churches and faith communities – there is a clear need for collaboration at the level of policy development and joint funding. For professional workers, a high priority is for joint training and for close cooperation in working practices, and for recruitment of workers reflecting the ethnic make up of the local communities. Such co-operation seems even more difficult today than it was ten years ago.

## Parents as family workers

Whilst professional workers have an important role in parent education an increasing number of projects and services point to the value of peer group support. The playgroup movement, family groups, parent education schemes, many informal antenatal and parent and toddler groups, home-visiting schemes and telephone helplines have all demonstrated that parents themselves, given adequate training and ongoing support, are well able to lead groups, visit homes and offer support to other parents. Where parents are involved in this way, the professional role may need to be re-defined to include the provision of training and support, or to act as a catalyst in helping to start new schemes, rather than always taking responsibility for running the scheme. Care must be taken, however, that parents are not exploited, and that adequate payment is provided for what can be a demanding and time consuming job.

## Responding flexibly to different needs

The importance of flexibility and sensitivity in responding to the needs of parents and prospective parents, and of starting from the concerns and interests of individuals, has already been noted. The needs of individual parents will change throughout the life cycle, and no two parents – or their children- will be completely alike. Whilst a mature, confident parent may simply want to meet other local parents and perhaps attend a weekly discussion group on relationships with the family, a young single mother on benefit may need support in seeking a job or better practical and emotional support before beginning to explore some of the skills of parenting. For those experiencing severe difficulties, the most effective approaches may provide high quality education for the children, support for the parents, as well as work with parents and children together. The growth in the number of specialist support schemes testifies to the need for open access support to be supplemented by groups and services for particular groups of parents. In the last ten years there has been a much greater awareness of the need to ensure that parent education and support respects the ethnicity, religion, culture and language of individual families.

## Self-confidence and self-image

Key concepts at each stage of the lifecycle have been those of self-confidence and self-image. Our view of ourselves is significantly affected by the feedback we get from those around us and in this respect we have seen the importance of the ethos of the school and have looked at the crushing effect that professional 'expertise' has often had, albeit unwittingly, on many parents' views of their own capabilities. The best parent education schemes have found how important it is to value the experience that individuals bring to each situation, to build on their strengths, and to recognise the need to work with parents rather than do things to them. Effective relationships are built on partnership, mutual respect and a shared sense of purpose, with an emphasis on reciprocity that allows people to give as well as to receive – not on a judgemental view of inadequate parenting. This approach has important implications for the methods used in parent education, and for the training of those professionals who work with parents.

## Methods in parent education

The range of different approaches to providing support and education for parents was outlined in chapter 3. While the mass media undoubtedly reaches the largest number of people and is critical in helping to form attitudes and in conveying information, it can less successfully increase understanding or skills. Groups are particularly successful as a way of sharing experiences, making friends and learning from each other, and importantly, giving parents the confidence to question the 'experts'. But groups do require skilled leadership and such skills are not always readily available. Whilst informal groups may increase confidence, they may not always be as successful in developing skills, and a growing number of 'parent education' groups have been established since our last national survey. Structured behavioural approaches can be helpful but, if they are not handled sensitively, they may create problems by undermining confidence and creating dependency.

## Training

Ten years ago we commented on the fact that very few of those working with families have, through their training, an experience of seeing families as a whole, tending to focus either on some members – usually the children – or on pathology and dysfunction. Although in the time available to us we have not been able to investigate developments in training, we believe that this is still an area of concern and that some voluntary agencies are making greater progress in developing appropriate training than statutory agencies. It is important that family workers have skills in enabling, facilitating, listening, communicating and handling sensitive issues, and that they are aware of how their own attitudes, values and feelings will have an impact on the families with whom they work.

## Evaluation

We also commented in *The Needs of Parents* on how little we know about the effectiveness of these various approaches to parent education, and the same is largely true today. Although there is longitudinal research from the United States on the effectiveness of some programmes that are now being introduced in the UK, there is nothing comparable underway in this country. There have been some small scale objective studies, and many schemes have relied on self-reporting to show the satisfaction of parents who have been involved. But there have been no long-term follow ups of the recipients of parent education programmes, and no assessment of what approaches might suit which parents. There are a number of areas in which research is urgently required if policy makers are to be persuaded to shift resources into preventive work of this kind. What skills are required in parenting and how is parental competence acquired? Which approaches are most successful in changing patterns of behaviour that are unhelpful to family functioning? If the main objectives of parent education are gains in knowledge, enhanced skills, changed attitudes, changed practice, increased confidence – then which approaches work best and how can outcomes for children be measured? How can cognitive development be allied to affective development, taking account of parents' experiences and feelings as well as their intellectual grasp of issues? Which programmes work for which parents, and which strategies are appropriate for the most vulnerable families? What do parents actually need during the life cycle and when do they need it – what are the 'touchpoints' for them? There are also questions about what are the key skills and attributes required of group leaders/facilitators, and whether parents or professionals are best suited to this role.

## Status of parenting: of fathering as well as mothering

Perhaps the most obvious change that has taken place since we wrote ten years ago has been the changing roles of men and women, in the home and in the workplace. Despite the impact of both unemployment and of the increasing numbers of women returning to work, parenting is still too often seen as mothering, and indeed is still largely done by mothers. This is evident in the way parent education and support is offered, in those who take advantage of it, and in the media coverage of parenting issues, where men as fathers were either ignored or seen as 'baddies' who neglected or abused their families. The need to see parenting as a shared responsibility, and to involve boys and men in preparation, education and support for parents is crucial, both for the health of families, and in order to raise the low status of parenting in Britain. Motherhood is idealised and yet denigrated; fatherhood is still largely ignored. Greater equality of opportunity has left many women struggling to excel as workers, whilst their roles and abilities as mothers are undervalued. If shared parenting were a reality, and if men's roles as fathers were seen to be as important as their roles as workers, this might go some way towards giving parenting the value it deserves.

# Agenda for action

We conclude with a definition of parent education based on a synthesis of the best programmes that we have seen, and with a number of guidelines for action. Many of these are similar to those we made in *The Needs of Parents* but there is now a much clearer interagency agenda, and many overlaps with the objectives of health promotion and prevention programmes. We have attempted to link the recommendations, wherever possible, to the specific requirements of recent legislation and government guidance.

## General recommendations

1.  **A coherent national family policy should be developed, creating a framework within which parent education and support can be provided locally, but also ensuring that social, employment, education, health, housing and economic policies support families in bringing up their children.**

    Action       Treasury
                 Department of Social Security
                 Department of Employment
                 Lord Chancellor's Department
                 Department of Health
                 Department for Education
                 Department of Environment

2.  **Parent education and support should be available to all who wish to take advantage of it.**

We define parent education, and its aims and objectives as follows:

- Parent education and support comprises a range of educational and supportive measures which help parents and prospective parents to understand their own social, emotional, psychological and physical needs and those of their children and enhances the relationship between them; and which create a supportive network of services within local communities and help families to take advantage of them.

- It should be available to all parents and prospective parents, boys as well as girls, young men as well as young women, fathers as well as mothers.
- It is a lifelong process and as such will have a different emphasis at different stages of the life cycle.
- Its emphasis should be on individuals' roles and relationships in the here and now, as well as on their future roles and relationships.
- The overall aim of parent education is to help parents develop self-awareness and self-confidence and improve their capacity to support and nurture their children.

It should do this by:

- providing people with access to **information and knowledge** about human health and development; different stages of child development, marriage and family life; sources of help within the community, including welfare rights and benefits;
- helping them develop **social skills**; in understanding themselves and relating to others; in communicating;in making decisions and accepting responsibility for them; and **practical skills** in managing a home and family;
- offering opportunities and encouragement in **understanding** how to apply this information and these skills in relation to their own needs, desires, life-styles, personal characteristics and potential;
- helping them to identify their own **values and attitudes** and acknowledge how these affect the way in which children are brought up;
- supporting the development of a **range of services** through schools, churches, community institutions and health agencies, and enabling parents to use them.

Parent education should be based upon the **general principles** noted in chapter 3, and in particular that:

- there is no single right way of parenting, no blueprint for a perfect family, and diverse family patterns should be respected;
- the ability to parent reflects each individual's level of self-confidence and sense of worth. Education and support

should therefore acknowledge, value and build on parents' and prospective parents' existing skills, experience and abilities;

- programmes should be available to fathers and mothers, and be sensitive to the diverse social, ethnic and cultural backgrounds of families;
- in order to fulfil their obligations, parents need adequate social and economic support.

3. **A cross-departmental group, chaired by the Minister with responsibility for family issues, and working in collaboration with the All Party Parliamentary Group on Parenting, should review ways in which the recommendations in this book might be taken forward**

    Action      Secretary of State for Health
                         All Party Parliamentary Group
                         on Parenting

4. **A forum or consortium of organisations concerned with parent education should be set up to support a coordinated approach to education and support for parents and to help to raise the status of parenting, working closely with the All Party Parliamentary Group on Parenting.**

    Action      voluntary organisations
                         local authorities
                         health authorities

5. **Local authorities, health authorities, voluntary organisations and the churches and other faith communities should work together to create a coordinated approach to preparation, education and support for parents in each area, with a stronger commitment to prevention rather than crisis work with families**

The approach we have outlined in this book impinges on the responsibilities of many different agencies: health authorities and trusts are responsible for health promotion, health care, antenatal clinics and classes; education authorities, schools, adult and further education establishments and the youth service for education for family life and parent education; social service departments for family support when children are 'in need'; and voluntary and self-help organisations and the churches make an important contribution at each stage of the lifecycle. In looking at the implementation of the Children Act and the Community Care Act, the Audit Commission (1994) notes the need for closer collaboration between universal and targeted services and recommends strategic joint planning in assessing need, and that providers work jointly to both assess need and provide services. Had education services been included in the study, they would clearly have been part of this joint approach.

It is therefore further **recommended that:**

6. **each agency working with families in a local area designates a lead officer to work towards a coordinated approach locally;**

7. **the local authority and health authority work collaboratively to develop a joint policy on preparation, education and support for parents, in association with voluntary organisations, churches and faith communities, parents and other interested bodies;**

8. **a network of interagency projects, such as the Job for Life project which took a lifecycle approach to preparation and support for parents, be set up in local communities;**

9. **more specific recommendations below are taken into account through this collaborative mechanism.**

> **Action**     local authorities
>                health services
>                voluntary organisations
>                churches and faith communities

10. **There are certain core elements which should be a part of the training of all those working with families. It is therefore recommended that the training of health, education and social work personnel who will be working with families should include the elements noted below:**

   • opportunities to understand their own **attitudes, values and feelings** about marriage, family life and parenthood and develop sensitivity to those with whom they work, and who may hold different values and attitudes from their own;

   • an extension of their **knowledge** about and **understanding** of family patterns, human and child development, and relationships;

   • development of their **skills,** in teaching and particularly in the sensitive and enabling approaches required for working with groups; and in working with parents and with colleagues from different professional backgrounds.

> Action       Teacher Training Agency
> Central Council for Education and
>     Training in Social Work
> Council for Awards in Children's
>     Care and Education
> UK Central Council for Nursing,
>     Midwifery and Health Visiting

11. **Research studies should be funded to increase our understanding of parent education.**

These should look at the comparative effectiveness of different approaches to parent education and support; at the skills involved in parenting and how they are acquired; at the skills required in leadership of parent education schemes and at how leadership affects the schemes; at the materials currently available; at which approaches work for which families; and at what parents say they need and use at different stages of the life cycle.

> Action       government departments
> Economic and Social Research Council
> funding agencies

12. **It is recommended that the All Party Parliamentary Group on Parenting and the Parent Education Forum should meet with representatives of the media to discuss new initiatives to parent education and family support.**

A major task is to change public attitudes towards parenting as the most important role that most of us perform; and to support the view that to seek support or look to improve skills and understanding is not an admission of failure. This requires the concerted support of many agencies, but television, radio and the press have a particularly important role to play.

> Action       BBC
> ITC
> representatives of the press
> All Party Parliamentary Group on
>     Parenting

# Education for family life: work with children and young people in schools, further education and the youth service

13. **Family life education should be part of a coordinated approach**

to personal, social and health education in primary and secondary schools, in further education and in residential settings such as residential children's homes and Young Offender Institutions.

14. **Schools should appoint a lead teacher to coordinate the work that is already going on through sex education, personal and social education and in other curriculum areas.**

This should ensure that all young people have access to a course which equips them with:

- **skills** in understanding themselves, in communicating with and relating to others, and in handling conflict;
- **opportunities** for developing self-confidence and for discussing values and attitudes;
- **knowledge** about human and particularly child development, methods of contraception, about family life and parenting, and about how to find out and use such resources as may be available;

in order that they can make balanced and informed decisions about the choices that affect their own lives.

15. **There should be optional subjects for those who wish to specialise in child development.**

These options should be so organised that they present genuine choice to boys and girls alike. The child development option should include opportunities for working with and observing young children.

16. **Family life education should be sensitive to the family backgrounds, cultures and faiths of the children and young people and wherever possible the parents of the pupils for whom it is to be offered, and the pupils themselves, should be consulted.**

17. **Family life education should be based on the needs, interests, experience and abilities of the pupils here and now rather than focus on the practical skills of child care which are more appropriate later in the life cycle.**

Action        governors and heads of schools

18. **In their inspection of the moral and spiritual aspects of the school, OFSTED should be encouraged to assess the extent to which these recommendations are being implemented.**

Action        Office for Standards in Education

19. **In-service training and continuing support should be available to all members of staff working in this area of the curriculum.**

They may find themselves not only dealing with unfamiliar content, but also using new methods of teaching, particularly informal group discussion.

> Action    schools and LEA advisors

20. **The youth service should be given a clearer role in the provision of family life education as described above.**

> Action    National Youth Agency
> Department for Education

21. **Health authorities, in meeting the targets of Health of the Nation to reduce teenage pregnancies by half, should support schools and youth agencies in this aspect of their family life education curriculum.**

> Action    health agencies

# Preparation for parenthood: pre-conceptual care, pregnancy and the transition to parenthood

Schemes and services should be available in each local area to comply with the aims of parent education, before, during and after pregnancy.

These should:

- provide prospective parents with sufficient information to enable them to make appropriate choices about parenthood;
- involve prospective fathers as well as mothers;
- give realistic information about parenthood, as well as about pregnancy and childbirth;
- provide opportunities for couples to talk with each other and with other couples about the experience of parenthood, childbirth, fatherhood and motherhood.

22. **Health purchasers and providers should consider the model specification on p132-3 as a basis for providing high quality information and education throughout pregnancy, labour and the early months of parenting. This should be extended to include pre-conceptual information and care.**

> Action    health agencies
> voluntary organisations

23. **GPs and health visitors should be informed of every confirmation of pregnancy in their area in order to make available information on diet, smoking, drugs and so on.**

    Action      GPs and health visitors

24. **Antenatal clinics should introduce efficient appointments systems, provide creche facilities for young children, more privacy, personal attention, and more explicit information, appropriate to the language and culture of expectant parents.**

25. **Antenatal clinics should take the opportunity provided by health checks to provide antenatal education.**

    Action      GPs
                obstetric staff

26. **Antenatal clinics and classes should make every effort to reach those who do not make full use of the services, particularly young parents, lone parents, parents from black and minority ethnic groups, disabled women and their partners, drug-using parents, adoptive parents.**

27. **Care should be taken to ensure that antenatal clinics and classes are as accessible as possible.**

This might include the setting up of walk-in clinics, evening and weekend clinics and classes, mobile or local community based services; and that they are more relevant to the needs of individual parents, by providing opportunities to meet others with newly born babies, and to share feelings and anxieties about pregnancy, childbirth and parenthood.

    Action      health professionals
                voluntary organisations

28. **All prospective and new parents should be given information about the availability of antenatal and postnatal education and groups and the names and roles of the various professionals involved in their care.**

29. **Continuity of care between and antenatal and postnatal stages should be improved.**

The transition to parenthood is a critical time as new relationships are developed, and existing ones are reassessed.

    Action      health agencies

# Education and support for parents

30. **A range of schemes and services should be available in each local area which meet the overall aims of parent education and support.**

Most of these should be open access; some will need to be targeted on those with particular needs. For parents of young children these should:

- provide parents with support and information to enable them to have some measure of control over their lives and to retain their individuality as people and as a couple;
- provide support for parents who may feel depressed or isolated;
- enable parents to make use of services available within the community;
- increase parenting skills so parents can enjoy their children and become models of good parenting to their own children;
- support and develop parents' self-confidence in making decisions about their children's future.

For parents of older children it should also:

- provide information and support to enable parents to understand their adolescent children and develop appropriate 'coping' strategies;
- enable parents to 'allow' their children to leave home;
- provide parents with sufficient information that they may understand and participate in educational and employment decisions.

31. **The local authority and health authority should develop a corporate policy on parent education** (see above).

This could perhaps build on the Children Act review of services for children under eight, and the children's services plans. This should establish what already exists, and assess the need for new services in relation to the expressed needs of parents.

32. **Education, social services and health authorities should work collaboratively to assess need and target specialist resources.**

   Action         local authorities
                  health authorities

33. **High priority should be given to work with parents of children**

under the age of one, and particularly the first few months after birth (see above).

34. **Support projects, including family centres and schools, should work towards becoming real community resources, offering parents opportunities to increase their understanding of and involvement in their children's development, and to continue their own personal growth through adult education. The role of adult education, and the skills of adult educators and community educators are critical to the development of parent education.**

> Action          adult and community education
> local authorities
> voluntary organisations
> schools

35. **There is a pressing need for parent education for parents of school age children.**

This would include increasing parents understanding of what is 'normal' development for each age group; providing oppor- tunities for discussing issues relating to their children's education, health, employment and so on, and looking at changing relationships within the family. Schools are well placed to provide facilities for such courses.

> Action          voluntary organisations
> schools

36. **Resources should be made available to voluntary and self-help organisations to establish parent education schemes appropriate to their needs.**

Whilst voluntary schemes have a key role to play in the provision of services for families, they should supplement and not substitute for statutory services.

> Action          local authorities
> health authorities
> central government

37. **Information should be made available in an appropriate and accessible way to all parents on all existing supportive and education services.**

> Action          local authorities
> health authorities

38. **Information and advice should be made available to all couples at the registration of birth, marriage and divorce.**

> Action       Registrar General

39. **Training should be made available for parents who wish to lead groups, become involved in home visiting schemes, or run other support services.**

> Action       voluntary agencies
> local authorities

40. **Training of those who work with children (particularly teachers) should include training to work with parents.**

This should include skills in involving parents more closely in their children's schooling.

> Action       Teacher Training Agency
> In-service training institutions

We conclude with words similar to those that we used ten years ago, which we feel are as apposite today as they were then. Bringing up children in the 1990s is a demanding and at times difficult task. It requires not only inner resources of empathy, resilience, confidence and appropriate skills and knowledge, but also the external resources of support provided by a caring community. Whilst the majority of parents manage well for most of the time, many would welcome further opportunities for increasing their knowledge, understanding and enjoyment of family life. It is clearer now than it was ten years ago that 'good enough' parenting leads to more confident parents who bring up more confident children, that access to appropriate support services are crucial, and that some of the skills of parenting can be learned. It is also more evident that 'good enough' parenting saves money, as is clear from renewed interest in the links between parenting skills and children and young people's behaviour (sometimes anti-social and criminal) and their attainment in school. If society continues to have high expectations of parents then it must create policies which enable them to balance the demands of parenthood and employment; and it must also provide opportunities for young men and women to make realistic choices about becoming parents; and provide an adequate network of information support and education for fathers and mothers as and when it is needed. As Mia Pringle, the Bureau's first director (1975) said nearly twenty years ago, 'Modern parenthood is too demanding and complex a task to be performed well merely because we have all once been children.'

# Appendix I: Organisations and individuals who contributed information

| | |
|---|---|
| Adult Literacy Basic Skills Unit | Alan Wells |
| All Party Parliamentary Group on Parenting | Jeanne le Bars |
| Artemis Charitable Trust | Richard Evans |
| Association of Inter-Church Families | Ruth Reardon |
| Avon Educational Psychology Service | Tonia Robinson |
| Baby Life Support Systems | Sue Linnett |
| Barnardo's | Mike Jarman |
| Bastiani, John | |
| British Agencies for Fostering and Adoption | Jill White |
| British Association for Early Childhood Education | Cynthia James |
| British Broadcasting Corporation | Angie Mason |
| British Paediatric Association | K L Dodd |
| Calderdale Association for Parents | Janet Hall |
| Calouste Gulbenkian Foundation | Simon Richey |
| Canterbury & Thanet Community Health Care | Fay Godby |
| Carlton Television | Halina Kierknc |
| Catholic Bishops Working Party | Peter Desmond |
| Centre for Fun and Families, Leicester | David Neville |
| Centre for Policy Studies | |
| Child Accident Prevention Trust | Louise Pankhurst |
| Child Poverty Action Group | Sally Witcher |
| Children in Wales | Catriona Williams |
| Children's Society | Ruth Gardner |
| Church of Jesus Christ of Latter Day Saints | |
| City Lit Institute | Diana Stoker |
| Clyne, Peter | |
| Commission for Racial Equality | Jane Lane |
| Community Education Development Centre | John Rennie |
| Community Mothers Programme | Brenda Molloy |
| Contact-A-Family | Harry Marsh |
| 45 Cope Street | Kate Billingham |
| Cornwall Parent Link | Roz Plasted, |
| | Rosemary Hogg |
| Council for Disabled Children | Philippa Russell |

| | |
|---|---|
| Crime Concern | Jon Bright |
| De Montfort University | Carole Sutton |
| Demos | |
| Devon Local Education Authority | Tanny Stobart |
| Devon Parent Network | |
| Devon Schools Psychological Service | Peter Jones |
| Down's Syndrome Association | Anna Khan |
| Drumchapel High School, Glasgow | Margaret Kinsella |
| Early Childhood Development Unit | Walter Barker |
| Early Education Support Agency, Leeds | Heather Marsland |
| East Sussex County Council Playlink | Brian Gill |
| Education 2000, Leeds | Julia Timmins |
| Education Extra | Kay Andrews |
| Effective Parenting Programme | Elizabeth Hartley-Brewer |
| | Lorraine Hills |
| End Physical Punishment of Children | Peter Newell |
| Evans, Clare | |
| Everyday Problems in Childhood | Hugh Clench |
| Exploring Parenthood | Carolyn Douglas |
| | Elizabeth Howell |
| Family Care, Edinburgh | Jennifer Speirs |
| Family Caring Trust | Michael Quinn |
| Family Centre Network | Ian Vallender |
| Family Life & Marriage Education Group | |
| Family Life Education Ecumenical Group | Peter Desmond |
| Family Mediation Scotland | Mandy Haeburn-Little |
| Family Planning Association | Sheenagh Day |
| Family Policy Studies Centre | Ceridwen Roberts |
| Family Rights Group | Mary Ryan |
| Family Service Units | Adah Kay |
| | Jane Wiffin |
| Families Need Fathers | David Cannon |
| Foundation for the Study of Infant Deaths | Jane Silvester |
| General Synod of the Church of England, | |
|    Board for Social Responsibility | Alison Webster |
| Gingerbread | Mary Honeyball |
| Guys Hospital, Bloomfield Centre | Maggie Mills |
| Hackney Home-Start | Thelma Stephens |
| Haringey Home Intervention Scheme | David Silverman |
| Health Education Authority | Karen Ford |
| Health Visitors' Association | Margaret Buttigieg |
| Healthy Child Project | |
| Home Early Learning Project | Julia Timmins |
| Home Link | Maria McCann |
| Home-Start UK | Margaret Harrison |
| IKEA | |
| Institute of Criminology, Cambridge | David Farrington |

| | |
|---|---|
| International Year of the Family | Veronica Ashworth |
| Jehovah's Witnesses | |
| Joseph Rowntree Foundation | Janet Lewis |
| Kahn, Tim | |
| Kids' Clubs Network | Lesley Phillips |
| Larkfield Family Centre | Norma Gill |
| Leach, Penelope | |
| Lichfield Diocesan Association for Family Care | Paddy Vidal-Hall |
| Life | Nuala Scarisbrick |
| Maternity Alliance | Christine Gowdridge |
| Maudsley Hospital | Sue Jenner |
| Media Awareness Project | Jane Harvey |
| Meet-A-Mum Association | Bryony Hallam |
| Mencap | Mary Dickins |
| Methodist Church Division of Education and Youth | David Gamble |
| Mothers' Union | Roger Cozens |
| Multiple Births Foundation | Elizabeth Bryan |
| National Association for the Welfare of Children in Hospital | Pauline Shelley |
| National Association for Maternal and Child Welfare | Benita Target |
| National Childbirth Trust | Suzanne Dobson |
| National Childminding Association | Gill Haynes |
| National Council for One Parent Families | Sue Slipman |
| National Family Trust | Richard Whitfield |
| National Foster Care Association | Marion Lowe |
| National Playbus Association | Andrea Allez |
| National Portage Association | Mollie White |
| National Society for the Prevention of Cruelty to Children | Eileen Hayes |
| National Stepfamily Association | Erica De'Ath |
| National Youth Agency | Janet Paraskeva |
| NCH Action for Children | Bob Smart |
| NEWPIN | Carey Foster |
| | Anne Jenkins |
| NIPPERS | Janet Palmer |
| Northern Ireland Preschool Playgroup Assoc. | Siobhan Fitzpatrick |
| Oakworth Postnatal Depression Group | Vicky Young |
| Office for Standards in Education (OFSTED) | Joan Sartain |
| ONE-plus-ONE | Penny Mansfield |
| Open University | Mick Jones |
| Oxford Family Skills Project | Yo Davies |
| | Ivana Klimes |
| | Annette Mountford |

Oxford University, Department of Applied
  Social Studies and Social Research                Teresa Smith
Parent-Infant Project (PIPPIN)                      Mel Parr
Parentline/OPUS                                     Carol Baisden
Parent Network/Parent Link                          Jacqui Pearson
                                                    Barbara Morgan
Parents & Co                                        Lucy Draper
Parents as Teachers                                 Pam Holton
Parents Against Injustice                           Sue Amphlett
Parents Helpline, Brighton                          Mary Dunmore
Parents in Crisis                                   Moira McMillan
Portsmouth Area Family Concern                      Eileen Jones
Pre-school Playgroups Association                   Margaret Lochrie
Priority Area Playgroups                            Jane Roach
Quarriers, Larkfield Family Centre                  Norma Gill
Rathbone Society                                    Jeanette Clark
RELATE                                              Jan Laithwaite
Royal Society of Arts                               Lesley James
Save the Children Fund                              Bill Bell
Schools Health Education Unit                       John Balding
SCOPE                                               Geoff Poulton
Scottish Council for Single Parents                 Sue Robertson
Scottish Pre-school Play Association                Moira Ferguson
Sex Education Forum                                 Rachel Thomson
Sheffield City Council                              Mary Markham
Southend Health Services                            Kevin Hewitt
Stillbirth and Neonatal Death Society               Sarah Scott
St Neots Youth and Community Centre                 Pam Taylor
Strathclyde Psychological Service                   H Edwards
                                                    L Townsend
Surrey Educational Psychology Service               Sonya Hinton
Tavistock Institute of Marital Studies              Christopher Clulow
Teenage Parenthood Network                          Suzanne Audrey
Toy Libraries Association/Playmatters                Glenys Carter
Trust for the Study of Adolescence                  John Coleman
Under Fives Support Service, Peterborough
Utting, David
Westwood & Ravensthorpe Family Project,
  Peterborough                                      Kathy Tomlinson
What about the Children?                            Doreen Goodman
Young Families Now, Aberdeen                        Marion Flett
Young Minds                                         Steve Flood
Young Mums Education Trust
Young Women's Christian Association
Youth Aid                                           Lucy Ball
Veritas Basic Parenting Programme                   Michael Quinn
Waltham Forest Local Education Authority            Titus Alexander

# Appendix 2: Resources for parent education and support

In addition to the many books and articles on parent education listed in the bibliography, a number of organisations have produced lists of books and audiovisual material for use in parent education, and some have published materials for use in group discussion. Many of these materials will be available locally from health education units or teachers' centres.

## Published materials

### The ABC of Behaviour: Troubleshooting for Parents of Young Children
Sonya Hinton, 1994.
A booklet to help parents work out their own solutions to everyday problems.

Right from the Start Publications, Room 189B, County Hall, Kingston-upon-Thames, KT1 2DJ.

### Approaching Parenthood: a resource for parent education
D Braun and A Schonveld, 1993.
Aims to support practitioners in the development of parent education. The research carried out for *Life Will Never Be The Same Again* (Combes and Schonveld, 1992) has been distilled into a range of parent education materials capable of use in a variety of settings.

Health Education Authority, Hamilton House, Mabledon Place, London, WC1H 9TX.

### Birds, Bees and Babies
Materials for workshops in pre-school groups and primary schools.

National Childbirth Trust, Alexandra House, Oldham Terrace, Acton, London, W3 6NH.

*Birth to Five*
A guide to the first five years of being a parent, given free to all first time mothers.

Health Education Authority, Hamilton House, Mabledon Place, London, WC1H 9TX.

### Centre for Fun and Families
Videos, booklets and training materials on skills required to run group programmes for parents experiencing communication and behaviour difficulties with children and young families.

25, Shanklin Drive, Knighton, Leicester, LE2 3RH.

*Coping with Kids*
Based on Lee Canter's Assertive Discipline Course for Parents published in the USA, the parents book, materials and videos are available only to trained leaders through Behaviour Management Ltd.

Tonia Robinson, Educational Psychologist, South Bristol Area Team, Merrywood Boys School, Daventry Road, Knowle, Bristol, BS4 1QQ.

*Education for Citizenship*
1991. A resource pack for Key Stage 3 containing more than 50 student-centred cross-curricular activities, covering various topics including families.

The Children's Society, Edward Rudolf House, Margery Street, London, WC1X 0JL.

*Education for Parenthood*
A resource pack launched by the Children's Society in 1994.
The pack provides a parenthood curriculum linked to the National Curriculum. Its five sections cover exploring what it means to be a parent, the qualities parents need, parent/child relationships, rights and responsibilities, and health and development.

The Children's Society, Edward Rudolf House, Margery Street, London, WC1X 0JL.

*Everyday Problems in Childhood (EPIC)*
An open learning course for parents of young children, developed by educational psychologist Hugh Clench. Discussion materials on temper tantrums, aggression, sleep problems, eating, dressing, going out, separation.

The Parent Company, P.O. Box 1005, Brighton, BN1 3NA.

**Family Caring Trust Veritas Parenting Programme**
Books, tapes and videos for use in parent discussion groups.
   *Basic Parenting Programme*
   *Teen Parenting Programme*
   *Married Listening Programme*
   *Parenting and Sex Programme*
   *Parent Assertiveness Programme*
   *Young Adult Programme*

Michael Quinn, Family Caring Trust, 44, Rathfriland Road, Newry, Co. Down, BT34 1LD.

*Family Groups and Parenthood (Life Foundations Volume 4)*
Barnard and others, 1993. General editor Professor Richard Whitfield.
A collection of teaching resources for use in PSE for young people aged 14-21, in a variety of settings. The topics are intended to be covered in 25 sessions, and include an examination of the pressures of parenthood and the different phases of parenting. These materials are well established and widely used, both in schools and in other settings where young people are in groups.

NES Arnold, Ludlow Hill Road, West Bridgford, Nottingham, NG2 6HD.

*Families Like Ours*
A resource pack for primary schools in Scotland, 1993.
A similar pack for secondary schools is planned.

Family Mediation Scotland, 127 Rose Street, South Lane, Edinburgh, EH2 4BB.

*Help! I'm a Parent* (video)
1994. A video and written material for church leaders, church groups, parents and families.

Church Pastoral Aid Society, Athena Drive, Tachbrook Park, Warwick, CV34 6NG.

*IMPACT Maths materials*

IMPACT Supplies, P.O. Box 1, Woodstock, Oxon, 0X20 1HB.

*Keeping Kids Safe*
1993. A resource of activities and information for parents' groups.

Child Accident Prevention Trust, 18-20 Farringdon Lane, London, EC1R 3AY

*Living with Teenagers and* **Parents of Teenagers**

RELATE, Herbert Gray College, Little Church Street, Rugby, Warwickshire, CV21 3AP

*Managing Difficult Children*
Eight booklets for parents, using a behavioural approach, covering such issues as observing and recording behaviour, dealing with the consequences, rewards and penalties, sleeping problems.

Carole Sutton, Department of Health and Community Studies, de Montfort University, Scraptoft Campus, Leicester, LE7 9SU.

*New Lives and New Lives Together*
1993. A postnatal pack available for the cost of postage only.

The Maternity Alliance, 15 Britannia Street, London, WC1X 9JP.

**PACT (Parents and Teachers and Children Working Together)**
**PICC (Parental Involvement in the Care Curriculum)**
Information on both of these from Roger Hancock and Sarah Gale, Hackney Educational Psychology Service, Woodberry Down Centre, Woodberry Grove, N4 2SH.

**Open University**
Several of the Open University parent education packs and courses are now out of print, and a new Parenting and Under Eights project is underway developing new materials. The following however, are still available:
  *Pregnancy and Birth*
  *Living with Babies and Toddlers*
  *Parents and Teenagers*
  *Parents Talking: The Developing Child*
  *Parents Talking: Family Relationships*

Department of Community Education, Open University, Walton Hall, Milton Keynes, MK7 6AA.

**Parent Education Project**
Leaflets on feeding, play and sleep developed for a project run by health visitors and psychologists.

Southmead Health Education Department, Gloucester House, Southmead Hospital, Bristol, BS10 5NB.

### Parent Network/Parent Link

Booklets for use in parent discussion groups on being a parent, feelings, labels, being a helper, whose problem is it?, reflective listening, needs and wants, challenging. Also *The Parents Book* by Ivan Sokolov and Deborah Hutton, Thorsons 1988.

Parent Network, 44-46 Caversham Road, London, NW5 DDS.

### Parents as Co-educators

1993. A handbook and discussion materials for teachers.

Community Education Development Centre, Lyng Hall, Blackberry Lane, Coventry, CV2 3JS.

### Portsmouth Area Family Concern

Resource materials for use with parent discussion groups.
*Positive Parenting Packs 1 and 2.*
1. *Parenting Isn't for Cowards*
2. *Families – Fun or Frenzy?*

Portsmouth Area Family Concern, 30 Hillside Avenue, Waterlooville, P07 5BB.

### Positive Parenting: raising children with self-esteem
Elizabeth Hartley-Brewer, 1994.
A book to 'empower and encourage' parents, focusing on self-esteem, self-confidence and self-reliance. Materials for group leaders and parent discussion groups in preparation.

Cedar Books, Michelin House, 81 Fulham Road, London, SW3 6RB

### Primary School Workbook: teaching sex education within the national curriculum
Gill Lenderyou, 1993.
This practical guide to teaching sex education in primary schools, includes a discussion of the key issues, exercises, background notes and handouts.

Family Planning Association, 27-35 Mortimer Street, London, W1N 7RJ.

*Religion, Ethnicity and Sex Education: exploring the issues*
Rachel Thomson for the Sex Education Forum, 1993
The pack presents seven religious 'perspectives' on sex, sexuality and sex education (Anglican, Hindu, Islamic, Jewish, Methodist, Roman Catholic and Sikh). It also includes a discussion of equal opportunities, legal and National Curriculum requirements for sex education.

Sex Education Forum, 8 Wakley Street, London, EC1V 7QE

**School Home Investigations in Primary Science (SHIPS)**

Association for Science Education, College Lane, Hatfield, Hertfordshire.

*Teenage Parenthood*
An education pack focusing on 'unplanned, premature parenthood', to be used as part of a wider social and sex education curriculum.

Bristol YWCA, 76 Oldbury Court Road, Bristol, BS16 2JG.

*Teenagers in the Family*
Teenagers under Stress
Teenagers and Sexuality

Trust for the Study of Adolescence, 23 New Road, Brighton, East Sussex, BN1 1WZ.

*The New Pregnancy Book*
A guide to pregnancy, childbirth and the first few weeks with a new baby.

Health Education Authority, Hamilton House, Mabledon Place, London, WC1H 9TX.

*The Really Helpful Directory: services for pregnant teenagers and young parents*
This directory lists approximately 350 separate projects for young mothers, 130 of them being residential, 50 educational, 30 antenatal/parentcraft provision and 140 support and information projects. Published jointly with the Maternity Alliance. 1993

Trust for the Study of Adolescence, 23 New Road, Brighton, East Sussex, BN1 1WZ.

### Time for Children

A report of a curriculum development project which aimed to support teachers in identifying ways of integrating family education and the personal and social development of students into the National Curriculum.

Community Education Development Centre, Lyng Hall, Blackberry Lane, Coventry, CV2 3JS.

### Us and the Kids

Contains ideas and resources for parent groups, covering activities, photographs of family situations in many parts of the world, and of many types of family unit.

Development Education Centre, Gillett Centre, Selly Oak Colleges, Bristol Road, Birmingham, B29 6LE. 1991

### Values, Cultures and Kids

Dorit Braun, 1991, Stanley Thornes

A handbook of approaches and resources for teaching about family education within a multicultural society.

### Video Directory on Parenting

Mental Health Film Council, 1991

A comprehensive list of audio-visual material on parenting. An up-to-date list can be obtained from the database for a search fee.

Mental Health Film Council, Resource Centre, 359 Holloway Road, London N7 6PA.

### What is a Family?

1990. The pack consists of black and white photographs of different images of family life. The materials have been designed to raise issues of stereotypes, family structures and roles and relationships in the family.

Development Education Centre, Gillett Centre, Selly Oak Colleges, Bristol Road, Birmingham, B29 6LE.

### Working with Parents for Change

A package of materials developed by educational psychologists for use by early childhood educators, focusing on a parent group work approach to managing difficult behaviour.

Sales and Publications Department, Strathclyde University, Jordanhill Campus, 76 Southbrae Drive, Glasgow.

### *Your Baby, Your Choice*

A birthplan teaching aid which is intended for use in an antenatal group, and incorporates individual birth plans to help women understand the choices available to them.

The Maternity Alliance, 15 Britannia Street, London, WC1X 9JP.

# References

Adams, L (1982) 'Consumers' views of antenatal education', *Health Education Journal*, 41 (1) 12-16

Adler (1930) *The Education of Children*. New York, Greenberg Publishing

Adult Literacy Basic Skills Unit (1993) *Parents and Their Children: the intergenerational effect of poor basic skills*. ALBSU

Allan, J (in press) 'Parenting education: constraints and possibilities', *Children & Society*, 8.3

Amin, K and Oppenheim, C (1992) *Poverty in Black and White: deprivation and ethnic minorities*. Child Poverty Action Trust and Runnymede Trust

Atkinson, A B (1993) 'Beveridge, the national minimum, and its future in a European context', *Welfare State Programme discussion paper WSP/85*. London School of Economics

Audit Commission (1994) *Seen But Not Heard: developing community child health and social services for children in need*. HMSO

Bagilhole, B (1994) *Evaluation of Charnwood Home-Start*. University of Loughborough, Department of Social Sciences

Baginsky, M (1993) *Parent Link in Waltham Forest: an evaluation*. Baginsky Associates

Ball, C (1994) *Start Right: the importance of early learning*. Royal Society of Arts

Ball, J 'Postnatal care and adjustment to motherhood' *in* Robinson S and Thomson, A eds (1989) *Midwives, Research and Childbirth*, 1, Chapman and Hall

Barker, W and Anderson, R (1988) *The Child Development Programme: an evaluation of process and outcomes*. University of Bristol, Early Childhood Development Unit

Barker, W, Anderson, R and Chalmers, C (1992) *Child Protection: the impact of the Child Development Programme*. University of Bristol, Early Childhood Development Unit

Barnard, P and others (1993) *Life Foundations Volume 4*. Family

Groups and Parenthood/Marriage. NES Arnold/National Family Trust

Bastiani, J (1993) 'Parents as partners: genuine progress or empty rhetoric?' *in* Munn, P *ed. Parents and Schools*. Routledge

Bastiani, J (1993) *Directory of Home-School Initiatives in the UK*. Royal Society of Arts

Bavolek, S J and Comstock, C M (1983) *Nurturing Program for Parents and Children 4-12 Years*. Eau Claire, Family Development Resources Inc, Wisconsin, USA

Bavolek, S (1990) 'Parenting: theory, policy and practice', *Research and Validation Report of the Nurturing Programmes*. Eau Claire, Family Development Resources Inc, Winconsin, USA

BBC TV (1993) *QED. The Family Game*. BBC publications

BBC TV (1994) *Spoiling the Child?* BBC2 16 March

Bernard, J (1976) *The Future of Marriage*. Pelican

Bettelheim, B (1987) *A Good Enough Parent*. Thames and Hudson

Biehal, B and others (1992) *Prepared for Living? A survey of young people leaving the care of three local authorities*. Leaving Care Research Project, University of Leeds. National Children's Bureau

Billingham, K (1989) '45 Cope Street: working in partnership with parents', *Health Visitor*, 62, 5, 156-157

Binning, S (1994) 'Breaking the patterns', *Nursery World*, 6 January

Blackburn, C (1991) *Poverty and Health: working with families*. Open University Press

Booth, W and Booth, T (1994) *Parenting under Pressure: mothers and fathers with learning difficulties*. Open University Press

Bradshaw, J (1993) *Household budgets and living standards*. Joseph Rowntree Foundation

Bradshaw, J and Holmes, H (1989) *Living on the Edge: a study of the living standards of families in Tyne & Wear*. Child Poverty Action Group

Brannen, J and Moss, P (1991) *Managing Mothers: dual earner families after maternity leave*. Unwin Hymac

Brannen, J and others (1994), *Young People, Health and Family Life*. Open University Press

Braun, D (1991a) *Values, Cultures and Kids*. Stanley Thornes

Braun, D (1991b) *Time for Children*. Community Education Development Centre

Braun, D and Eisenstadt, N (1990) *What is a Family? Photographs and Activities*. Development Education Centre, DEC Publications

Braun, D and Schonveld, A (1992) *Preparation for Parenthood: myth or reality*. Community Education Development Centre

Braun, D and Schonveld, A (1993) *Approaching Parenthood: a resource for parent education*. Health Education Authority

Brazleton, B (1993) *Touchpoints*. Viking

Brierley, P (1993) *Reaching and Keeping Teenagers*. Monarch

Briscoe, M (1989) *Health Visitor*, 62, 11, 336-338

British Paediatric Association (1990) *Report of the Joint Working Party on Professional and Parent-Held Records used in Child Health Surveillance*. British Paediatric Association

British Social Attitudes Survey (1989). Gower

Brown, G (1989) 'A lone parent group in Yorkshire', *Health Visitor*, 62, 6, 187-188

Bullock R, Little, M and Millhams, S (1993) *Going Home: the return of children separated from their families*. Dartmouth Publishing

Burghes, L (1994) *Lone Parenthood and Family Disruption: the outcomes for children*. Family Policy Studies Centre

Burgoyne, J and Clark, D (1984) *Making a Go of It. A Study of Stepfamilies in Sheffield*. Routledge

Burnell, A (1993) *What Do We Know About Relationships Between Parents and Children and Where Things Go Wrong?* Exploring Parenthood

Burnell, A and Goodchild, J (forthcoming) *Developing Work and Family Services: a case study*. Exploring Parenthood

Caddle, D (1991) 'Training for fatherhood', *Home Office Research and Statistics Department Research Bulletin*, 30, 35-39 (Parenthood training courses in young offender institutions)

Caesar, G, Smith, C and Berridge, D (1993) *Study of Pre-school Projects in Barnardo's London Division. Report on the Ferncliff Centre, Hackney*. Barnardo's

Cameron, R J ed. (1982) *Working Together: portage in the UK*. NFER Nelson

Campling, J (1993) 'Unemployment and the labour market, Social Policy Digest', *Journal of Social Policy*, 22, 3, 402

Cannan, C (1992) *Changing Families, Changing Welfare*. Harvester Wheatsheaf

Canter, L and Canter, M (1988) *Assertive Discipline for Parents*. Harper and Row

Canterbury and Thanet Community Healthcare (1991) *Evaluation of First Steps Groups*.

Carpenter, V and Yeung, K (1986) *Coming In From the Margins: youth work with girls and young women*. Youth Clubs UK

Centre for the Study of Social Policy (1990) *Helping Families Grow Strong. New directions in public policy*. Papers from the colloquium on public policy and family support. USA

Chandler, T 'Working with fathers in family centres' *in* Phil Lee *ed.* (1993) *Changing Men and Masculinity and Caring* (provisional title). Routledge and Kegan Paul

Chase-Lansdale, P L and Hetherington, E M 'The impact of divorce on life-span development. Short and long-term effects', *in* Baltes, P B, Featherman, D L and Lerner, R M *eds* (1990) *Life Span Development and Behaviour*, 10, Baum Associates

Cherlin, A J (1992) *Marriage, Divorce, Remarriage*. Harvard University Press

Chevannes, M (1989) 'Child rearing among Jamaican families in Britain', *Health Visitor*, 62, 48-51

Childcare Links (1990) *Making Childcare Links*. Childcare Links

Children Act Advisory Committee (1992, 1993) *Annual Reports*.

Children's Committee (1980) *The Needs of Under-Fives in the Family*. HMSO

Children's Society (1991) *Education for Citizenship*. The Children's Society

Chisholm, D (1989) 'Factors associated with late booking for antenatal care in Central Manchester', *Public Health*, 103 (6) 459-466

Choices in Childcare (1994) *The Guide: setting up and running a children's information service*. Choices in Childcare

Clark, D *ed.* (1991) *Marriage, Domestic Life and Social Change, Writings for Jacqueline Burgoyne*. Routledge

Clench, H (1993) 'EPIC: an example of empowerment', Paper given to National Portage Conference, Keele September 1993

Cleveland Report (1988) *Report of Inquiry into Child Abuse in Cleveland, Cm412*. HMSO

Clulow, C (1982) *To Have and To Hold, Marriage, the First Baby and Preparing Couples for Parenthood*. Aberdeen University Press

Clulow, C and Mattinson, J (1989) *Marriage Inside Out, Understanding Problems of Intimacy*. Pelican, Penguin Books

Cockett, M and Tripp, J (1994) 'Children living in re-ordered families', *Joseph Rowntree Findings*, No.45

Cohen, B (1990) *Caring for Children*. Family Policy Studies Centre

Coleman, J 'Understanding adolescence today: a review' *in* Pugh G *ed.* (1993) *Thirty Years of Change for Children*. National Children's Bureau

Combes, G and Schonveld, A (1992) *Life Will Never Be the Same Again: learning to be a first-time parent*. Health Education Authority

Commission for Racial Equality (in press) *From Cradle to School: a practical guide to racial equality in early childhood provision*. Revised edition

Commitee of Enquiry into Discipline in Schools, DES and Welsh Office (1989) *Discipline in Schools*. Elton Report, HMSO

Committee on Child Health Services (1976) *Fit for the Future* (Court Report). HMSO

Community Education Development Centre (1992) *Preparation for Parenthood: myth or reality?* Community Education Development Centre

Community Education Development Centre (1993) *Parents as Co-Educators: a handbook for teachers*. Community Education Development Centre

Conway, J (1988) *Prescription for Poor Health: the crisis for homeless families*. LFMC/MA/SHAC/Shelter

Cook, A James, J and Leach, P (1991) *Positively No Smacking*. Health Visitors' Association and EPOCH

Cooper, C '"Good enough", border line and "bad enough" parenting', in Adcock, M and White, R (1985) *Good Enough Parenting: a framework for assessment*. British Association for Adoption & Fostering

Cooper, J (1993) 'The origins of the National Children's Bureau' *in* Pugh, G ed. (1993) *Thirty Years of Change for Children*. National Children's Bureau

Cousins, N (1986) 'Getting along with the lads', *Youth Service Scene*, 127, 8

Cowan, C P and Cowan, P A (1992) *When Partners Become Parents: the big life change for couples*. USA Basic Books

Cowan P and others 'Becoming a family' *in* Cowan, P and Heatherington, M eds (1987) *Family Transitions*. LEA

Cox, A D (1993) 'Preventive aspects of child psychiatry', *Archives of Disease in Childhood*, 68, 691-701

Cox, A, Pound, A and Puckering, C 'NEWPIN: a befriending scheme and therapeutic network for carers of young children', *in* Gibbons J ed. (1992) *The Children Act 1989 and Family Support: principles into practice*. HMSO

Cox, M (1985) *An Enquiry into Education for Parenthood within the Southend District*. Southend Health Authority

*Crime Concern* (in preparation) Family Task Group report

Cullinan, R (1991) *Health Visitor*, 64, 12, 412-414

Cummings, E M and Davies, P (1994) 'Maternal depressions and child development', *J Child Psychol. Psychiat*, 35, 1, 73-112

Cunningham, C and Davis, H (1985) *Working with Parents: frameworks for collaboration*. OU Press

Curtice, L (1989) 'Talking about how difficult we find it', *Health Visitor*, 62, 11, 343

Daines, B and Gill, B (1993) *Playlink Schemes – an evaluation*. East Sussex County Council

Dalli, C (1992) 'The rationale behind National's PAFT programme and why it raises concerns', *New Zealand Journal of Educational Studies*, May

Dally, A (1982) *Inventing Motherhood*. Burnett Books

Davidson, N (1988) 'A crisis of masculinity', *Youth and Society*, 134, 10-11

Davies, R B and others (1991) *The relationship between a husband's unemployment and his wife's participation in the labour force*, Mimeo *in* Irwin and Morris (1993)

Davis, R (1988) 'Learning from working class women', *Community Development Journal*, 23, 2

Dawson, N and McHugh, B (1986) 'Application of a family systems approach in an education unit', *Maladjustment and Therapeutic Education*, 4, 2

Dearing, R (1994) *The National Curriculum and its Assessment: final report*. School Curriculum and Assessment Authority

De'Ath, E and Slater, D (1992) *Parenting Threads, Caring for Children When Couples Part*. Stepfamily Publications

Dembo, M H, Sweitzer, M and Lauritzen, P (1985) 'An evaluation of group parent education: behavioral, PET and Adlerian programs', *Review of Educational Research*, 55, 2, 155-200

Demo, D H and Acock, A C (1992) 'The impact of divorce on children', *Journal of Marriage and the Family*, 50

Dennis, N and Erdos, G (1993) *Families without Fatherhood*. Choice in Welfare Series, No 12, Institute of Economic Affairs

Department of Health and Social Security (1974a) *The Family in Society: dimensions of parenthood*. HMSO

Department of Health and Social Security (1974b) *The Family in Society: preparation for parenthood*. HMSO

Department of Health and Social Security (1978) *Violence to Children: a response to the first report from the select committee on violence in the family (1976-77)*. HMSO Cmnd 7123

Department of Health and Social Security (1980) *Reply to the Second Report from the Social Services Committee on Perinatal and Neonatal Mortality*. HMSO. Cmnd 8084

Department for Education (1993) *Education Act 1993: sex education in schools*. Department for Education

Department of Education and Science (1977) *Education in Schools: a consultative document*. HMSO Cmnd 6869

Department of Education and Science (1985) *Better Schools*. HMSO

Department of Education and Science (1988) *The Education Reform Act 1988*. HMSO

Department of Health (1991) *1990 Report of the Chief Medical Officer on the State of the Public Health*. HMSO

Department of Health (1992) *The Health of the Nation, A strategy for Health in England, White Paper Cm 1986*. HMSO

Department of Health (1993) *Adoption: the future, White Paper, Cm 2288*. HMSO

Department of Health (1993) *Changing Childbirth, Parts I and II*. HMSO

Department of Social Security (1993a) *Households below Average Income, A statistical Analysis 1979-1990/91*. HMSO

Department of Social Security (1993b) *Income Support – 1992 Annual Statistical Enquiry*. Press Release 24 May

Development Education Centre and Community Education Development Centre (1991) *Us and the Kids. Ideas and resources for parent groups*. DEC Publications

Di Salvo, P and Skuse, T (1993) *Really Helpful Directory: services for pregnant teenagers and young parents*. Trust for the Study of Adolescence

Dimmock, B ed. (1992) *A Step in Both Directions? The Impact of the Children Act 1989 in Stepfamilies*. National Stepfamily Association

Dinkmeyer, D and McKay, G (1982) *The Parents Handbook – Systematic Training for Effecting Parenting*. Circle Pines, American Guidance Service

Doherty, W and Ryder, R (1980) 'Parent effectiveness training: criticisms and caveats', *Journal of Marital and Family Therapy*, 6 , 4, 409-19

Dormor, D J (1992) *The Relationship Revolution*. One Plus One

Douglas J ed. (1988) *Emotional and Behavioural Problems in Young Children: a multidisciplinary approach to identification and management*. NFER Nelson

Draper, J and others (1981) *Early Parenthood Project Report of the First Year*. Hughes Hall

Dreikurs, R and Soltz, V (1964) *Happy Children: a challenge to parents*. New York, Hawthorn

Dumon, W (1991) *Families and Policies, Evolutions and Trend in 1989-1990*. Brussels, European Observatory on National Family Policies

Dybwad, G (1952) 'Fathers Today: neglected or neglectful?', *Child Study*, 29 (1) 3-5

Easen, P Kendall, P and Shaw, J (1992) 'Parents and educators:

dialogue and development through partnership', *Children & Society*, 6, 4, 282-296

Edwards, P and Townsend, L (1993) 'Group work is the key', *Nursery World*, 29 April

Edwards, R (1992) 'Co-ordination, fragmentation and definitions of need: the new Under Fives Initiative and homeless families', *Children & Society*, 6, 4, 336-352

Einzig H (1994) *Briefing on Parenting Education and Support*. International Year of the Family, Family and Relationships Group

Eurobarometer (1990) *The Family and Desire for Children*. European Commission

European Commission Childcare Network (1990) *Men as Carers for Children*. Community of European Communities

Evans, F 'The Newcastle Community Midwifery Project: the evaluation of the project', *in* Robinson, S and Thompson, A E (1991) *Midwives, Research and Childbirth*, Vol II, Chapman and Hall

Exploring Parenthood (1994) *Social Audit Report on Provision of Family Services*. Exploring Parenthood (in preparation)

Exploring Parenthood (1992) *Responsible Parenting Requires a Responsible Society*. Report of a symposium, October 1992

Eyken, W van der (1982) *Home-Start: a four-year evaluation*. Home-Start

Family Mediation Scotland (1993) *Families Like Ours*. Family Mediation Scotland

Farrington, D and West, D 'The Cambridge study in delinquent development: a long term follow up of 411 London males' *in* Kaiser, G and Kerner, H *eds* (1990) *Criminality: personality, behaviour and life history*. Springer Verlag, Berlin

Ferri, E (1984) *Stepchildren: a national study*. NFER Nelson

Ferri, E (1993) *Life At 33: the fifth follow-up of the National Child Development Study*. National Children's Bureau

Ferri, E and Saunders, A (1991) *Parents, Professionals and Pre-school Centres: a study of Barnardo's provision*. National Children's Bureau

Finch, J (1983) 'Can skills be shared? Preschool playgroups in disadvantaged areas', *Community Development Journal*, 18, 3

Fine, M *ed.* (1980) *Handbook of Parent Education*. Academic Press

Fleming, J and Ward, D (1992) *For the Children to be Alright their Mothers Need to be Alright. An alternative to removing the child*. The Radford Shared Care Project. University of Nottingham, School of Social Studies

Forehand, R and McMahon, R (1981) *Helping the Non-Compliant Child: a clinician's guide to parent training*. Guildford Press

Foundation for the Study of Infants Deaths (1993) *Newsletter 45*

Fox Harding, L (1991) *Perspectives in Child Care Policy.* Longman

Freeman, M and Hemmings, A (1994) *The Room To Be Me Project: an evaluation report.* University of Sussex

Funder, K, Kinsella, S and Courtner, P (1992) 'Stepfathers in children's lives', *Family Matters*, 31, Australian Institute of Family Studies

Gamble, D (1994) 'Parenting courses: the self-help option?', *Concern*, spring

Garnett, L (1992) *Leaving Care and After.* National Children's Bureau

Gibbons, J (1990) *Family Support and Prevention: studies in two areas.* National Institute for Social Work

Gibbons, J ed (1992) *The Children Act 1989 and Family Support: principles into practice.* HMSO

Gibbons, J and Thorpe, S (1989) 'Can voluntary support projects help vulnerable families? The work of Home-Start', *British Journal of Social Work*, 19, 189-202

Gill, A (1989) 'Putting fun back into families', *Social Work Today*, 4 May

Gill, N (1992) Larkfield Family Centre Project: Evaluation Report – December 1992 (unpublished)

Gillies, E and Chaudry, M (1984) 'Health education sessions on early antenatal and pre-conceptual health: a pilot study', *Health Visitor*, 57, 3, 81-82

Ginott, H (1965) *Between Parent and Child, New Solutions to Old Problems.* Pan Books

Goldschmied, E and Jackson, S (1994) *People Under Three: young children in day care.* Routledge

Gordon, T (1975) *Parent Effectiveness Training.* New York, Peter Wyden

Graham, H (1994) 'The changing financial circumstances of families with chidren', *Children & Society*, 8.3

Grant (forthcoming) *Report of Moyenda Project.* Exploring Parenthood

Hague, G and Malos, E (1993) 'Local authority responses to women and children escaping from domestic violence', *Joseph Rowntree Foundation Findings*, No.85

Hansard, 24 June 1992, col. 459-462. The Lord Bishop of Coventry

Harman, D and Brim, O (1980) *Learning to Be Parents: principles, programs and methods.* Sage Publications

Hartley-Brewer, E (1994) *Positive Parenting.* Cedar

Hartley-Brewer, E and Hills, L (1994) *Facilitators Manual: guidelines for running coffee and chat sessions.* For Barnet/Hertfordshire/Nuffield pilot

Haskey, J (1987) 'Social class differentials in remarriage after divorce', *Population Trends*, 47, 34-42

Haskey, J (1989) 'Families and households of the ethnic minority and white populations of Great Britain', *Population Trends*, Autumn, HMSO

Health Education Authority (1992) *Birth to Five*. Health Education Authority

Health Education Authority (1993) *A Survey of Health Education Policies in Schools*. HEA/NFER

Health Education Authority (1992) *Today's Young Adults*

Health Education Authority (1993) *New Pregnancy Book*. Health Education Authority

Health Education Authority/MORI (1989) *Health Education in Schools*

Health Visitors' Association (1993) Press release 1 October 1993, *Funding Squeeze Threatens Child Health Services*. Health Visitors' Association

Her Majesty's Inspectorate (1991) *A Survey of the Education of Children Living in Temporary Accommodation*. HMSO

Herbert, M (1987) *Behavioural Treatment of Children with Problems*. Academic Press

Hewitt, P and Leach, P (1993) *Social Justice, Children and Families*. The Commission on Social Justice, IPPR

Hewitt, K and others (1991) 'Parent education in preventing behaviour problems', *Health Visitor*, 64, 12

Highmore, R and McCann, M (1989) 'Breathing space for parents', *Scottish Child*. Aug/Sept, 12-13

Hill, P (1993) 'Recent advances in selected aspects of adolescent development', *Journal of Child Psychology and Psychiatry*, 34, 69-100

Hills, J (1993) *The Future of Welfare, A guide to the debate*. Joseph Rowntree Foundation

Hinton, S (1987) *A Study of Behaviour Management Workshops for Parents of Nursery School Children*. Unpublished thesis, Institute of Education, University of London

Hinton, S (1994) *The ABC of Behaviour: troubleshooting for parents of young children*. Start Publications

Hoffman, L 'The value of children to parents and child-rearing patterns' *in* Kagitcibasi C ed. (1987) *Growth and Progress in Cross-cultural Psychology*. Berwyne, Swets North America Inc

Hogg, C and Harker, L (1992) *The Family Friendly Employer, Examples from Europe*. Daycare Trust

Hohmann, M, Barnet, B and Weikart, D (1979) *Young Children in Action: a manual for pre-school educators*. Ypsilanti: High Scope Educational Research Foundation

Holden, J (1989) *British Medical Journal*, 298 (6668) 223-226

Holman, R (1992) 'Family Centres', *Highlight No. 111*. National Children's Bureau

Holman, R (1983) *Resourceful Friends*. The Children's Society

Hope, P (1994) *Education for Parenthood*. The Children's Society

House of Commons Health Committee (1992) *Sessions 1991-92. Maternity Services*. HMSO

Hudson, F and Ineichen, B (1991) *Taking it Lying Down: sexuality and teenage motherhood*. Macmillan

Ihinger–Tallman, M and Pasley, K (1987) *Remarriage*. Sage

Ineichen, B and Hudson, F (1994) 'Teenage Pregnancy', *Highlight 126*. National Children's Bureau

Irwin, S and Morris, L (1993) 'Social Security or economic insecurity? The concentration of unemployment (and research) within households', *Journal of Social Policy*, 22, 3, 349-372

Jackson, B (1984) *Fatherhood*. Allen and Unwin

Jackson, S 'Great Britain', *in* M Lamb ed. (1987) *The Father's Role, Cross-cultural Perspectives*. Larence Erlbaum Associates

Jackson, C (1992) 'Community mothers: trick or treat?' *Health Visitor* 65, 6, 199-201

Jackson, D (1993) *Do Not Disturb, The Benefits of Relaxed Parenting for You and Your Child*. Bloomsbury

Jain, C (1985) *Attitudes of Pregnant Asian Women to Antenatal Care*. West Midlands Regional Health Authority

Jenner, S (1992) 'The assessment and treatment of parenting skills and deficits: within the framework of child protection', *ACPP Newsletter*, 14, 5

Jenner, S and Gent, M (1993) 'Evaluating the contribution of a parent training technique to a parenting assessment package for parenting skills and deficits in the context of child protection', *JCPP Newsletter*

Johnson, Z Howell, F and Molloy, B (1993) 'Community mothers' programme: randomised controlled trial of non-professional intervention in parenting', *British Medical Journal*, 29 May 1993, Vol. 306, 1449-1452

Jonathan, R 'Parental rights in schooling' *in* Munn, P ed. (1993) *Parents and Schools*. Routledge

Joseph, Lord (1991) *The Importance of Parenting*. Centre for Policy Studies

Joshi, H (1991) 'The cash opportunity cost of childbearing, and approach to estimation using British data', *Population Studies*, 44, 41-60

Kahn, T (1994a) 'Back to school for practical parenting', *Observer*, January 23

Kahn, T (1994b) 'Less Chalk and More Talk', *Independent*, 10 February

Kahn, T (1994c) *Monitoring the Media, February 1994*, Report to the National Children's Bureau

Katz, A (1994) 'The family is fine...but under pressure', Sainsbury's Magazine, May

Kiernan, C (1993) *Survey of Portage Provision 1992/93*. National Portage Association

Kiernan, K 'The family: formation and fission' *in* Joshi, H *ed*. (1989) *The Changing Population of Britain*. Basil Blackwell

Kiernan, K (1992) 'The impact of family disruption in childhood on transitions made in young adult life', *Population Studies*, Vol 46

Kiernan, K and Estaugh, V (1993) *Cohabitation, Extra-marital childbearing and social policy*, Occasional Paper 17, Family Policy Studies Centres

Knight, B and Osborn, S (1992) *Parents, Families and Crime Prevention*. Unpublished report for the Home Office

Kolvin, I and others (1990) 'Continuities in Deprivation'. ESRC/DHSS Studies *in Deprivation and Disadvantage*, 15, Avebury

Konner, M (1991) *Childhood*. Little, Brown

Kumar, V (1993) *Poverty and Inequality in the UK: the effects on children*. National Children's Bureau

Kurtz, Z, Thornes, R and Wolkind, S (1994) *Services in England for the Mental Health of Children and Young People: a national survey for the Department of Health*. Unpublished

*Labour Force Survey 1990 and 1991* (1992) HMSO

Lamb, M E 'Fathers and child development: an integrative overview' *in* Lamb, M E *ed*. (1981) *The Role of the Father in Child Development*. Wiley and Sons, New York

Lamb, M *ed*. (1987) *The Father's Role – crosscultural perspectives*. Lawrence Erlbaum Associates

Lang, P *ed*. (1988) *Thinking About Personal and Social Education in the Primary School*. Blackwell

Leach, P (1994) *Children First*. Michael Joseph

Le Masters, E E (1957) *Parenthood as Crisis Marriage and Family Living*, 19, 352-355

Leira, A (1993) 'Mothers, markets and the state: a Scandinavian model?' *Journal of Social Policy*, 22, 3, 329

Lenderyou, G (1993) *Primary School Workbook: teaching sex education within the national curriculum*. Family Planning Association

Lewis, C, Newson, E and Newson, J 'Father participation through childhood and its relation to career aspirations and delinquency', *in* Beaill, N and McGuire, J *eds* (1992) *Fathers: psychological perspectives*. Junction Books

Lewis, C and O'Brien, M *eds* (1987) *Reassessing Fatherhood: new observations on fathers and the modern family*. Sage

Lewis, C 'A feeling you can't scratch?: the effect of pregnancy and birth on married men', *in* Beaill, N and McGuire, J *eds* (1982) *Fathers Psychological Perspectives*. Junction Books

Lewis, J M and others (1976) *No Single Thread: psychological health in family systems*. Brunner/Mazel

Lindell, S (1988) 'Education for childbirth: a time for change', *Journal of Obstetrics, Gynaecology and Neonatal Nursing*, 17, 2, 108-111

Lindsell, S and Pithouse, A (1993) *Gwent Family Centre Strategy. North Gwent Family Centre. Final Report September 1993*. University of Wales College of Cardiff School of Social and Administrative Studies. Unpublished

Lloyd, P (1983) 'Postnatal groups: what format do mothers want?', *Health Visitor* 56, 9, 337-338

Lloyd, T (1985) *Work with Boys*. National Youth Bureau

Lloyd, T (1986) 'New ways of working with boys', *Youth Service Scene*, 120, 5

Lord Chancellor's Department (1993) *Looking to the Future. Mediation and the Grounds for Divorce*. Cmnd 2424, HMSO

Lutz, P (1983) 'The stepfamily: an adolescent perspective', *Family Relations*, 32, 367-75

Lund, K and Nilsson, N E (1987) *Growing Up Together*. Orebro, Sweden Mikael Junior High School

Macleod, F (1984) *Home Based Early Learning Projects: evaluation report*. Community Education Development Centre

Madeley, R and others (1989) 'Nottingham mothers stop smoking project – baseline survey of smoking in pregnancy', *Community Medicine*, 11 (2) 124-130

Mansfield, P and others (forthcoming) *Person, Partner, Parent*. Macmillan

Mansfield, P and Collard, J (1988) *The Beginning of the Rest of Your Life? A Portrait of Newly-wed Marriage*. Macmillan

Maternity Services: health committee second report, House of Commons Paper 29-1 (1992). HMSO

Maximé, J 'The importance of racial identity for the psychological well-being of the young black child', in Pugh, G *ed.* (1991) *Quality and Equality for Under Fives*, Conference Report, National Children's Bureau

Mayall, B (1986) *Keeping Children Healthy*. Allen and Unwin

Mayall, B (1990) 'Childcare and childhood', *Children & Society*, 4, 4, 374 -385

McCabe, F and others (1984) *Antenatal Education in Primary Care: a survey of general practitioners, midwives and health visitors*. Centre for Mass Communication Research, University of Leicester

McCleary, G F (1933) *The Early History of the Infant Welfare Movement*. H K Lewis

McConville, A (1989) 'Setting up a parenting group', *Health Visitor*, 6 (11) 338-339

McGaw, S (1993) 'The Special Parenting Service – supporting parents with learning difficulties', *Disability, Pregnancy and Parenthood International*, No 4, 8-10

McGaw, S and Sturmey, P (1993) 'Identifying the needs of parents with learning disabilities: a review', *Child Abuse Review*, 2, 101–117

McGaw, S and Sturmey, P (1994) 'Assessing parents with learning disabilities: the parental skills model', *Child Abuse Review*, 3, 1

McGlaughlin, A and Empson, J (1979) 'Mother plus child = future', *Community Care*, 16 August, 277,25.

McIntosh, J (1987) *A Consumer Perspective on the Health Visiting Service*. Department of Child Health and Obstetrics, University of Glasgow

McIntosh, J (1988) 'A consumer view of birth preparation classes: attitudes of a sample of working class primaparae', *Midwives Chronicle*, January 8-9

McKee, L and O'Brien, M eds (1982) *The Father Figure*. Tavistock

McKnight, A and Merrett, A (1986) 'Availability and acceptance of health education among socially 'at risk' pregnant women attending health centres in Belfast', *Family Practice*, 3 (2) 85-91

McKnight, A and Merrett, A (1987) 'Alcohol consumption in pregnancy – a health education problem', *Journal Royal College of General Practitioners*, 37 (295) 73-76

McRae, S (1993) *Cohabiting Mothers: changing marriage and motherhood?*, Policy Studies Institute

Methodist Division of Education and Youth, NCH and Network (1994) *Partners in Parenting: parents, families and the Church*. NCH

Michaels, G Y and Goldberg, W A eds (1988) *The Transition to Parenthood: current theory and research*. Cambridge University Press, New York

Miedzian, M (1992) *Boys Will Be Boys: breaking the links between masculinity and violence*. Virago

Milner, D (1983) *Children and Race: ten years on*. Ward Lock Educational

Ministry of Health (1932) *Final Report of the Departmental Committee on Maternal Mortality and Morbidity*. HMSO

Mitchell, A (1985) *Children in the Middle: living through divorce*. Tavistock Publications

Mosley, J (1993) *Turn Your School Round*. Wisbech, Learning Development Aids

Moss, P (1992a) *in* Hogg, C and Harker, L, *The Family Friendly Employer, Examples from Europe*. Day Care Trust

Moss, P 'Perspectives from Europe' *in* Pugh G *ed*. (1992) *Contemporary Issues in the Early Years*. Paul Chapman

Moss, P and others (1986) Marital relations during the transition to parenthood, *Journal of Reproductive and Infant Psychology*, 4, 57-67

Munro, J (1988) 'Parentcraft classes with Bengali mothers', *Health Visitor* 61, 2, 48

Myers, R (1992) *The Twelve Who Survive: strengthening programmes of early childhood development in the third world*. Routledge

National Association of Citizen's Advice Bureaux (1994) *Child Support One Year On. CAB evidence on the first year of the child support scheme*. NACAB

National Youth Agency (1991) *Planning and Evaluation in a Time of Change: Report of the Third Ministerial Conference for the Youth Service*. National Youth Agency

National Children's Bureau (1992) *Child Facts 2 – Children's Homes*. National Children's Bureau

National Childbirth Trust (1991) *NCT Teachers Annual Returns 1990: outreach*. NCT

National Childbirth Trust (1992) *Annual Report*

National Childminding Association (1986) *Childminding: materials for learning and discussion*. National Childminding Association

National Curriculum Council (1990) *Curriculum Guidance 5: health education*. National Curriculum Council

National Curriculum Council (1993) *Spiritual and Moral Development – a Discussion Paper*. National Curriculum Council

New, C and David, M (1985) *For the Children's Sake: making childcare more than women's business*. Penguin Books

Newell, P (1989) *Children are People Too: the case against physical punishment*. Bedford Square Press

Newham Parents' Forum (1988) *A Treasured Experience? What women said about Newham Maternity Hospital*. Newham Parents' Forum

Newson, J and Newson, E 'Cultural aspects of child-rearing in the English speaking world' *in* Richards, M P M *ed*. (1985) *The Integration of a Child into a Social World*. Cambridge University Press

O'Connor, L (1990) 'Education for parenthood and the national curriculum: progression or regression?', *Early Child Development and Care*, 57, 85-88

O'Dell, S Flynn, J and Benlolo, L (1977) 'A comparison of parent training techniques in child behaviour modification', *Journal of Behaviour Therapy and Experimental Psychology*, 8, 261 – 268

O'Dell, S 'Progress in parent training' *in* Hersen, M Eisler, R and Miller, P eds (1985) *Progress in Behaviour Modification*, 19, Academic Press

Office of Population Censuses and Surveys (1989) *The Prevalence of Disability Among Children*. HMSO

Office of Population Censuses and Surveys (1993) *Stillbirths and Neonatal Deaths 1992*. OPCS Monitor DH3 93/1. OPCS

Office of Population Censuses and Surveys (1994) *General Household Survey 1992 London*. HMSO

OFSTED (1994) *Framework for the Inspection of Schools*

Open University (1983) *Pre-school Playgroups Association Pack P598*. Open University

Open University (1992) *Parenting and Under 8s Project Proposal*

Open University (1994) *Personal Communication*

Open University Community Education (1986) *A Review of a Collaborative Health Education Programme* 1976 – 1986. A report for the Health Education Council, Open University

Open University of Scotland (1984) *Prisoners, Parents and Children: a report on parent education projects at Saughton and Barlinnie prisons*

Oppenheim, C (1993) *Poverty: the facts*. CPAG

Organisation for Economic Cooperation and Development/Centre for Educational Research and Innovation (1982) *The Educational Role of the Family: a thematic analysis of existing country policies, positions and programmes*. (CERI/ERF/82.01)

Osborn, A F (1990) 'Resilient children. A longitudinal study of high achieving socially disadvantaged children', *Early Child Development and Care*, Vol 62

Page, D (1993) 'New housing association estates: emerging problems', *Joseph Rowntree Foundation Findings*, No.84

Paraskeva, J 'Youth work and informal Education' *in* Coleman, J and Warren-Adamson, C eds (1992) *Youth Policy in the 1990s: the way forward*. Routledge

Parent School Partnership (1992) *PSP and Parents*. Liverpool City Council Education Department

Parentline (1993) *How Can We Help? 100 calls analysed*. Parentline

Parr, M (1993) *Research and evaluation report of the Parent-Infant Project: background to project and study one (1989-1992)*. PhD Thesis in preparation. University of East London, Psychology Department

Patterson G (1982) *A Social Learning Approach vol 3, Coercive Family Processes*. Eugene Oregon, Castalia

Pearce, J (1991) *Families and Friends, How to Help Your Child Enjoy Happy Relationships*. Thorsons

Perkins, E (1988) *45 Cope Street: the first 18 months November 1986-May 1988*. Nottingham

Perkins E and Morris B (1981) 'Should we prepare for parenthood?' *Health Education Journal*, 40, 4, 107 – 110

Pfannenstiel, J and Seltzer, D (1989) *New Parents as Teachers: evaluation of an early parent education program*, Early Childhood Research Quarterly, 4, 1-8

Pfannenstiel, J Lambson, T Yarnell, V (1991) *Second Wave Study of the Parents as Teachers Program*. St Louis, Parents as Teachers National Center Inc

Phillips R 'Newham parents centre: parents as partners in education' *in* Wolfendale, S (1992) *Empowering Parents and Teachers*. Cassell

Phillips, A (1993) *The Trouble with Boys, Parenting the Men of the Future*. Pandora

Philpot, T and Ward, L (forthcoming) *Values and Visions: changing ideas in services for people with learning difficulties*. Butterworth-Heinemann

Phoenix, A (1991) *Young Mothers*. Oxford

Pickvance, C and Pickvance, K (1992) 'The effect of housing costs on young people's lifestyles', *Joseph Rowntree Foundation Findings*, No.68

Pilling, D (1990) *Escape from Disadvantage*. Falmer Press

Pleck, J (1981) *The Myth of Masculinity*. Cambridge

Pleck, J (1984) *Changing Fatherhood*. Unpublished manuscript cited *in* Lamb (1987)

Pollock, S and Sutton, J (1985)' Fathers' rights, women's losses', *Women's Studies International Forum*, 8 (6), 539-9

Portsmouth Area Family Concern (1992) *Positive Parenting Packs, 1, Parenting Isn't for Cowards; 2. Families – fun or frenzy?*

Pound, A, Ulanowsky-Rose, C and Whitfield, R (1993) 'Family groups and parenthood', *Life Foundations Vol. 4*, Nottingham Group

Pound, A and Mills, M (1985) 'A pilot evaluation of NEWPIN, a home-visiting and befriending scheme in South London', *ACPP Newsletter*, 7,4

Powell, D (1990) 'Home visiting in the early years: policy and program design decisions', *Young Children*, September 65-73

Prendergast, S and Prout, A (1986) *Knowing and Learning About Parenthood*. Health Education Council

Pring, R 'Personal and social education in the primary school', *in* Lang, P ed. (1988) *Thinking about Personal and Social Education in the Primary School*. Blackwell

Pringle, Mia Kellmer (1975) *The Needs of Children*. Hutchinson

Prout A (1988) *Health Visitor*, Vol 61, No 3, 92-94

Public Utilities Access Forum, (1990) *Payment Direct for Water, Electricity and Gas, A Discussion Paper*. May

Puckering, C and others (in press) *Mellow Mothering: process and evaluation of group intervention for distressed families*

Pugh, G ed. (1980) *Preparation for Parenthood*. National Children's Bureau

Pugh, G ed. (1993) *Thirty Years of Change for Children*. National Children's Bureau

Pugh, G and De'Ath, E (1984) *The Needs of Parents: policy and practice in parent education*. Macmillan for the National Children's Bureau

Pugh, G and De'Ath, E (1987) *Working Towards Partnership in the Early Years*. National Children's Bureau

Pugh, G and Poulton, L (1987) *Parenting as a Job for Life*. National Children's Bureau

Quine, L (1991) 'A hard day's night', *Community Care*, 29 August

Quinn, M and Quinn, T (1988) *What Can a Parent Do? Some Practical Skills to Help Parents be More Responsible and More Effective*, 2nd edition. Family Caring Trust

Quinn, M and Quinn, T, (1992) *Being Assertive: ways of respecting others but not letting yourselves be walked on*. Family Caring Trust

Richards, M and Dyson, M (1982) *Separation, Divorce and the Development of Children: a review*. Paper for the DHSS

Richman, N and Goldthorpe, W O 'Fatherhood, the social construction of pregnancy and births', *in* Kitzinger, S and David, J eds (1978) *The Place of Birth*. Oxford University Press

Robertson, J and Robertson, J (1982) *A Baby in the Family*. Penguin Books

Robinson, T (1994) *Coping with Kids: assertive discipline for parents*. Leaflet from Avon Education Department Psychology Service

Robinson, M and Smith, D (1993) *Step by Step: focus on stepfamilies*. Harvester/Wheatsheaf

Rocheron, Y and Dickinson, R (1990) 'The Asian mother and baby campaign: a way forward in health promotion for Asian women?' *Health Education Journal*, 49, 3, 128-133

Rocheron, Y, Dickinson, R and Khan, S (1989) *The Evaluation of the*

*Asian Mother and Baby Campaign: synopsis.* Centre for Mass Communication Research, University of Leicester

Rogers, C R (1951) *Client Centred Therapy.* Boston, Houghton Mifflin

Rogers, C R (1961) *On Becoming a Person: a therapists view of psychotherapy.* Boston, Houghton Mifflin

Rousseau, J J (1762) *Emile ou l'Education.* Amsterdam, London

Rowe, J and Mahoney, P (1993) *Parent Education: guidance for purchasers and providers.* Health Education Authority

Rowe, G and Whitty, G (1993) *Times Educational Supplement,* 9 April 1993, 8

Russell, P 'Supporting Families' *in* Philpot, T and Ward, L eds (forthcoming) *Values and Visions: Changing ideas in services for people with learning difficulties.* Butterworth-Heinemann

Russell, P and Flynn M, (1991) *National Development Team Workshop for Parents – Castle Priory College, Wallingford.* Council for Disabled Children, National Children's Bureau

Rutter, M (1974) 'Dimensions of parenthood: some myths and some suggestions', *The Family in Society, Dimensions of Parenthood.* HMSO

Rutter, M 'Stress, coping and development: some issues and some questions', *in* Garmezy, N and Rutter, M eds (1983) *Stress, Coping and Development in Children.* McGraw Hill, New York

Rutter, M and Madge, N (1976) *Cycles of Disadvantage.* Heinemann

Rutter, M (1987) 'Psychological resilience and protective mechanisms', *American Journal of Orthopsychiatry,* 57, 316-331

Schaffer, R (1977) *Mothering.* Fontana/Open Books

Schaffer, R (1990) *Making Decisions About Children.* Blackwell

Schieffelin, B and Ochs, E 'A cultural perspective on the transition from prelinguistic to linguistic communication' *in* Woodhead M, Carr, R and Light, P eds (1991) *Becoming a Person.* Open University Press

Schmidt Neven, R (1990) *The New Explorers:a psychodynamic approach to parenting in a changing society.* Full Circle

Schweinhart, L, Barnes, H and Weikart, D (1993) *Significant Benefits: the High/Scope Perry Preschool Study through age 27.* Ypsilanti, Michigan, High/Scope Press

Sefi, S (1988) 'Health visitors talking to mothers', *Health Visitor* 61, 7 – 10

Sex Education Forum (1992) *A Framework for School Sex Education.* National Children's Bureau

Shinman, S (1987) *Under Fives Initiative Final Report.* Home-Start Consultancy

Silverman, D And Stacey, M (1989) 'Listen to the parents', *Special Children,* February 1989

Simpson, B and others (1993) *Post-Divorce Fatherhood: discussion paper.* Family and Community Dispute Research Centre, Newcastle

Simpson, R and Walker, R (1993) *Europe, For Richer or Poorer?* CPAG Publications

Skynner, R and Cleese, J (1983) *Families and How to Survive Them.* Methuen

Smith, C ed. (1994) *Developing Effective Aftercare Projects.* The Royal Philanthropic Society

Smith, C and van der Eyken, W (1990) *Information Services for Parents of Under Fives. Final Evaluation Report.* Institute of Child Health, University of Bristol. Department of Health and Social Security

Smith, C and Vernon, J (forthcoming) *Children, Parents and Day Nurseries: meeting the challenge of child care in the nineties.* National Children's Bureau

Smith, D (1989) *Taking Shape: developments in youth service policy and provision.* National Youth Bureau

Smith, M (1988) *Developing Youth Work: informal education, mutual aid and popular practice.* Open University

Smith, P and Berridge, D (1994) *Ethnicity and Childcare Placements.* National Children's Bureau

Smith, T (1993) *Family Centres and Bringing up Young Children: six projects run by The Children's Society.* The Children's Society

Snelling, J (1989) *Health Visitor,* Vol. 62, 83.

*Social Trends 23* (1993) Central Statistical Office

Sokolov, I and Hutton, D (1988) *The Parents Book.* Thorsons

Sommer, D (1993) *Fatherhood and Caring: who cares? in the equality dilemma.* Copenhagen, Danish Equal Status Council

SSAC (1990) *Direct Deductions and Water Charges,* Paper to the Secretary of State for Social Security by the Social Security Advisory Committee, 25 October 1990

Statham, J (1994) *Childcare in the Community.* Save the Children Fund

Stevenson, J ed. (1989) *Health Visitor Based Services for Preschool Children with Behaviour Problems,* Occasional Paper 2, Association of Child Psychology and Psychiatry

Stewart, A and Ring, W (1991) 'What about adopters?', *Health Visitor,* 64, 9, 297-299

Sutton, C (1992) 'Training parents to manage difficult children: a comparison of methods', *Behavioural Psychology,* 20, 115 – 139

Sutton, C (1994) 'Parent education and training: a seriously neglected field', *Children UK,* 1, 14

Taylor, A (1985) 'Antenatal classes and the consumer: mothers' and fathers' views', *Health Education Journal,* 44, 2, 79 – 82

Teague, A (1993) 'Ethnic Group: first results from the 1991 Census', *Population Trends*, 72, 12-17, HMSO

Teenage Parenthood Network (1992) *Too Much Too Young*, No 7, 2-3

Thompson, A (1982) *Experience and Participation: report of the review group on the youth service in England*. HMSO

Thomson, R and Scott, L (1992) *An Enquiry into Sex Education*. National Children's Bureau for Sex Education Forum

Thomson, R ed. (1993) *Religion, Ethnicity and Sex Education: exploring the issues*. National Children's Bureau for Sex Education Forum

Thornes, B and Collard, J (1979) *Who Divorces?* Routledge and Kegan Paul

Topping, K (1986) *Parents as Educators: training parents to teach their children*. Croom Helm

Topping, K and Wolfendale, S eds (1985) *Parental Involvement in Children's Reading*. Croom Helm

Treasury (1993) Tables D1, 2.1 and 2.5

Triseliotis, J 'Open Adoption', *in* Mullender, A ed. (1991) *Open Adoption, the Philosophy and Practice*. Practice Series 19. BAAF

Utting, D, Bright, J and Henricson, C (1993) *Crime and the Family, Improving Child-rearing and Preventing Delinquency*. Family Policy Studies Centre

Verdon, F (1980) 'Some reflections', *in* Pugh, G (1980)

Voluntary Organisations Liaison Council for Under Fives and National Children's Bureau Early Childhood Unit (1992) *Organisations Concerned with Young Children and Their Families: a national directory*. VOLCUF/National Children's Bureau

Walczak, Y and Burns, S (1984) *Divorce: the child's point of view*. Harper and Row

Walker, J 'Divorce, remarriage and parental responsibility', *in* De'Ath, E ed. (1982) *Stepfamilies: What Do We Know? What do we need to know?* Stepfamily Publications

Walker, J Simpson, B and McCarthy, P (1991) 'The housing consequences of divorce', *Joseph Rowntree Fundings*, No.25

Wallace, L (forthcoming) *Comprehensive Home-Start Initiative for Parental Support*. University of Leeds, Department of Adult and Continuing Education

Wallerstein, J S and Kelly, J (1980) *Surviving the Break-Up. How Children and Parents Cope with Divorce*. McGrant McIntyre

Warren, C (1990) *The Potential for Parent Advocacy in Family Centres*. M Phil thesis. University of Southampton

Wedge, P and Prosser, H (1973) *Born To Fail?* National Children's Bureau and Arrow Books

Weikart, D 'Organising delivery of parent education' *in* Fantini, M D and Cardenas, R (1980) *Parenting in a Multicultural Society*. New York, Longman

Westmacott, E and Cameron, R J (1982) 'Selling behavioral psychology to parents and teachers', *AEP journal*, 5, 9

Whalley, M (1994) *Learning to be Strong*. Hodder and Stoughton

White, L K and Booth, A (1985) 'The quality and stability of remarriages: the role of stepchildren', *American Sociological Review*, Vol. 50, No.5

White, P (1994) *Information Shops in Action*. National Youth Agency

Willetts, D (1993) 'The Family', *WH Smith Contemporary Papers*, No.14

Williams, E (1993) 'Informative years' *Times Educational Supplement*, 18 June

Williams, T and Roberts, J (1985) *Health Education in Schools and Teachers Education Institutions*. University of Southampton Health Education Unit

Wilson, H (1987) 'Parental supervision re-examined', *British Journal of Criminology*, 20, 3, 203-235

Wolfendale, S (1992) *Empowering Parents and Teachers: Working for children*. Cassell

Wood, D (1982) 'The DHSS Cohort Study of Unemployed Men. WP1.' *Men registered as unemployed in 1978 – A Longitudinal Study*. DHSS

Woodhead, M 'Psychology and the cultural construction of children's needs' *in* James A and Prout A, *eds* (1990) *Constructing and Reconstructing Childhood*. Falmer

Wynn, M and Wynn, A (1981) *The Prevention of Handicap of Early Pregnancy Origin: some evidence for the value of good health before conception*. Foundation for Education and Research in Childbearing

Young, M and Willmott, P (1973) *The Symmetrical Family*. Pelican

Youth Work Advisory Group, Scotland (1987) *Project on Fatherhood*. Youth Work Advisory Group

Youth Clubs UK (1987) *Getting Started: a practical guide to work with girls and young women*. Youth Clubs UK, 1987

# INDEX

The index covers the Introduction and Chapters 1 to 7. It does not include Appendices and References. Entries are arranged in letter-by-letter order (hyphens and spaces between words are ignored). Principal page references are printed in **bold** type.